10/11

P9-CKV-245

OFF
STAFF MEALS FROM
THE
AMERICA'S TOP RESTAURANTS
MENU

MARISSA GUGGIANA

welcome
BOOKS

Contents

Introduction 12

OPPOSITE: Line cook Tyler Kanaval sauces up his chicken-fried duck legs at Blackbird.

OPPOSITE: AOC's line cook, Sara Saxonberg, dresses her tostadas with pico de gallo.

Introduction

The greatest twinning of meaning in this book is that between restaurant-staff meals and the meals you have with your family. Staff meal has nuances of function, but at its core, it is a time for the health of a staff to develop. Like dinner for many families, it is the only time that everyone is together in an unstructured way. When service begins, the front of house and the kitchen cleave into separate hierarchies and then staff peels off, one by one, as work ends. A family unit, or a staff *en totale*, has its own character, but it doesn't survive if you don't feed it dinner. And like many family meals I remember from my surly teenage years, there can be awkward moments, unsuccessful casseroles, ungrateful eaters; but you come to the table. Every night. The practice becomes the meaning.

Those are postprandial thoughts, though. The urge that created this book was to taste what cooks make for one another. Menu items are to Thanksgiving dinner as staff meal is to Tuesday supper. Unlike just any Tuesday supper, these meals have the nimbleness of tested skill, passion, and food knowledge. It's like gazing into your pantry with 3-D glasses. The recipes are all wonderful on their own but they are also buoyant techniques that hold the weight of available ingredients, seasonality, time limitations, and other constraints. These are recipes created by constraints. Equations solved by giving "x" the value of a chef's skills.

My mandate in writing this book was to find the places that treat staff meal as an honor and a practice in grace, not as a chore. It was certainly an adventure in gratitude for me; I was greeted by open back door after open back door at so many admirable kitchens. I purposefully sought out farm to table restaurants, because my life in food has taught me that taste begins at conception. Almost every single restaurant in this book considers the local produce and livestock an extension of their kitchen. The few exceptions, the less ingredient-centric menus, were selected because they have purpose in their community as a gathering place or guardian of food traditions and local history. A restaurant that values their farmers and their community, you can discreetly assume, will respect their staff.

All the selections for *Off the Menu* have a well-developed relationship to staff meal. Some chefs, like Jamie Bissonnette of Boston's Toro and Amanda Cohen of Dirt Candy in New York City, use the meal to break the fourth wall of the kitchen, sharing their menus through Twitter and a blog, respectively, as a peek under the skirt for cooks and foodies. Some chefs, like Blue Hill at Stone Barns' Dan Barber or Osteria Stellina's Christian Caiazzo, use the ritual to extend their community by breaking bread with farmers, winemakers, and other contributors to the cause. Russell Moore at Camino in Oakland, California, thinks of staff meal as an elevation of staff dignity, everyone eating in the dining room and preparing food calibrated to the same quality as menu items. And then there are chefs like Linton Hopkins at Restaurant Eugene in Atlanta who explained that staff meal is a sort of testing ground. If you can't throw together a meal for your peers from the contents of the pantry, then you're not truly a chef. There were studious staff meals, like that conducted by Sean Rembold at Marlow & Sons in Brooklyn, and raucous, Bacchanalian staff meals, like the pasta dinner helmed by Ethan Stowell at Tavolàta in Seattle.

Each of these meals carried the character of the group as a whole. Though I am sure they have ebbs and flows and may be a bit looser when they're not being photographed (fewer high heels and more swearing, I'd imagine), I could read something profound about what it takes to put out great food. Along with skill, there is the building of a culture that makes the food. The particularity of that culture is nowhere more present than at staff meal, where you can see that it isn't just the linens or the decision to serve an *amuse-bouche* or whether the servers wear ties, that makes the culture of a restaurant. It is the philosophy and the way the staff absorbs that philosophy and expresses it. And in a subtle but cumulative way, the forging of that happens at staff meal.

The personal experience of making this

book has its own narrative arc. In counterpoint to the grandeur of fine dining is my life on the road. For six weeks I carried a camera bag and one tote bag full of a laptop and my meager pile of interchangeable outfit parts. Through a winter so gruesome it brought city-shuttering snowstorms to Atlanta, I trudged. Beyond the sometimes-beat feeling of being broke and homesick, there were the illuminated pleasures of meeting extraordinary chefs in perfect restaurants. Unlike the hundreds of other interviews I have conducted, capturing staff meal is a time trial. To eat, photograph, and connect with the staff, as well as the chef, is a task in itself, but to do it in the fifteen to forty-five minutes that generally comprise a staff meal is a thrilling challenge. The dinner bell would ring and I would be shooting, noting, and talking in a fascinated frenzy. No matter what seedy motel or Chinatown bus awaited me after a shoot, I left every workday feeling joyful and lucky, carrying a version of that post-work high I remember from my days as a server.

When I look through the cookbooks at bookstores, as I often do, I notice relatively few that don't fit the mold of high-profile chefs sharing recipes from their menus. These kinds of books come from a supportive infrastructure of sous chefs and assistants. It is expensive and demanding to make any book, and the diminution of publishing only increases the cost and decreases the appetite for risk. But it is truly rare to have the support to spend a year traveling, researching, and letting ideas develop. These recipes had never been written down, they aren't reheated leftovers. The outcome of this book was unknown at the beginning. Would we end up with a hundred recipes of bland baked chicken thighs or the gorgeous individual expressions of personal taste that we have here? The profiles, recipes, and ruminations come from a spirit guided by curiosity, not marketability. To eat in the dining rooms of these great American restaurants is a personal pleasure, but to sit with the chefs in the most unbuttoned hour of their creative life is an honor and a story worth sharing.

—MG

PAGES 16–17: Chef Jamie Bissonnette (right) with the staff at Toro.

Abattoir

Abattoir is the French word for "slaughterhouse" and the name of a restaurant in Atlanta. The amplified rusticity of the place echoes its origins as a slaughterhouse and its link to a time when cooking was a tool to eat what was available, and not the fanciful fabrication of meals that exist outside of seasons and localities. Meat is the starting point of the food here, animals brought in straight from an *abattoir* to Abattoir.

Like Bacchanalia, this restaurant is owned by Anne Quatrano, but the menu is driven by executive chef and partner Joshua Hopkins. This was one of the staff meals that became a family meal, drawn out by a conversation that lingered until it was done, instead of at the beckoning of work. We talked particularly about the role of food critics. *Yelp* is a dirty word in most restaurants, since so many have been stung by a comment that can take on more weight than it merits when the critiques are all given equal bearing. A too-long delay for water may be an anomaly and may be of little importance, but it can drag down the stature of the restaurant in its ratings. Beyond Yelp, the scrutiny of food has become an industry. Are amateurs, who are diners, after all, unqualified to make statements that can damage a reputation? And what is the role of the expert in a culture where so many are foodies or foodie-wannabes? Regardless, Abattoir receives high marks.

At the table, I am clearly in expert hands. Glazed chicken with fried rice, green salad with house-made kimchee, bacon cookies, and the coup de grace—chicharrones that are served in large sheets, which you break off at your own discretion. The fried pork fat is a study in texture; there is an art to achieving lightness and crispness and then seasoning them sweet and hot to add dimension to the richness of the fat, relieved of its moisture. The Hopkinses' dog paces enough to remind us of his presence every time a piece is broken off and then curls back up in his spot.

The restaurant is kept dark, between meals as we are, and the only light is from a far bank of windows and the low hanging fixtures above the farm table where we eat. It feels like nothing else exists—not even the whir of the dishwasher distracts us. This food is the trick to that and it has the same effect at home when I prepare it myself.

OFF THE MENU

Soy-and-Honey-Glazed Chicken

Skillet-Fried Rice

Kimchee and Lettuce Salad

Brown Sugar Bacon Cookies

Suggested beer:
Southern Tier
422 Pale Wheat Ale or
Sierra Nevada Kellerweis

TOP LEFT: Chef Josh Hopkins displays chicharrones. BOTTOM RIGHT: Brad Winkler, server, digs into soy-and-honey-glazed chicken.

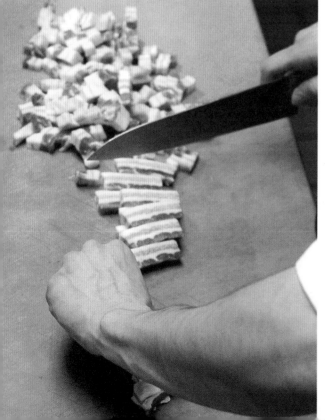

Soy-and-Honey-Glazed Chicken

Growing up, we had chicken, rice, and greens so many nights that it was a private joke amongst my siblings. Chef Joshua Hopkins revamps this trio by reminding me that a little glaze on the chicken or some kimchee on the salad can change your experience of the meal.

1 cup chicken stock

½ cup soy sauce

2 tablespoons honey

8 boneless chicken thighs, roasted, or rotisserie chicken, chopped

1 tablespoon minced ginger

1 bunch cilantro, coarsely chopped

1 small jalapeño, thinly sliced

In a large sauté pan, bring the stock, soy sauce, and honey to a simmer. Reduce the sauce for about 10 minutes. Add the chicken and increase heat to high. Continue to cook, rotating the chicken until it has absorbed almost all of the sauce. Remove from the heat and add the ginger, cilantro, and jalapeño. Toss to cover and serve immediately.

Serves 6

Skillet-Fried Rice

This is a beatiful side dish as it is presented here, but will also stand up as an entree. The bacon fat and eggs give it heft enough to pin your appetite.

1 pound bacon, large diced
Canola oil for frying
3 cups cooked long-grain rice
4 eggs, scrambled, divided
2 tablespoons soy sauce
2 cups scallions, sliced small
2 teaspoons fresh lemon juice

In a medium skillet over medium-high heat, cook the bacon until crisp. Transfer to paper towels and reserve the fat.

Heat two 12-inch skillets on high heat; coat with a mixture of bacon fat and canola oil. When the oil begins to smoke, divide the rice between the skillets and allow to cook without moving the pans for 1 minute. Add half the eggs to each skillet. After 30 seconds, flip the rice and eggs, cook for 1 minute more, and then divide the soy sauce, bacon, scallions, and lemon juice between the skillets. Cook for 2 more minutes, stirring occasionally. Serve immediately.

Serves 6 to 8 as a side

Kimchee and Lettuce Salad

Making kimchee is one of the easiest fermentation processes. The intensity of its flavor will slap any dish awake, and it will reside happily in your refrigerator for months.

1 small head napa cabbage
Salt
4 cloves garlic, minced
2 tablespoons minced ginger
2 tablespoons fresh lime juice
½ cup Korean chili flakes
2 tablespoons granulated sugar
1 cup fish sauce
¼ pound shaved carrot
¼ pound shaved daikon radish
1 cup scallions, chopped into 1-inch pieces
1 pound young lettuce greens

A few days ahead, wash the napa cabbage, chop into large 1-inch pieces and salt liberally. Leave in a cool, dry place in a tightly wrapped container for 24 hours.

After 24 hours, rinse off the salt. In a food processor, combine the garlic, ginger, lime juice, chili flakes, and sugar, and purée. Add the fish sauce slowly to form a paste; taste and adjust the seasoning. Combine the cabbage, carrot, radish, and scallions with the chili paste. Toss with lettuce just before serving.

Serves 6 to 8 as a side

Brown Sugar Bacon Cookies

Save this recipe for company, because you will get a lot of mileage out of the concept. The bacon adds the right saltiness to make these excellent, with just enough unexpected umami. You can also substitute some butter for rendered bacon fat, which I have done when a baking urge strikes and there's no other fat in the house.

3 cups all-purpose flour
1 teaspoon baking soda
1 teaspoon salt
2 sticks unsalted butter, room temperature
1 cup firmly packed light brown sugar
1 cup granulated sugar
2 eggs
½ cup bacon, rendered and chopped fine

Preheat the oven to 325°F. Sift together the flour, baking soda, and salt. Set aside.

In a large mixing bowl with a paddle attachment, cream together the butter and sugars on medium speed for 1 minute until light and fluffy, scraping the sides as necessary. Mix for 1 more minute, then scrape the sides again. Add the eggs one at a time on medium speed until incorporated.

Reduce the speed to low and add the flour mixture a little at a time. Once incorporated, turn the speed to medium for 30 seconds. Scrape the sides of the bowl and fold in the bacon by hand so that it is evenly distributed.

Scoop with an ice-cream scoop onto Silpat- or parchment-lined sheet pans, flattening each cookie slightly with the back of a spoon, and bake for 14 to 18 minutes, rotating twice, until golden brown.

Makes 2½ to 3 dozen medium-sized cookies

~ Joshua Hopkins ~

ABATTOIR (ATLANTA, GA)

Executive chef and partner Joshua Hopkins has been with Anne Quatrano and Clifford Harrison's restaurant group since 2005. He began at Bacchanalia and now runs Abattoir. He started his culinary career with Maverick Southern Kitchens, and he stays true to his love of regional food.

What was your favorite food as a kid?
Triscuits, banana peppers, and mayo.

What was the first meal you made that you were proud of?
The meal I made for Christian Chemin during my first apprenticeship, which made me realize how much I loved to cook.

What three adjectives describe your cuisine?
Simple, regional, and meaty.

What book most influences your food, cookbook or otherwise?
Cooking by Hand by Paul Bertolli.

What is your favorite ingredient?
Vinegar.

What music do you like to hear when you cook?
Jazz or punk.

What is your favorite hangover meal?
Hash browns, country ham, pork, and eggs.

What is your favorite midnight snack?
Goldfish crackers and pickles.

What restaurant in the world are you most dying to try?
Tetsuya's in Sydney, Australia.

What kitchen utensil is most indispensable to you?
My paring knife.

Who do you most like to cook for?
Friends that are chefs at other restaurants.

If you could do one other job, what would it be?
Photojournalist.

What do you most value in a sous chef?
Organization and thirst for knowledge.

What food trend would you erase from the annals of history?
TV dinners.

What one food would you take with you to a desert island?
Beer-soaked pizza.

What is your favorite guilty-pleasure treat?
Oatmeal-raisin cookies.

What most satisfies your sweet tooth?
ChikaLicious Dessert Bar in New York.

What would you eat at your last meal, if you could plan such a thing?
French fries with mayonnaise.

Cheeseburger or foie gras?
Cheeseburger.

What's your favorite place (and what is your favorite thing to order) for:

A splurge meal?
Urasawa in Beverly Hills.

Late-night/after-work meal?
Café Agora in Atlanta for gyros.

A cup of coffee?
Octane Coffee Bar in Atlanta for a black coffee with a shot of espresso.

A greasy-spoon meal?
Silver Skillet in Atlanta.

Hamburger craving?
Bocado Restaurant in Atlanta.

Bread desire?
Star Provisions in Atlanta for ciabatta.

Groceries?
Buford Highway Farmers' Market in Atlanta for herbs, fruits, and vegetables; Whole Foods for meat; Star Provisions in Atlanta for bread, fish, and cheese; and Kroger in Atlanta for Triscuits and Goldfish.

AOC

LOS ANGELES, CA

In *Angeleno* magazine's Top 10 LA Restaurants of All Time—which includes Spago and Josie—Suzanne Goin and Caroline Styne hold two spots: both their restaurants Lucques and AOC are in the pantheon. AOC is named for the *Appellation d'Origine Côntrollée*, which is the governing body of France's wine industry, setting rules for what percentage of syrah grapes can be present in a Châteauneuf du Pape and other matters that I simultaneously think are supercilious and wonderful.

My staff meal at AOC is without pomp. Tostada Tuesday is a tradition that engenders titillation from the staff. Simply put, make-your-own meals are fun. Especially when they come from the kind of spirited kitchen that occasionally takes a short soccer break after family meal. The kind of food that wins James Beard awards is different from the kind of food that a family wants for dinner. To me, eating out is often a pleasure like a museum visit—it seeds inspiration and shifts in perspective. If my perspective were shifted every night, I would hardly have one. Simple food that is prepared well and meets nutritional needs is not a capitulation at dinner, it is right. Staff meal, like home cooking, is less mental. You may not feel yourself compelled to describe the effect of a particular herb but you will probably want seconds.

AOC is often described as architectural. It is angular and designed without give; you are aware of the space because it doesn't yield to embellishments. There are two bars: one for drinking from the acclaimed wine list and one for the cheese and charcuterie tippler, fitted out with a glass-doored, reach-in cooler that showcases some of the offerings.

We sit at the second bar, the tableau of long-cured perishables in contrast to the freshly prepared staff meal. AOC is a magnifying glass, looking closely at ingredients and wines by offering them with focus. The dishes are small plates with a few ingredients that both explain something about one another through contrast and also transcend differences to become something new: most famously, bacon-wrapped dates with a slip of Parmesan cooked in the wood oven, and a terrine of foie gras served with sweet-and-sour prunes. And behind the kitchen door, Tostada Tuesday is put away, hardly a leftover in sight.

OFF THE MENU

~

Ground Beef Tostadas
with Pico de Gallo

Pot Beans

Cabbage Salad

Suggested wine:
Lang & Reed North Coast
Cabernet Franc 2009

Ground Beef Tostadas
with Pico de Gallo

This is the meal I dreamed of as a child. I would have gladly eaten this six days a week (and on the seventh day, pizza). This is the chef's version of a laid-back dinner, made festive through self-assembly and homemade meat and beans.

Pico de Gallo
4 ripe red tomatoes, diced
1 yellow onion, small diced
2 or 3 jalapeños, seeded and finely chopped
½ cup chopped fresh cilantro
½ teaspoon dried Mexican oregano
½ cup lime juice
Kosher salt and freshly ground black pepper

1 pound ground beef
½ yellow onion, small diced
½ tablespoon fresh thyme
1 clove of garlic, finely chopped
½ teaspoon dried Mexican oregano
½ teaspoon paprika
½ teaspoon cumin seed, toasted and ground
Pinch of cayenne
½ cup chopped fresh cilantro
½ cup chopped fresh parsley
Kosher salt and freshly ground black pepper
Canola oil, about 3 cups, for frying
6 corn tortillas

In a medium-sized bowl, combine all pico de gallo ingredients, cover, and refrigerate for an hour before serving.

In a large cast-iron skillet over high heat, cook and crumble ground beef for about 15 minutes. Once the beef starts to turn brown, add the onion, thyme, and garlic. Stir and cook for 5 minutes. Lower heat to medium low, stir in dry spices, and cook for 15 to 20 minutes, until the beef is cooked through and nicely browned. Stir in cilantro and parsley, check for seasoning, and drain off any excess fat.

Add canola oil to ¼-inch depth in a large cast-iron skillet. Heat to medium high, and using tongs, dip a tortilla into the oil. Once the tortilla starts to get a bit of color, turn it over and fry the other side. When golden brown on both sides, transfer to a large tray lined with paper towels to drain excess oil. Repeat with the rest of the tortillas. Sprinkle a bit of kosher salt on each tostada while still hot.

To serve, arrange ground beef, fried tostadas, and pico de gallo in separate bowls for guests to assemble themselves. Add favorite salsas, guacamole, and queso fresco as options.

Serves 6

——— Pot Beans ———

**This is a standard to know by instinct. The beans should give you no resistance,
so let them cook until they are easily smashed. If you need to add more liquid,
do so, it's a shame to lose the bottom third of a pot of beans to scorching.**

1 pound dried pinto beans
¼ cup extra-virgin olive oil
½ yellow onion
½ tablespoon fresh thyme
1 bay leaf
1 arbol chili

Rinse beans and discard any small stones. Soak beans overnight in cold water. In a stockpot over high heat, combine olive oil, onions, thyme, bay leaf, and chili. Cook until onions are translucent, about 5 minutes, and then add the beans. Stir well and add 3 quarts of water. Bring to a boil, lower heat, and simmer until beans are tender, about 40 minutes to an hour.

Serves 6 as a side

——— Cabbage Salad ———

**Cabbage, lime, and cilantro form one of the great love triangles of the kitchen.
This salad elevates the affair with red onion and mayonnaise.**

1 pound green cabbage, cored
   and thinly sliced
1 pound red cabbage, cored and
   thinly sliced
½ red onion, thinly sliced
¾ cup lime juice
Kosher salt and freshly ground
   black pepper
½ cup mayonnaise
½ cup fresh cilantro
¼ cup chopped fresh parsley

In a large bowl, toss the cabbage, red onion, lime juice, salt, and pepper. Combine well, then add the mayonnaise and herbs. Toss again, making sure everything is incorporated. Taste for acidity and seasoning.

Serves 6 as a side

~ Suzanne Goin ~

AOC (LOS ANGELES, CA)

Suzanne Goin's restaurants—AOC, Lucques, Tavern, and The Hungry Cat, are all in the food-culture equivalent of syndication, garnering awards and new fans year after year, including James Beard Foundation's Best New Chef California and three stars for Lucques from the *Los Angeles Times*.

What was your favorite food as a kid?
Shrimp cocktail and chocolate mousse—always eaten together.

What was the first meal you made that you were proud of?
Roger Vergé's steak with peppercorns, currants, and Armagnac.

What three adjectives describe your cuisine?
Rustic, sensual, and personal.

What book most influences your food, cookbook or otherwise?
One book? That is very hard (impossible): Chez Panisse, Richard Olney, Eric Ripert, there are too many to name.

What chef do you most admire?
Russell Moore of Camino in Oakland.

What is your favorite ingredient?
Olive oil.

What music do you like to hear when you cook?
I don't like music when I'm at work, but at home I go through phases—Ravel, Wilco, Radiohead, among others.

What is your favorite hangover meal?
Bacon, eggs, sticky bun, and a lot of coffee.

What is your favorite midnight snack?
Farro, black rice, cavolo nero, currants, and pine nuts.

What restaurant in the world are you most dying to try?
Restaurante Martín Berasategui in Spain.

What kitchen utensil is most indispensable to you?
Mortar and pestle.

Who do you most like to cook for?
My regular customers.

If you could do one other job, what would it be?
I honestly can't think of anything I'd rather do.

What do you most value in a sous chef?
Dedication to me and to the craft.

What one food would you take with you to a desert island?
A pig.

What is your favorite guilty-pleasure treat?
Sticky bun with bacon on top.

What most satisfies your sweet tooth?
Chocolate-covered honeycomb.

What would you eat at your last meal, if you could plan such a thing?
Steak, tomato salad, grilled bread, burrata, olive oil, and arugula salad.

Cheeseburger or foie gras?
Cheeseburger.

What's your favorite place (and what is your favorite thing to order) for:

Happy hour?
The Hungry Cat in Los Angeles, for a Luke's lemonade and a dozen clams.

A splurge meal?
Le Louis XV in Monte Carlo, France.

Breakfast?
Du-par's in Los Angeles, for pancakes.

A late-night/after-work meal?
Gjelina in Venice, California, and order lots of salads and a pizza.

A greasy-spoon meal?
Zankou Chicken, locations all over Los Angeles. I like the shawarma and falafel.

Ice cream?
Mashti Malone's on La Brea in Hollywood.

Chocolate?
Valerie Confections in Los Angeles for toffee.

Aquavit

Aquavit is a Scandinavian restaurant named after a Scandinavian alcohol and offering deeply Scandinavian food. So, of course, the staff meal is cut from the same cloth. At Aquavit I am told that Scandinavian home cooking is influenced by German food, while the fine dining is more influenced by French cuisine. I wouldn't place this meal anywhere outside the Nordic territories.

Food can convey you to another time or place instantly, smell being such a powerful translation of memories. The hearty veal stew with heavy dill is an intense indicator of origin. I've never been to that part of Europe but I have this romantic vision of it, very après-ski. Something like what the 1970s fondue craze was evoking. This dish is a perfect reminder of why I love cookbooks. I make stew all the time; it is one of the most unsurprising things to come out of my kitchen for anyone who eats with me regularly. But I never use dill or cream. Not because I don't like either of those ingredients, they just haven't become second nature. And they completely own the dish. So if someone was bored of my bourguignon, they may just be bowled over by a blanquette. And I don't even

---

OFF THE MENU

Veal Blanquette in Dill

Banana Bread
with Tosca Topping

Suggested wine:
Calera Mills Pinot Noir 2002
or Stonestreet Alexander
Valley Chardonnay 2007

---

have to learn a new technique.

Cold parts of the world have a certain stoicism, and I saw that in the staff at Aquavit. Of course, there were employees from all over the globe, as there are in most New York kitchens, but many of the cooks spoke Swedish with Chef Marcus Jernmark, who was handsome and straight backed, like an off-duty war hero. It was the most polite of all the staff meals I joined. The front of house staff sits on one side of the dining room and the kitchen staff on the other side, all at tables brought in for the meal, so there is room for everyone without disturbing the place settings for that evening's service. While food was consumed, the lineup was conducted. For the kitchen, this involved running through the inventory for menu items: *Is there enough dough already prepared? What is left of the fish that was on special last night?*

A server in her forties prayed before she ate and Swedish sprinkled around the room. I listened and ate the last piece of banana bread I had hidden for myself earlier, knowing desserts always go fastest in a crowd. Next time I prepare this recipe, I will travel back to this moment.

TOP RIGHT: Chef Marcus Jernmark finally reaches the end of the food line.

Veal Blanquette in Dill

Chef Marcus recommends serving this dish with boiled fingerling potatoes and a good salad with apples and carrots. The vinegar and dill make the stew cheering in winter and appropriate in other seasons.

2 pounds veal stew meat
1 medium carrot, peeled and diced
1 medium parsnip, peeled and diced
1 medium yellow onion, peeled and diced
1 bouquet garni: fresh parsley, thyme, and bay leaf tied together
4 cups vegetable stock
1 cup chicken stock
1 cup heavy cream
3 tablespoons white wine vinegar
2 tablespoons granulated sugar
Salt and freshly ground black pepper
1 tablespoon cornstarch
½ cup chopped fresh dill

Fill a large bowl with water and ice and set aside. Fill a medium saucepan halfway to the top with lightly salted water and bring to a boil. Add the meat and blanch until water returns to a boil. Transfer the meat to the prepared ice-water bath. Drain the meat and set aside.

In a large Dutch oven over medium-high heat, combine the meat; chopped carrot, parsnip, and onion; bouquet garni; and stocks, and bring to a simmer. Cover and cook for 45 minutes, skimming off fat that rises to the surface at regular intervals. Then add the cream, vinegar, sugar, salt, and pepper, and continue to simmer until the meat is tender, about 1½ hours longer.

Add the cornstarch and cook the blanquette until thickened, about 5 minutes; the sauce should coat the back of a spoon. Adjust seasonings to taste. Add the dill, stir through, and serve.

Serves 4 to 6

Banana Bread with Tosca Topping

A classic catharsis for turning bananas, this quickbread by pastry chef Emma Bengtsson is given a decadent crown of tosca. The caramel technique could also be applied to other desserts. Brownies tosca, anyone?

2¼ cups granulated sugar

2 sticks unsalted butter,
   cut into 1 inch cubes

3 large eggs

2¾ cups all-purpose flour

½ teaspoon salt

1 teaspoon baking soda

1½ cups very ripe
   bananas, puréed

½ cup ripe bananas,
   mashed

Tosca Topping

1 cup heavy cream

¾ cup corn syrup

1 cup granulated sugar

1¾ sticks unsalted butter

1¾ cups slivered almonds

Preheat the oven to 350°F. Beat the sugar and butter together in the bowl of an electric mixer until fluffy. Add the eggs to the bowl one at a time, making sure each egg is fully incorporated before adding the next.

Combine the flour, salt, and baking soda, and sift. With the mixer on a low speed, add a third of the dry ingredients until the batter is evenly combined, then add half of the banana purée. Scrape down the bowl and mix until blended. Continue to alternate the addition of dry ingredients with the banana purée, scraping down the bowl to insure a smooth mixture. Gently fold in the mashed bananas, and pour the batter into a greased 9 x 13-inch pan. Spread the batter with a spatula.

Bake the banana bread for 20 minutes, rotate the pan, and bake for an additional 20 minutes until a skewer comes out clean. Allow the bread to cool in the pan before adding the Tosca.

While the banana bread is in the oven, make the Tosca. Stir together the cream, corn syrup, sugar, and butter in a medium pot, and bring the mixture to a boil. Continue to cook the caramel on high heat until it reaches 245°F on a candy thermometer. Remove from heat and gently fold in the almonds. With the banana bread cool and still in the pan, pour the Tosca on top, and spread with a spatula until the top of the bread is evenly coated. Return the loaf to the 350°F oven and bake until the Tosca is bubbling and golden brown, anywhere from 5 to 15 minutes. Let cool. Run a paring knife around the edges before unmolding the bread from the pan.

Serves 15 to 20

~ Marcus Jernmark ~

AQUAVIT (NEW YORK, NY)

Marcus Jernmark has the grace and pride of a world-class athlete. He was one of the top hockey goalkeepers in Sweden before his life as a chef, and now he heads the best Swedish kitchen in New York. Outside Aquavit, he has traveled the world promoting Swedish foods with a project called Culinary Sweden.

What was your favorite food as a kid?
Swedish pancakes on Thursdays, and a silly dish called Afrikana: it's beef tenderloin in a curry cream sauce served with mango chutney, banana and peanuts—it's totally wrong but it's delicious.

What was the first meal you made that you were proud of?
Maybe it's strange, but I don't think I've ever felt pride when it comes to cooking. I get pleasure and satisfaction from cooking.

What book most influences your food, cookbook or otherwise?
The French Laundry Cookbook. It has a culinary mindset I agree with, and it will be on my shelf for years to come.

What chef do you most admire?
I admire loyal chefs who have worked their way up, people who have been elevating their career through devotion to the restaurant and the owner. Daniel Humm and Jonathan Benno come to mind.

What is your favorite ingredient?
I'm split between artichokes and langoustine.

What music do you like to hear when you cook?
Carla Bruni. It's good when I want to relax. It's in French and since I don't speak French there isn't much to think about. Otherwise, I listen to hip-hop.

What is your favorite hangover meal?
Potpie and rich Thai food.

What is your favorite midnight snack?
Fish stew, usually at the end of service.

What restaurant in the world are you most dying to try?
Fäviken, Magnus Nilsson's restaurant in northern Sweden.

Who do you most like to cook for?
My guests here at Aquavit. That's what I'm here to do and that's what I want to do.

If you could do one other job, what would it be?
Hockey goalie or sommelier.

What do you most value in a sous chef?
Loyalty, understanding quality, dependability, and good people skills.

What food trend would you erase from the annals of history?
I think that every food trend is somewhat good to learn from. However, there are certain fast-food trends that haven't brought anything to the table. Another one is fusion: there are people who do fusion well, but I think they are in the minority.

What one food would you take with you to a desert island?
Potatoes.

What is your favorite guilty-pleasure treat?
Swedish candy.

What most satisfies your sweet tooth?
I'm a cookie guy: cookies and pastries. I don't think there's anything better than a good Danish from our AQ Kafé.

What would you eat at your last meal, if you could plan such a thing?
I'm addicted to shellfish, so it would have to be a lot of Champagne and seafood. That's all I need. Oh, and charred meat—the crust of a grilled rib eye—with a large side béarnaise for dipping.

Cheeseburger or foie gras?
The cheeseburger to eat and the foie gras to cook.

What's your favorite place (and what is your favorite thing to order) for:

A splurge meal?
Eleven Madison in New York City, I had one of my best food experiences there.

A late-night/after-work meal?
The pub around the corner from Aquavit.

Groceries?
Fairway in New York City—it's the only place I feel I won't get robbed, and they have good quality.

Bacchanalia

Bacchanalia is part of chefs-owners Anne Quatrano and Clifford Harrison's Atlanta foodscape, a suite of businesses that are all finely wrought and loved in their city. Abattoir, another of the restaurants in this book, is also in the group. Annie, as Ms. Quatrano is affectionately invoked by those who know her, is a matriarch. Everywhere I went in this city, her name was tumbling out of mouths, leaping through conversations.

Bacchanalia shares a building and ownership with Star Provisions, which is a gourmet larder. Each category of artisanal, and, generally, locally produced or homemade product is housed in its own little nook with its own experts and its own environment: a to-go counter, a *charcutier*, a main hall with tables and curated objects of varying practicality, like pig sculptures and excellent cookbooks and perfect dish towels.

Step past Star Provisions and you are in Bacchanalia, a serious restaurant with a theatrically framed kitchen that glistens through a paned window. The kitchen is platonically full of hanging copper pots and a long line of head-down cooks.

In the twilight of staff meal, though, there is only executive chef Daniel Porubiansky, assembling

> **OFF THE MENU**
>
> Bánh Mì Sandwich
>
> *Suggested beer:*
> Tiger Beer or a
> Japanese White Ale

bánh mì for his crew. As we talk, he slices the pork belly in perfect increments.

The staff meal is served at Star Provisions; Bacchanalia's dining room rests inert and ready for service. Frances Quatrano, the GM, takes a stage manager's pause to line the trays up and straighten a cap here, an apron there. In many restaurants, this sort of direction can feel fussy and, worse, exclusive. But it all felt collaborative and familial. And sitting down to a meal with a staff is an infallible litmus test for happiness. All of the cooks spoke freely and respectfully, so handsome in their crisp whites.

From rampant cross-country traveling, I can say that there remains a character to different places. Whenever I cross the Mason-Dixon, a knot unwinds. The hospitality and politesse of the South are tangible and manifest. Even with a meta-sense of themselves, there is still something uncontrived and sweet about Southerners. These cooks, unruffled by having their caps straightened by a lady, had such reserve and thoughtfulness. Perhaps, like most cooks, they went back into the kitchen and swore like sailors on leave, but when they ate staff meal with me, they sat up straight and waited their turn to talk.

Bánh Mì Sandwich

This Vietnamese sandwich is a street-food craze in America, as it has long been in Vietnam. The combination of juicy, tender pork belly and the salty, crunchy veggies is heady. Bánh mì is traditionally served with a slather of paté, but this version relies on pork belly and mayonnaise to provide the savory fat to balance the herbaceous, salty condiments.

2 to 3 pounds pork belly, about 2 inches thick
¼ cup maple syrup
4 crusty demi-baguettes
Mayonnaise (page 40)
Pickled Carrots, Radish & Chilies (page 40)
Picked leaves of basil, cilantro, and mint
1 red onion, thinly sliced

Marinade
1 cup soy sauce
⅓ cup fish sauce
¼ cup maple syrup
4 cloves garlic, crushed
2 jalapeños, coarsely chopped
2 inches ginger, coarsely chopped
¼ cup coarsely chopped fresh cilantro
¼ cup coarsely chopped fresh basil

Sauce
1 cup soy sauce
⅔ cup honey
⅓ cup fish sauce
2 tablespoons ginger
4 cloves garlic
1 jalapeño

Mix the marinade ingredients together and marinate the pork in the refrigerator for 2 hours.

Preheat the oven to 300°F. In a heavy-bottomed pot or Dutch oven, cook the pork belly in the marinade for 2 to 3 hours until tender, basting once or twice during braising.

Pulse the sauce ingredients in a blender and strain. Set aside.

When the pork belly is tender, remove the meat from the pot, add ¼ cup of maple syrup to the cooking juice, and reduce by a quarter on the stove over medium-high heat. Turn the oven up to 425°F. Glaze the belly with the maple-syrup mixture and cook in the 425°F oven for 15 minutes, until crispy and brown.

To assemble, slice the demi-baguettes into halves and toast. Spread the mayonnaise on the bread, add slices of warm pork belly, top with the pickled vegetables, and drizzle with the sauce. Top with picked herbs and slices of onion.

Makes 4 sandwiches

BOTTOM RIGHT: Frances Quatrano sets up staff meal.

Mayonnaise
4 egg yolks
3 tablespoons lemon juice
½ teaspoon Dijon mustard
⅓ teaspoon salt
2⅔ cups peanut oil

In a food processor or blender, combine the egg yolks, lemon juice, mustard, and salt. Turn the processor on high and slowly drizzle the oil into the mixture. Refrigerate the mayonnaise until ready to use.

Makes about 3 cups

Pickled Carrots, Radish, and Chilies
1 cup granulated sugar
1 cup champagne vinegar
1 teaspoon salt
2 carrots, peeled and sliced in rounds
1 large black radish, julienned
2 jalapeños, thinly sliced

In a medium saucepan, heat 1 cup of water, the sugar, vinegar, and salt until the sugar dissolves. Cool and pour over the carrots, radish, and jalapeños. Cover and refrigerate for 2 days.

Makes about 1½ cup

~ Anne Quatrano ~

BACCHANALIA (ATLANTA, GA)

Chef Anne Quatrano is best known for breathing new life into Atlanta's fine dining scene. She and her husband (chef partner Clifford Harrison) live about an hour's drive from the city with their free-range chickens, pigs, goats, and James Beard Foundation's Discovery Chefs of the Year awards.

What was your favorite food as a kid?
Pop-Tarts.

What was the first meal you made that you were proud of?
Eggplant Parmesan.

What three adjectives describe your cuisine?
Clean, balanced, and precise.

What book most influences your food, cookbook or otherwise?
The Chez Panisse Menu Cookbook by Alice Waters.

What chef do you most admire?
Lidia Bastianich.

What is your favorite ingredient?
Fresh herbs.

What music do you like to hear when you cook?
The Rolling Stones.

What is your favorite hangover meal?
Cinnamon toast.

What is your favorite midnight snack?
Thin Mint Girl Scout Cookies.

What restaurant in the world are you most dying to try?
Noma in Copenhagen.

What kitchen utensil is most indispensable to you?
Small offset spatula.

What is your favorite pot?
A two-quart sauce pot.

Who do you most like to cook for?
My paternal grandfather.

If you could do one other job, what would it be?
An architect.

What do you most value in a sous chef?
Enthusiasm.

What food trend would you erase from the annals of history?
Towering.

What one food would you take with you to a desert island?
Prosciutto baguette.

What is your favorite guilty-pleasure treat?
Affogato with ice cream from Johnston Family Farm in Newborn, Georgia.

What most satisfies your sweet tooth?
Meringue cookies from Star Provisions.

What would you eat at your last meal, if you could plan such a thing?
A fresh egg.

Cheeseburger or foie gras?
This is not a fair question . . .

What's your favorite place (and what is your favorite thing to order) for:

Splurge meal?
Per Se in New York City.

A cup of coffee?
Stumptown cappuccino at the Ace Hotel New York.

A greasy-spoon meal?
Pastrami and rye and a side of mustard from Katz's Delicatessen in New York City.

Hamburger craving?
Abattoir in Atlanta.

Bread desire?
Acme Bread Company in San Francisco.

Blackbird

Paul Kahan's name figures heavily in every restaurant conversation in Chicago. It can't be helped—the man covers the waterfront. He is executive chef and partner at Avec, Big Star, Blackbird, the Publican, and soon, the Publican Butcher Shop. As I am the president of a meat plant, the author of a meat cookbook, and the cofounder of The Butchers Guild, our conversation melts easily into talk of carcasses and ranchers and the logistics of getting an animal from the field to the meat counter. Heaven. Kahan is obviously as excited by the minutiae as he is by the glory.

"We have a tradition here that on a cook's last day, they can prepare whatever they like for their last meal." Who is leaving today? I wonder. This meal has to be someone's fantasy. "We always have duck on the menu, so sometimes we have a bunch of legs left over," chef David Posey explains. This is the premise for Blackbird's iteration of chicken and waffles,

> ## OFF THE MENU
>
> Chicken-Fried Duck Legs
>
> Coleslaw
>
> Belgian Waffles
>
> Chess Pie
>
> *Suggested wine:*
> Francis Tannahill Dragonfly
> Gewurztraminer 2007

which is glorious. Any of the elements of this meal would be useful to master: perfect waffles ("There are two styles of waffles in Belgium," Kahan explains. This is the Liège, as opposed to the Brussels); braised and deep-fried duck legs, the technique for which could be applied to other poultry; mayonnaise-rich slaw; and, oh, the house-made syrup with braising liquids from the duck, which is so sweet and savory in the same instant that you want to keep going back to it.

Family meal is often an outlet for cooks to try something different from the menu. I ask if there have ever been any unsuccessful efforts in staff meals past. I am rewarded with a giggly reminiscence of "beef kneecaps," a gelatinous mess of fatty failure. While this supper is a departure from the nightly menu, the fastidiousness of the preparation is definitively Blackbirdian. This is superb Southern food, prepared by one of the best restaurants in the country.

TOP LEFT: Chef Paul Kahan operating as waffle quality controller.
BOTTOM RIGHT: Pastry chef Patrick Fahy catches up on news during his break.

Chicken-Fried Duck Legs

This meal is a reminder that techniques can go farther than their original intent. The pearl sugar in the waffles creates explosions of sweetness that spark in the richness of the duck legs and jus syrup. The coleslaw is a tangy mingler amongst the sweet and savory.

1 tablespoon fennel seed

4 bay leaves

10 sprigs thyme

2 tablespoons olive oil

4 whole duck legs, feet chopped off to expose the bone

1 head fennel, medium diced

1 onion, medium diced

3 stalks celery, medium diced

1 head garlic, peeled and smashed

Salt and freshly ground pepper

2 cups red wine

Chicken stock to cover duck legs, about 4 cups

About 1 cup maple syrup

2 cups all-purpose flour

2 cups cornstarch

2 tablespoons salt

1 teaspoon cayenne pepper

2 cups buttermilk

Canola oil for frying

Favorite hot sauce

Preheat your oven to 300°F. Make a bouquet garni: place the fennel seed, bay leaves, and thyme on a piece of cheesecloth, gather, and tie.

Heat the oil in a sauté pan large enough to hold legs in one layer over medium-high heat and brown the duck legs, skin side down, until almost burnt, about 10 to 15 minutes. Turn over and sear the meat side about 2 minutes. Remove from the pan and add the vegetables, bouquet garni, salt, and pepper. Cook for 3 to 5 minutes, stirring often, making sure to get no color on the vegetables and scraping the bottom of the pan to loosen the brown bits from the duck. When the vegetables are tender, add the wine, bring to a boil, lower the heat, and simmer about 5 minutes, to reduce the wine by half. Transfer the vegetables and wine to a baking dish and add the duck legs on top. Pour in stock so the legs are three-quarters covered. Cover the dish with foil and place in the oven. Braise until tender, about 1½ to 2 hours. Uncover, let cool, cover, and refrigerate overnight.

The next day, remove the top layer of fat, warm the braising liquid, and remove the duck legs. Strain the liquid and place in a pot. Reduce the liquid over medium heat to about 1 cup. Season with salt. Add an equal amount of maple syrup to the sauce. Keep warm while you fry the duck.

Mix flour, cornstarch, salt, and cayenne in a large container. Place buttermilk in another large container. Drain the braised duck legs of excess liquid, dredge in flour mixture, and tap off excess flour. Place the legs in the buttermilk and let them soak for 1 minute. Take the legs out of the buttermilk and drain off excess. Place the legs in flour again and coat. Remove from flour and shake off excess. Fry in a deep fryer or a pot of oil heated to 325°F until golden brown and crisp. Serve with Belgian Waffles and top wth Coleslaw and hot sauce.

Serves 4

—— Coleslaw ——

This coleslaw is the mortar for the waffles and chicken-fried duck legs. Or prepare it as a picnic apparatchik, loyal to any dish served on a lawn.

1 head green cabbage, thinly
  shredded
1 red onion, sliced thin
1 green apple, julienned
3 tablespoons granulated sugar
3 tablespoons apple cider vinegar
1 tablespoon celery seed
Salt
Mayonnaise

In a large bowl, mix all the ingredients except the mayonnaise. Let sit out for 3 hours to soften the vegetables. Drain off excess liquid and add mayonnaise to desired creaminess.

Serves 4 as a side

—— Belgian Waffles ——

Perfect Belgian waffles with the extravagance of pearl sugar. Make these on their own for brunch with sausages and syrup or preserves and a sprinkling of confectioners' sugar.

4 eggs
1¾ cups warm 100°F water
4 cups all-purpose flour
1½ teaspoons kosher salt
2 tablespoons granulated sugar
½ ounce fresh cake yeast
1¾ cups whole milk, 100°F
1¾ sticks unsalted butter,
  melted and cooled
Nonstick cooking spray
8 to 10 tablespoons pearl sugar
Confectioners' sugar, for topping

In a large bowl, whisk together the eggs and warm water. In a separate bowl, whisk together the flour, salt, and sugar. Add the yeast to the milk, stir to dissolve, and set aside. Whisk flour mixture into the egg mixture and stir until smooth. Whisk in the butter and stir to combine. Whisk in the milk mixture and stir. Pour the batter into a large plastic container and let it stand at room temperature until it starts to bubble and foam, about 10 to 45 minutes, depending on the room temperature.

Heat a waffle iron according to the manufacturer's instructions and spray with cooking spray. Ladle the batter into the waffle iron—it is better to overfill—and sprinkle about 1½ teaspoons of pearl sugar per waffle over all of the batter (this makes waffles extra crunchy). Close the iron and cook until golden brown and crunchy. Dust with the confectioners' sugar.

Makes 15 to 20 waffles

Chess Pie

A Southern dessert that some say gets its name from the old telephone game—turning "just pie" into "chess pie." This chess pie from pastry chef Patrick Fahy is not just pie, but the epitome of basic pieness: a buttery crust with a brown-sugar custard filling.

Piecrust

1 cup all-purpose flour

1⅓ sticks unsalted butter, cold and diced

⅛ teaspoon salt

⅓ cup ice water

Filling

½ cup granulated sugar

½ cup brown sugar

½ cup buttermilk

1 stick unsalted butter

2 whole eggs

2 egg yolks

1 tablespoon cornmeal

½ teaspoon freshly grated nutmeg

1 teaspoon apple cider vinegar, optional, to cut the sweetness

Put the flour, butter, and salt into a food processor and pulse until pea-sized pieces have formed. Gradually add ice water until the dough just comes together. Turn out onto a floured surface and wrap in plastic wrap. Let it rest for 1 hour, then roll out the dough into a circle slightly larger than your pie shell. Line the shell by pressing the dough into it. Don't forget to leave a little more crust than you think is necessary, as the dough will shrink when it bakes. Leave the pie shell in the freezer to chill.

Preheat the oven to 325°F. Combine all filling ingredients, including the optional vinegar, in a mixing bowl. Place the bowl in the top of a double boiler; whisk until smooth and warm, and the sugar has dissolved. Remove from heat and let cool for 10 minutes. Pour the mixture into the chilled pie shell and bake for 45 minutes or so, until the center is set and the top is golden brown. Transfer the pie to a rack and let cool before serving.

Serves 6 to 8

Paul Kahan

BLACKBIRD (CHICAGO, IL)

Paul Kahan's resume is bigger than this paragraph will allow, but in brief, he is the executive chef and partner at Blackbird as well as Avec, the Publican, Big Star, and soon, the Publican Butcher Shop. His restaurants are a food scene all their own.

What was your favorite food as a kid?
Grilled cheese with Jays potato chips stuffed inside.

What was the first meal you made that you were proud of?
Egg-and-cheese omelet.

What three adjectives describe your cuisine?
Seasonal, clean, and soulful.

What chef do you most admire?
Alice Waters.

What is your favorite ingredient?
Alliums—all kinds.

What music do you like to hear when you cook?
I own about 8,500 albums encompassing different musical styles. For example: Iggy Pop when I'm happy, Dexter Gordon on a rainy day, and Motörhead when I'm feeling feisty.

What is your favorite hangover meal?
Chilaquiles with eggs.

What is your favorite midnight snack?
Popcorn.

What restaurant in the world are you most dying to try?
Michel Bras in Laguiole, France.

What kitchen utensil is most indispensable to you?
Kuhn Rikon vegetable peeler.

Who do you most like to cook for?
My wife.

If you could do one other job, what would it be?
A mechanic—could be auto, airplane . . .

What do you most value in a sous chef?
Personal and professional integrity.

What food trend would you most like to erase from the annals of history?
The Food Network and "Celebrity Chefdom."

What one food would you take with you to a desert island?
Roasted chicken.

What is your favorite guilty-pleasure treat?
Double cheeseburger with grilled onions and crispy hash browns from the Diner Grill in Chicago.

What would you eat at your last meal, if you could plan such a thing?
Italian food from the Piedmont region.

Cheeseburger or foie gras?
Cheeseburger.

What's your favorite place (and what is your favorite thing to order) for:

A splurge meal?
Great Lake in Chicago.

A cup of coffee?
Intelligentsia on East Randolph Street in Chicago.

Groceries?
Green City Market in Chicago.

Kitchen equipment?
Northwestern Cutlery Supply in Chicago.

Ice cream?
Snookelfritz at the Green City Market in Chicago.

Chocolate?
Mindy's Hot Chocolate in Chicago.

Blue Hill at Stone Barns

TARRYTOWN, NY

Blue Hill at Stone Barns is situated within Stone Barns Center for Food and Agriculture, a not-for-profit working farm and education center promoting sustainable practices. The restaurant's menu is steeped in the same philosophical principles. When you dine there, the server will navigate the available ingredients and your proclivities, to help Chef Dan Barber and his kitchen prepare a meal that is, quite literally, just for you.

Staff meal at Blue Hill at Stone Barns is, in its own way, just as unique, aesthetic, and thoughtful. It takes place in a glass room that overlooks the pastoral grounds, with a long farm table that can always squeeze in one more. It is a table fit for a family wedding—or a restaurant staff of forty. Platters of fresh food are artfully arranged on an age-bowed wooden sideboard, and smartly dressed servers, managers, cooks, and busboys help themselves to whatever dishes the kitchen has prepared that day, just for them.

Staff meals are a perk of restaurant work, a natural gesture from a kitchen. But they are also an important time for the transmission of information. Once service begins, information from the front and back of the house passes from employee to employee like a game of telephone. At staff meal, the chef can tell everyone at one time what needs telling: menu details, new wines, VIP guests on the reservation list. A professional kitchen is like an emergency room with lower stakes: extremely fast-paced and dependent on constant prioritizing and re-prioritizing. Staff meal is a glorious lull.

At Blue Hill at Stone Barns, this lull takes place after much of the side work has been done. In the kitchen, this is called "prep." In the front of the house, it means setting tables, ironing tablecloths, executing details you might never specifically notice except that you will leave with a sense of exceptional care having been taken on your behalf.

After the ceremony of side work is mostly completed, the entire staff moves from solitary acts to a team priming for the guests. On Thursdays, family meal involves communing with Stone Barns Center's farmers and visiting wine purveyors and others that inform the meals. But every day offers vital information in a restaurant that demands a great deal of food knowledge and passion from every last person.

The day I visited, we ate a farm-driven meal of scrambled eggs with pesto, beet salad, and apple crisp. Rustic and simple, but perfect in the absolute diligence of technique.

OFF THE MENU

~

Scrambled Eggs
with Cured Meat "Ends"

Roast Beets with Pine Nuts,
Arugula, and Feta

Apple Crisp

Suggested wine:
Hermann J. Wiemer
Riesling 2009

Scrambled Eggs
with Cured Meat "Ends" and Pesto

If you can cook perfect scrambled eggs like Adam Kaye, the kitchen director, you need to cook little else. This dish illustrates the best way to do frugality: turn leftovers into a decadent meal using just a bit of technical prowess.

Winter Greenhouse Pesto

3 cups tightly packed salad greens such as arugula, chopped romaine leaves, and mache

2 cups roughly chopped herbs such as chives, parsley, and tarragon

½ clove garlic, minced

1 tablespoon pine nuts, very lightly toasted

1 tablespoon finely grated Parmesan cheese

1 cup grapeseed oil

Salt and freshly ground black pepper

8 eggs

½ cup heavy cream

Salt and freshly ground black pepper

½ tablespoon olive oil

1 cup small diced cured meat "ends" such as salami, coppa, speck, and pancetta

1 tablespoon unsalted butter

1 tablespoon chopped chives

Bring a large pot of well-salted water to a boil. Blanch the salad greens quickly and shock immediately in a bowl of ice water. When cool, remove and squeeze out all excess water. Roughly chop the blanched greens and place in the bowl of a blender with the herbs, garlic, pine nuts, and cheese. With the motor of the blender running on high speed, slowly add the oil until you have a thick green purée. Adjust seasoning with salt and pepper. Transfer the pesto to a container and refrigerate.

In a large bowl, beat the eggs with the cream. Lightly season with salt and pepper.

Heat the oil in a medium sauté pan over medium heat. Add diced meats and render for 10 minutes until crisp, stirring often. Add eggs directly to the pan, reduce the heat to low, and gently cook, stirring constantly, until the eggs coagulate into a creamy scramble. Stir in butter and chives and adjust seasoning with salt and pepper. Serve with the pesto.

Serves 6 to 8

Roast Beets with Pine Nuts, Arugula, and Feta

There is a lesson here that is useful to be reminded of again and again: let the ingredients be. The complexity in this salad comes from the conversation between quality ingredients, simply enhanced with a dash of flavorings.

2 pounds red beets, trimmed and washed

3 tablespoons olive oil

Freshly ground white pepper

1 tablespoon chopped shallots

2 tablespoons raspberry wine vinegar

1 tablespoon sherry vinegar

1 tablespoon good-quality maple syrup

1½ cups crumbled goat feta

¼ cup toasted pine nuts

3 cups baby arugula

Salt and freshly ground black pepper

Preheat the oven to 400°F. In a medium bowl, toss the beets with 1 tablespoon of olive oil and a generous sprinkling of salt and white pepper. Wrap beets together in aluminum foil and place on a baking sheet. Roast for about 1¼ hours, until the beets are tender. Remove them from the oven and cool. While still warm, peel the beets and chill.

Cut the beets into small wedges and toss with the shallots and remaining 2 tablespoons of olive oil, the vinegars, and maple syrup. Add the feta, pine nuts, and arugula, and mix gently. Season with salt and pepper and serve immediately.

Serves 6 to 8 as a side

Apple Crisp

A crisp is an apt expression of pantry cooking, which makes it a natural dessert for a staff meal. Though it is a forgiving and adaptive dish, you would do well to follow this version to the letter.

Apple Filling

2¼ pounds apples, peeled and cut
   into ½-inch dice
¼ cup chopped walnuts
⅓ cup granulated sugar
½ teaspoon cinnamon
⅛ cup rum raisins
⅛ cup dried figs

Crisp Topping

½ cup all-purpose flour
½ cup red fife flour
½ cup confectioners' sugar
1 stick unsalted butter, cut into ¼-inch cubes
3 tablespoons sliced almonds
Pinch of salt
¼ teaspoon ground cinnamon
¾ teaspoon vanilla extract

Preheat the oven to 375°F. In a medium bowl, combine the apple filling ingredients. Cover the bowl and allow to stand at room temperature for 30 minutes.

Put all the crisp topping ingredients in a medium bowl. Using fingertips, work the butter into the mix until it has a flaky consistency. Refrigerate for 30 minutes.

Transfer the fruit filling to a pie dish. Remove the topping mixture from the refrigerator and spread it evenly over the filling, breaking up the dough into small, grape-size pieces if necessary.

Bake for 30 minutes on the center rack of the oven until the crust is golden brown. Serve warm with ice cream, crème fraîche, or caramel sauce.

Serves 6 to 8

THE ESCOFFIER QUESTIONNAIRE

～ Dan Barber ～

BLUE HILL AT STONE BARNS (TARRYTOWN, NY)

Beyond the fervid success of two Blue Hill locations, Dan Barber is a very sharp and highly regarded public advocate for healthier food systems. His editorials appear regularly in the *New York Times* and he has spoken for audiences of import, such as the World Economic Forum, TED conference, and President Obama.

What was your favorite food as a kid?
"The Brookie"—half brownie, half cookie. My invention.

What was the first meal you made that you were proud of?
August of 1978—my first omelet.

What is your favorite ingredient?
Maybe a new breed of tomato, because they have to compete with everyone's idealization of heirlooms. There will always be a place for Brandywines and Green Zebras, but a great plant breeder can take the best genetics from those older varieties and make them even better.

What book most informs your food, cookbook or otherwise?
Margaret Visser's *Much Depends on Dinner.*

What chef do you most admire?
Michel Rostang. He's a brilliant chef from a whole line of brilliant chefs.

What music do you like to hear when you cook?
None.

What is your favorite midnight snack?
Before the drive home from Stone Barns, I reach for sweets, like handfuls of petits fours or cookies from the café. I crash about halfway to the city.

What kitchen utensil is most indispensable to you?
A spoon. I'm very particular about the spoons we use—both for plating the food, and for tasting it.

If you could do one other job, what would it be?
A bouquiniste—one of those street booksellers in Paris.

What do you most value in a sous chef?
I read that Warren Buffet once said: "In looking for people to hire, you look for three qualities: integrity, intelligence, and energy. And if they don't have the first, the other two will kill you." That's about right.

What food trend would you erase from the annals of history?
"Comfort food." All food should be comforting.

What one food would you take with you to a desert island?
GORP [Trail mix].

What would you eat at your last meal, if you could plan such a thing?
Pasta and tomato sauce, assuming I could also plan the season.

What's your favorite place (and what is your favorite thing to order) for:

Happy hour?
I just realized I've never been to a happy hour.

A greasy-spoon meal?
Los Dos Toros in the Denver Airport. If I have to have a layover, I want it there.

Bread desire?
Red fife brioche from Alex Grunert, Blue Hill pastry kitchen.

Bluestem

KANSAS CITY, MO

Bluestem is born of family. The owners, Colby and Megan Garrelts, are the chef and pastry chef, respectively. So it is fitting that their staff meal would have the love of a home-cooked gathering. It is, effectively, their own dinner table.

Bluestem is the first place you call for a big night out in Kansas City. The Bluestem menu is parsed into land and sea selections, so there is always a corner of cod or some scraps of scallops in the walk-in cooler for a seafood stew with some spunk. The coda to the meal is Milk Chocolate Trifle with Bananas, which must have been wrought from my most desirous dessert fantasies. Megan muses, "Dessert is nostalgia. It is a childhood romp through the candy store, the soda fountain, the ice cream parlor, or the cookie jar."

The Garrelts' restaurant has romance in it and the heft of their commitment to one another. Like any good marriage, it feels both eternal and ever-changing. This staff meal articulates the talents of both Colby and Megan and gives a peek into their cuisine.

OFF THE MENU

Tomato, Fennel and
Seafood Stew

Chocolate Banana Trifle

Suggested wine:
King Estate Signature
Pinot Gris 2009

Tomato, Fennel and Seafood Stew

Made from the trimmings left after preparing fish for Bluestem's dinner service, this stew is designed to bend and flex to the shortcomings of your seafood availability. Use what you have and let the citrus and fennel do the grunt work.

4 tablespoons olive oil

4 cloves garlic, peeled and smashed

2 onions, peeled and sliced

2 small fennel bulbs, trimmed and
   thinly sliced

2 cups white wine

2 cups orange juice

6 strips orange zest

¾ to 1 pound fingerling potatoes, sliced

Two 28-ounce cans whole peeled tomatoes,
   quartered, with juice

2 quarts seafood stock or clam juice

¾ to 1 pound shrimp, peeled and deveined

¾ to 1 pound cod, cut into 1-inch pieces

24 mussels, debearded and scrubbed

2 to 4 tablespoons crème fraîche

2 bunches Italian parsley, chopped

2 teaspoons lemon zest

Heat the olive oil in a large Dutch oven or heavy-bottomed pot over medium-high heat. Add the garlic, onion, and fennel and sauté until just brown, 5 to 10 minutes. Deglaze with the wine and reduce slightly. Add the orange juice, orange zest, potatoes, tomatoes with juice, and stock. Bring to a boil and simmer for about 30 minutes on medium-low heat. Add the shrimp and fish, and simmer for 3 minutes. Add the mussels; cover and steam until the shells open, about 3 minutes. Discard any unopened shells.

To serve, ladle the stew into individual bowls. Put a little crème fraîche on top, and garnish with parsley and lemon zest.

Serves 6 to 8

Chocolate Banana Trifle

A trifle is a composition of elements that requires no further baking, so it makes all the sense in the world to prepare it on those days when it is too hot to turn on the oven or too gorgeous outside to babysit a cake.

Chocolate Sponge Cake

⅓ cup cocoa powder

⅓ cup all-purpose flour

½ teaspoon ground cinnamon

¼ teaspoon ground cardamom

¼ teaspoon salt

9 eggs at room temperature, separated

1⅛ cups granulated sugar

2 tablespoons strong, hot coffee

For the chocolate sponge cake, preheat the oven to 325°F. Butter and line a jelly-roll pan with parchment paper. Sift the cocoa powder, flour, cinnamon, and cardamom together into a bowl. Add the salt and set aside.

In the bowl of a stand mixer fitted with a paddle attachment, beat the egg yolks on high speed until they achieve a thick ribbon state, approximately 5 minutes. Transfer the egg yolks to a larger bowl and set aside.

In a clean bowl of a stand mixer fitted with a whisk attachment, whip the egg whites on high speed until frothy, approximately 2 minutes. Add the sugar in a steady stream and continue beating until the egg whites form stiff—but not dry—peaks, approximately 3 minutes. Stir a dollop of the whipped egg whites into the egg yolks to lighten them. Gently fold the rest of the egg whites into the egg yolks in thirds, adding the coffee with the last third. Fold in the dry ingredients until well incorporated.

Pour the batter onto the parchment-lined jelly-roll pan and smooth the top with a large offset spatula. Slap the pan gently on the counter to get rid of any large air bubbles in the batter. Bake the cake for 12 minutes. It should be spongy and light. Cool the cake completely. Be careful not to touch the surface of the cake, which peels off easily.

continued on page 58

continued from page 57

Milk Chocolate and Banana Mousse
7 ounces dark chocolate
2 ounces milk chocolate
2 eggs plus 1 egg yolk
¼ cup granulated sugar
2 cups heavy cream, whipped to soft peaks
½ cup banana purée
¼ teaspoon cinnamon
2 teaspoons vanilla extract

Meringue
1 cup granulated sugar
½ cup egg whites

2 fresh, ripe bananas per serving, sliced
Sugar for coating

For the mousse, melt the chocolates over a double boiler; cool to room temperature. Whip the eggs, egg yolk, and sugar to ribbon stage until light in color and thick. Slowly incorporate the egg mixture into the chocolate in thirds. Fold the cream into the chocolate and eggs. Whisk together the banana purée with the cinnamon and vanilla. Fold into the chocolate mixture and chill to set. Transfer the mousse to a piping bag with a #4 tip and reserve until ready to assemble.

For the meringue, whisk together the sugar and egg whites in a double boiler or a heat-resistant bowl set over a low simmer until the sugar has dissolved and the mixture becomes frothy, about 3 minutes. Using a handheld electric mixer, whip the mixture on high speed until stiff peaks form, about 5 minutes. Transfer the meringue to a piping bag and use immediately.

To assemble: Using a ring cutter, slice the cake into rounds that will fit into individual glasses, or use one large glass serving bowl. Place one slice of cake on the bottom. Add to this a layer of sliced bananas and a layer of mousse; then add another layer of cake and more sliced bananas, and top with meringue. Using a small handheld torch, caramelize the meringue until it is light brown. Coat the remaining banana slices in granulated sugar, caramelize with the torch, and top the trifle with the caramelized bananas. Serve immediately.

Serves 4 to 6

Megan Garrelts and Colby Garrelts

BLUESTEM (KANSAS CITY, MO)

Colby and Megan Garrelts met in a five-star Chicago kitchen. Now their marriage lives most hours in the Bluestem kitchen, where they are co-owners and co-chefs, with Megan focusing on the dessert menu. They have received four stars from the *Kansas City Star*, a Best New Chefs nod from *Food & Wine*, and Colby has received five consecutive nominations for Best Chef Midwest from the James Beard Foundation.

What was your favorite food as a kid?
MG: Meatloaf and mashed potatoes.
CG: Spaghetti.

What was the first meal you made that you were proud of?
MG: Shake 'n Bake chicken.
CG: Thanksgiving turkey!

What three adjectives describe your cuisine?
MG: New varieties of American desserts.
CG: Clean, focused, fresh.

What book most influences your food, cookbook or otherwise?
MG: *The Last Course* by Claudia Fleming.
CG: Michel Bras' *Essential Cuisine.*

What chef do you most admire?
MG: Richard Leach/CG: Thomas Keller.

What is your favorite ingredient?
MG: Chocolate/CG: Fennel.

What music do you like to hear when you cook?
MG: Madonna/CG: Curtis Mayfield.

What is your favorite hangover meal?
MG: Brunch food.
CG: Chicken-fried steak.

What is your favorite midnight snack?
MG: Malt-O-Meal with brown sugar and raisins or other cereals.
CG: Chicken-fried steak.

What restaurant in the world are you most dying to try?
MG & CG: Michel Bras in Laguiole, France.

What kitchen utensil is most indispensable to you?
MG: Offset spatula and offset serrated knife/CG: Spoons.

If you could do one other job, what would it be?
MG: Veterinarian.
CG: Car builder.

What do you most value in a sous chef?
MG: Organization/CG: Silence.

What would you eat at your last meal, if you could plan such a thing?
MG: Osso buco with potatoes and green beans, and chocolate devil's food cake.
CG: Smoked pulled pork.

Cheeseburger or foie gras?
MG & CG: Cheeseburger.

What's your favorite place (and what is your favorite thing to order) for:

A splurge meal?
MG: Per Se in New York City.
CG: Alinea in Chicago.

Breakfast?
MG: Room 39 in Kansas City for quiche.
CG: Genessee Royale Bistro in Kansas City.

A late-night/after-work meal?
MG: Manifesto at the Rieger Hotel in Kansas City.

A cup of coffee?
MG & CG: Room 39 in Kansas City.

A greasy-spoon meal?
CG: Town Topic in Kansas City.

Ice cream?
MG & CG: Glacé in Kansas City.

Chocolate?
MG: Christopher Elbow Chocolates in Kansas City.

The Butcher & Larder

CHICAGO, IL

When I first met Rob and Allison Levitt two years ago, they were managing partners of a restaurant called Mado. They became so fastidious and passionate about bringing whole animals into their kitchen, and about working with the ranchers and farmers in the Chicago area, that their vision hardened into the diamond point of a butcher shop. Together they opened The Butcher & Larder in early 2011.

When the Levitts left Mado, they brought with them their relationships. The kitchen crew, the ranchers, and their customers all followed. The fourth wall of the kitchen has come down, and now customers who were diners can watch Rob breaking down a hindquarter of beef, preparing a brine or tying a roast. Customers are now part of the intimate camaraderie that forms among cooks who work long hours together under constant deadline. This amity generally takes the form of bawdy humor. It is warming to see this become part of the restaurant-customer relationship, rather than a hindrance to it. Finding that tableside talk always makes him feel self-consciously preening—something he is decidedly not—he warmed to his new counter role. I think Rob likes this part of his new life best of all: there is no back room or separation between the work and the presentation of the work.

One of the cooking lessons that comes through again and again in the making of staff meals is the thoughtful reuse of ingredients. This is as true at Butcher & Larder as it is in a restaurant. The butchering of meat leaves scraps or bits that can be made into ground meat or stew. Profitability—and ultimately, the survival of a butcher shop—often lies in the returns on those scraps, which can add up to half the edible weight of a side of beef.

The ground beef and stew meat are available in the meat counter, but the kitchen also prepares a daily sandwich, which elevates the less-valuable cuts and provides a creative outlet for the chef gene in the DNA of Butcher & Larder.

We ate our hot dog burgers with Jackson Coney sauce standing up behind the counter, talking about heavy metal and clowns and also about the successful integration of offal into the chili sauce. The meal was a playful use of some hot dog mix and other bits too scant to make it into the stuffer, which melded into a classic chili. And we chased it with a beer, us on one side of the counter, a contented customer on the other side, all having the same conversation.

OFF THE MENU

~

"Hot Dogs"
with Jackson Coney Sauce

Suggested beer:

Goose Island
Beer Company's
Willow Street Wit

"Hot Dogs"
with Jackson Coney Sauce

This is a gut bomb. But let's be honest, sometimes that is the only thing that will do. It is meaty and the Jackson Coney sauce has an old-fashioned appeal, with its high iron content and spice blend. The hot-dog mixture could actually become hot dogs, if you have a stuffer and a deep desire to impress everyone at the Fourth of July block party this year.

5 pounds lean beef, cubed
2 cloves garlic, finely minced
5 teaspoons sweet paprika
5 teaspoons smoked paprika
1¼ teaspoons ground clove
2 teaspoons powdered ginger
Salt
1 pound finely crushed ice
3 tablespoons olive oil
Yellow mustard, for topping
Diced white onion, for topping

Jackson Coney Sauce
2 pounds ground beef heart
2 tablespoons olive oil
1½ teaspoons cumin
1½ teaspoons chili powder
1½ teaspoons garlic powder
1½ teaspoons paprika
½ teaspoon salt

Grind the beef through the fine holes of a meat grinder. Mix in the garlic and spices, season with a little salt, and grind again through the fine holes. Mix in an electric mixer with the paddle for three minutes. Add the crushed ice and paddle until ice is emulsified and the mix is about 55°F. To taste, roll a small bit of the mixture in plastic and poach in simmering water. Taste and adjust salt. Set the mixture in the refrigerator.

Meanwhile, make the chili sauce. Grind the beef heart on medium grind. Heat the oil in a skillet over medium heat until shimmering. Add the meat and cook until light gray, about ten minutes. Add the spices, salt, and enough water to keep it very moist, like gravy surrounding the meat. Simmer for 1 to 2 hours, adding water regularly to keep the mixture loose.

When the chili is done, remove the hot-dog mixture from the fridge and form the meat into hamburger-size patties. Heat the oil in a large pan over high heat and fry the "hot dog patties" until brown and cooked through, about 3 minutes on each side. Serve patties in hamburger buns, topped with chili sauce, yellow mustard, and diced white onion.

Serves 12 to 16

～ Rob Levitt ～

THE BUTCHER & LARDER (CHICAGO, IL)

Rob Levitt and his wife, Allison, kissed the kitchen good-bye to open a butcher shop with a chef's perspective: locally raised meat cut to order, along with house-made sausages and cured meats. Before owning Mado, his last restaurant, Rob worked at Del Toro, North Pond, and 312 Chicago, as well as Park Avenue Café in New York.

What was your favorite food as a kid?
My mom's burgers and pizza at Barnaby's in Niles, Illinois.

What was the first meal you made that you were proud of?
An omelet for my dad.

What three adjectives describe your cuisine?
We don't really have a particular "cuisine," but I like to describe our goods as honest, responsible, and sustainable.

What book most influences your food, cookbook or otherwise?
Paul Bertolli's *Cooking by Hand*.

What chef do you most admire?
I most admire the small community of Chicago chefs that are really trying to be local and sustainable all year round.

What is your favorite ingredient?
I'm obsessed with unusual cuts of beef.

What music do you like to hear when you cook?
We listen to a variety of music in the shop. Everyone can add to the playlist. Personally, I listen to a lot of the Decemberists, but you are just as likely to hear KRS-1, Rush, or Motörhead.

What is your favorite hangover meal?
Pozole at Lula Café in Chicago.

What is your favorite midnight snack?
Ice cream, cold pizza, or left-over Chinese.

What kitchen utensil is most indispensable to you?
Boning knife.

If you could do one other job, what would it be?
Stay-at-home dad.

What do you most value in a sous chef?
The ones that really listen to me.

What food trend would you most like to erase from the annals of history?
Bacon. Just let it be bacon.

What one food would you take with you to a desert island?
Anything my wife baked. Seriously.

What is your favorite guilty-pleasure treat?
A Reese's Peanut Butter Cup milkshake from Baskin-Robbins.

What would you eat at your last meal, if you could plan such a thing?
A bit of really good country ham (probably from Benton's Hams out of Madisonville, Tennessee), some good bread, and lots of my wife's desserts.

Cheeseburger or foie gras?
Cheeseburger!

What's your favorite place (and what is your favorite thing to order) for:

Happy hour?
Goose Island Brewpub in Chicago.

A splurge meal?
Nightwood in Chicago, for everything!

Pastry?
Floriole Café and Bakery in Chicago, for croissants.

A late-night/after-work meal?
Avec in Chicago, for anything I haven't tried yet.

A cup of coffee?
If I have beans at home from Metropolis Coffee Company in Chicago, then I like to make it myself and bring the wife a cup.

A greasy-spoon meal?
Kuma's Corner in Chicago for a Kuma Burger with bacon, cheddar, and a fried egg, or a Solace—ten-ounce patty, braised sweet onions, bacon, and Gruyère on toasted rye.

Groceries?
I like to hit the Green City Market in downtown Chicago and see what the farmers are selling that day.

Chocolate?
Amadei chocolates from Tuscany.

Camino

Long before I'd ever enjoyed a meal at Camino, it was one of those places that kept turning up in my most intimate circles. *Meatpaper*, a magazine I help edit, once held a raucous cocktail and hors d'oeuvres shindig there, serving up crepinettes and other delicacies unrecognizable to any spell-checker and most eaters. I had also run into Camino in a field 45 miles north of the restaurant, at Green String Farm in Sonoma County, which has long operated in the vanguard of sustainability. I worked there in exchange for bags of produce, and met one of Camino's cooks and fellow volunteers, Kristen, who still travels those 45 miles once a week, every week, to spend a day working on the farm and gathering greens for the restaurant.

I collided with Camino yet again through friends who are Chez Panisse alums. Chez (shortened in the Bay Area foodie vernacular to its first word) is almost a college for a certain kind of idealistic young cook, ingredient driven and source savvy. Russell Moore (shortened to Russ in the Bay Area foodie vernacular), now chef/owner of Camino with his wife, Allison, was once the chef at Chez Panisse's Café. This makes him foodie-famous, and as I recently discovered firsthand,

> ## OFF THE MENU
>
> —
>
> Baked Clams with Chilies, Saffron, and Tomatoes
>
> Fried Farro with Dark Greens
>
> Honeycomb Candy
>
> *Suggested wine:*
> Unti Vineyards Rosé 2010

chef-famous. During my travels to make this book, chefs prodded me with more questions about Camino than any other restaurant I was profiling.

This curiosity is mainly not about Russ's pedigree or the farm-plucked meat and produce. It's about fire. Camino cooks their food over an open flame. Not like a pizza oven or a barbecue pit, but like a medieval fireplace in a large inn. "Alice [Waters] asked me if I knew how I was going to make it work. 'Yes, of course,' I told her. But I really didn't. I had planned and practiced but we weren't totally sure how we would handle busy nights."

It works brilliantly. The coals are in the center, radiating extreme heat. If there are more dishes than the middle pile of coals can reach, the coals are distributed more diffusely. When people tend a fire, they form a connection with it. We have all seen the fiendish observation of someone charged with warming the hearth or starting up the barbecue. This primal cooking adds a sheen of respect to anything that comes out of Camino's kitchen.

"We don't have crap here. We don't serve crap and we don't eat crap," says Russ, regarding the

relationship of the staff meal to the food served to guests. The pre-service buffet is made up of thirteen dishes: some just a few servings of a left-over dish, some served on heat-cracked dishware, some guilty pleasures ("We used to joke about French toast fingers but now it is one of the favorites."). The staff can order any drink off the menu, alcoholic or not, but it must be prepared just as finely as it would be for a guest. This functions as practice for service, but it's also a display of respect for the employees. In almost every shot of a kitchen staff eating in this book, you will see Tupperware filled with drinks, many with name tags taped to the sides. Nowhere else did I see cooks sitting down with tea service or a cocktail in a thin-stemmed 1940s-style martini glass.

The evening before, I'd had dinner at Camino with a friend and our dates, for a pre-Valentine's Day celebration (eat well, toast to love, and above all, avoid crowds and pink balloons). We tasted almost everything on the menu between us, seated beneath candlelit chandeliers and amidst other diners at the long, festive communal tables. Sitting at a family meal the next afternoon, with the restaurant almost empty and the sunlight gushing in, surrounded by Camino's lively staff and plates heaped with resplendent food, it felt every bit the feast as the previous night.

Baked Clams
with Chilies, Saffron, and Tomatoes

Camino makes this recipe with their own canned tomatoes, which is a glorious touch, if you get around to canning in late summer. This dish creates a spicy broth that begs to be sopped with the grilled bread and is well suited to sharing with friends who are close enough to not mind you dipping into the serving bowl.

1 spring onion or ½ bunch scallions

2 sprigs oregano

2 sprigs mint

2 chihuacle chilies, or substitute espelette, guajillo, or ancho

2 tablespoons olive oil

Small pinch of salt

2 bay leaves

4 cloves garlic, sliced thinly

Small pinch of saffron

1 cup chopped tomato

2 pounds manila or other small clams

½ cup white wine

Grilled bread

Slice the spring onion on the bias into large pieces (use all the green part if it looks good). Pick the leaves off of the oregano and mint and set aside. Mince or grind the chilies coarsely in a spice grinder.

Preheat the oven to 475°F. Heat a large sauté pan and add the olive oil, spring onion, and salt. Cook the spring onion over medium-high heat until it begins to brown slightly and soften, about 3 to 5 minutes. Add the bay leaves, garlic, chilies, and saffron. Continue cooking until the onion is soft, another 5 minutes. Add the oregano, mint, and tomato, and continue cooking over high heat. Fry the tomato for about 5 minutes, letting some of it stick to the pan, as this will improve the sauce. Once you have some color in the pan, add the clams, wine, and a splash of water.

Place the pan in the oven and cook until all the clams open up, about 5 to 10 minutes. Taste and adjust salt, and serve with plenty of grilled bread to mop up the sauce.

Serves 4

Fried Farro with Dark Greens

Farro Piccolo is only milled by Anson Mills, a cherished South Carolina source of grains. You can order it from their website, or find another farro varietal in your neck of the woods. This preparation is like fried rice but with all the nutritional robustness of farro.

1 cup Anson Mills
    farro piccolo
1 bunch dark greens: collard, kale, or
    broccoli rabe
3 tablespoons olive oil
1 spring onion or
    ½ bunch scallions
1 stalk green garlic or
    2 cloves garlic
A handful of fresh herbs: savory, marjoram,
    basil, anise hyssop

Preheat the oven to 375°F. Spread the dry farro on a sheet pan and toast it until a little brown, about 10 minutes. Toasting the farro will enhance the flavor.

Coarsely chop the dark greens. In a medium saucepan, bring 3 cups of water to a boil and add the greens. Cook over high heat for 5 to 8 minutes, drain, and set aside.

Combine the toasted farro with 2½ cups salted water in the saucepan. Bring to a boil, lower to a simmer, cover, and cook for 20 to 30 minutes. The cooking time will vary according to the variety of farro, whether there is some or all of the husk still on, and how long ago the farro was harvested. Drain the farro.

Heat a medium cast-iron skillet or other heavy-bottomed pan over a medium flame. Add 2 tablespoons of the olive oil, the spring onion, and garlic. Stir-fry for a few minutes, until the onion is just tender and beginning to brown. Add the farro along with the remaining tablespoon of oil and continue to fry to encourage browning, constantly stirring to avoid burning, about 6 or 7 minutes. After the farro is fried, add the herbs and about 2 cups (or more) of the cooked greens and warm through. Serve immediately. For a complete meal, serve farro with poached eggs or grilled or roasted meat.

Serves 4

Honeycomb Candy

This candy captures the earthy sweetness of the hive, which can instantly bring you back to a summer afternoon, real or imagined. It comes out in sheets of a caramely russet shade with a sheen. Chef Russell Moore suggests serving it with chocolate, which sounds almost too delicious.

1½ cups organic unbleached sugar
2 tablespoons honey
2 tablespoons agave syrup
1 tablespoon baking soda

Mix ¼ cup water, sugar, honey, and agave in a tall stockpot (be sure to use a tall pot as the mixture will bubble up when the baking soda is added). Wipe down the sides of the pot with a pastry brush dipped in water to unstick any sugar granules. Bring the mixture to a boil, insert a candy thermometer, and cook until the temperature reaches 300°F, stirring as little as possible. At 300°F, turn off the heat and carefully stir in the baking soda slowly, making sure to break up any lumps.

Pour the mixture onto a sheet pan lined with a Silpat or other silicone nonstick baking mat. Cool to room temperature, break into chunks, and store in an airtight container. The candy should keep for about 1 week.

Makes 14 ounces of candy

THE ESCOFFIER QUESTIONNAIRE

∼ Russell Moore ∼

CAMINO (OAKLAND, CA)

Russell Moore is executive chef and co-owner of Camino with his wife, Allison Hopelain. After 21 years at Chez Panisse, perhaps the most famous restaurant in the world, it is no simple effort to create food that exceeds all expectations.

What was your favorite food as a kid?
I always liked a giant bowl of wonton soup with lots of char siu in it.

What was the first meal you made that you were proud of?
I used to really gussy up the ole Rice-A-Roni with a fried egg, scallions, and Spam.

What three adjectives describe your cuisine?
Delicate, subtle, and partially burnt.

What book most influences your food, cookbook or otherwise?
Auberge of the Flowering Hearth by Roy Andries De Groot.

What chef do you most admire?
Tony Brush, Suzanne Goin, and Chris Bianco.

What is your favorite ingredient?
Scallions and chervil.

What music do you like to hear when you cook?
Nick Cave and the Bad Seeds (mostly the sad and dreary songs), Thin Lizzy, the Minutemen, and Bollywood soundtracks.

What is your favorite hangover meal?
Leftover paella with a poached egg.

What is your favorite midnight snack?
Vegetable-and-crackling-duck sandwich from staff meal at Camino.

What restaurant in the world are you most dying to try?
Every weird, single-dish-specialized restaurant in Korea.

What kitchen utensil is most indispensable to you?
Chinese ladle and sand pot (they work really well in the fire).

What do you most value in a sous chef?
Forward thinking, direct, not an ass-kisser.

What food trend would you most like to erase from the annals of history?
Plastic-bag cookery.

What one food would you take with you to a desert island?
Kimchee fried rice with an egg and lots of seaweed.

What is your favorite guilty-pleasure treat?
Tacos from great little places with questionable meat.

What most satisfies your sweet tooth?
Chunks of chocolate.

What would you eat at your last meal, if you could plan such a thing?
An epic Chinese banquet with foods I've never even heard of.

Cheeseburger or foie gras?
Honestly, I'm not so big on either.

What's your favorite place (and what is your favorite thing to order) for:

Happy hour?
I'm at Camino during happy hour. I'll be drinking Pu'er or Dragonwell tea.

A splurge meal?
Mission Chinese Food in San Francisco for a banquet!

Pastry?
Éclair from Tartine Bakery in San Francisco.

A late-night/after-work meal?
Ippuku in Berkeley for porridge and shochu.

A cup of coffee?
Tea. Lishan oolong from Far Leaves Tea in Berkeley.

Groceries?
Rainbow Grocery co-op in San Francisco.

Kitchen equipment?
Kamei Restaurant Supply in San Francisco for sand pots, Chinese ladles, and tea strainers.

Ice cream?
Ici Ice Cream in Berkeley.

Chocolate?
TCHO in San Francisco.

Cinque Terre

Cinque Terre is named after a coastal string of five fishing villages in the Italian Riviera. The restaurant, like much of the Slow Food movement, which originated in Italy, is a pearl formed around the grain of sand that is the Italian relationship to food. Cook what grows near you, in the season that it grows, learn from the old folks, don't waste, and please enjoy yourself. Chef Lee Skawinski is rightly praised for bringing small-town Italy to an American restaurant.

The scallops and lentils recipe served at Cinque Terre's staff meal could be at home on any Ligurian dinner table. The lentils with greens is a staple of all seasons in my home. Searing a few scallops makes the meal guest-worthy without adding more than a few minutes to the preparation. You could also plunk a few fat sausages on the lentils. In summer, I increase the ratio in favor of greens and I use whatever leafy produce looks most promising or fleeting from the farmers' market.

Chef Lee Skawinski's food, not excluding this recipe, is Ligurian without ornate conceit. In America, using local produce and protein is a novelty, not a practice. This recipe reminds me that the art of eating well is in no small measure the art of taking in the world around you, with pleasure.

OFF THE MENU

Seared Scallops
with Lentils and Spinach

Suggested wine:
A to Z Wineworks
Oregon Chardonnay 2005

Seared Scallops
with Lentils and Spinach

This has the primal element of a good dinner to serve guests: you can take a break and have a drink with your company once preparations are done and your lentils are simmering. You only need pop back in the kitchen for five minutes before serving. And scallops in season deserve a dinner party.

6 tablespoons olive oil
1 cup carrots, small diced
1 cup onion, small diced
1 cup celery, small diced
3 cloves garlic, chopped
3 cups lentils, triple rinsed
3 to 4 cups vegetable or
 mushroom stock
3 tablespoons apple cider vinegar
3 teaspoons chopped fresh herbs:
 chive, rosemary, parsley, and/or sage
Salt and freshly ground black pepper
6 slices bacon, cut into ½-inch pieces
3 shallots, chopped
1½ pounds spinach
2 pounds scallops

Add 2 tablespoons of the olive oil to a medium sauté pan and sauté carrot, onions, celery, and garlic over medium-high heat for 1 minute. Add the lentils and 3 cups of the stock, bring to a boil, cover and simmer until tender, about 25 to 35 minutes, adding more stock if necessary. To finish, add the cider vinegar, herbs, salt, and pepper; stir, cover, and set aside.

Sauté the bacon and shallots in a large sauté pan over medium heat until the bacon is crisp. Add, spinach until wilted, 4 to 5 minutes. Season with salt and pepper.

Season the scallops with salt and pepper. In a medium sauté pan heat 2 tablespoons of the olive oil over medium-high heat and sear the scallops for 2 or 3 minutes. Turn over and cook another minute. Remove from the heat—residual heat will finish cooking scallops.

To serve, divide the lentils into equal portions on six plates. Place sautéed spinach and bacon on top of lentils and top with the scallops. Drizzle with a bit of olive oil and serve immediately.

Serves 6

Commander's Palace

Commander's Palace is one of the most famous restaurants in the world. The grace with which they walked me through their seven dining rooms and the gardens made it seem almost choreographed. They are experts in sharing their story, as they are interviewed almost every day. The building is an ode to New Orleans' Garden District, a place that makes you sentimental for it, even in its presence.

Dottie Brennan is the matriarch of the family that has owned the restaurant since the 1970s, the latest in a legacy that is as old as New Orleans. Both Commander's Palace and Louisiana got their start in the 1880s and the lore in these walls is as thick as smoke. Dottie's sister Ella ran the restaurant until she died. I'm having my staff meal at Ella's table, which is a small booth in the kitchen where Ella could oversee the operation and hold meetings or taste a sauce. Not just anybody would get a seat at Ella's table; though as I charge through my serving of grillades and grits, I have to imagine the standards have loosened. The grits remind you that cooking well is not about fine dining. These grits are country food, but they are not any less complex for their heartiness. They are perfect. Grillades is fried pork that comes to New Orleans by

OFF THE MENU

Grillades and Grits

Pain Perdu
(or French Toast)

Suggested wine:
Plumpjack Winery
Cabernet Sauvignon 2008

way of Haiti and at Commander's Palace is served in a silky gravy.

With such a long timeline, the stories are not of one narrative, they're as varied as New Orleans itself. I hear about Ella's parents forbidding her to cycle past Commander's Palace as a little girl—long before her family owned it—because there was a high-brow brothel in the upstairs rooms; and about George Rico, who worked at Commander's Palace for forty years and was in Guinness World Records for receiving the largest known tip ever, of $40,000. I am told that the stuffed birds on the walls of the main dining room echo the Garden District tradition of having aviary wallpaper; and that locals used to will their jackets to the restaurant—which had a sport-coat dress code for the dining room—to supply any who arrived at dinner without one.

Each room feels like it exists now and also in some other time. It almost makes me feel like a well-fed ghost, the past more corporeal than the present. But things are still changing here; it is not a museum. After Katrina, the dress code was lightened so that jackets were no longer required. It is a rare dignity that remains constant, not the wallpaper.

TOP RIGHT: Nancy Pham delivers the balloons that festoon the coatroom every day of the year.
BOTTOM: Chef Tory McPhail eats in the usual chef manner, standing up in the kitchen.

Grillades and Grits

This Creole dish is a New Orleans brunch perennial. Like so many of my very favorite dishes, it was created to make use of cheaper, tougher cuts of meat. Tenderness is achieved by pounding and braising the meat. The creamy grits take on the flavor of the sauce and are satisfying enough to make up for less meat in the lean times.

2 pounds pork or veal cutlets,
   about 1 ounce each
1 cup all-purpose flour
Salt and freshly ground black pepper
1 stick unsalted butter
3 medium red bell peppers, julienned
3 stalks celery, cut thin on the bias
2 medium onions, thinly sliced
15 cloves garlic, thinly sliced
1 quart veal stock or chicken broth
2 large tomatoes, peeled, seeded,
   and chopped
8 cups milk
2 cups grits
1 bunch green onions, thinly sliced

Pound the cutlets into ¼-inch-thick pieces. Add the flour to a large bowl and season with salt and pepper. Dredge the medallions in the flour mixture, shake off excess flour, and set aside in another bowl. Reserve the flour.

Heat a large heavy-bottomed pot or Dutch oven over high heat and add 2 tablespoons of the butter. Brown the butter without burning, about 2 minutes. Add a quarter of the meat to the pot and cook 2 to 2½ minutes, until brown. Turn the meat over and brown the other side, about 1½ minutes. Remove the meat and scrape the bottom of the pan with a wooden spoon. Repeat with the rest of the meat in batches, adding 2 or more tablespoons of butter for each batch. Set aside.

Add peppers, celery, onions, and garlic to the pot. Stir, scraping the bottom of the pot with a wooden spoon, and season with salt and pepper. Cover and cook for about 8 minutes or until vegetables start to become tender and brown.

Add ¼ cup of the reserved seasoned flour to the vegetables. Stir and cook for about 1½ minutes, or until all the liquid is absorbed and the vegetables start turning darker brown, occasionally scraping the bottom with the wooden spoon. This will cook the flour and lend color to your sauce.

Add the stock; stir, scraping the bottom with the spoon. Bring to a boil, add the meat, and return to the boil. Add tomatoes, bring to a boil, and then lower the heat to a slow simmer. Taste to adjust seasoning, and cook for about 30 to 45 minutes, until the meat is tender and the sauce coats the back of a spoon.

While the meat is simmering, prepare the grits. In a large saucepan over high heat, bring the milk, seasoned with salt and pepper, to a simmer, stirring occasionally with a whisk. Be careful not to let the milk boil over or scorch. Gradually whisk in the grits until well blended with the milk. Boil the mixture for about 2 minutes. Adjust the seasoning, turn down the heat, and simmer for 2 to 3 minutes, whisking frequently, until the grits become thick. Cover, turn off the heat, and let rest for 10 minutes. Stir in 2 tablespoons of butter and season with salt and pepper.

To serve, add 4 pieces of meat to each plate with a generous amount of vegetables and sauce, and a serving of grits. Sprinkle with green onions.

Serves 8

Pain Perdu
(or French Toast)

The French call it "lost bread," because it ennobles stale bread. Not only is it a good use for two-day-old bread, but French toast made with stale bread is also actually better, by virtue of being lighter. Commander's Palace suggests topping it with honey melted into butter; or go *traditionnellement*: dust with confectioners' sugar and serve with a pot of preserves.

1 dozen eggs

1 cup milk

1 tablespoon vanilla extract

⅓ cup packed brown sugar

1 tablespoon ground cinnamon

½ teaspoon ground nutmeg

Salt and freshly ground black pepper

4 tablespoons unsalted butter

16 slices day-old French bread,
   cut ¾-inch thick on the bias

¼ cup confectioners' sugar

½ cup cane syrup, molasses, or honey butter

In a large bowl, whisk the eggs. Add the milk and vanilla, and whisk until well combined. In a separate bowl, mix the sugar, cinnamon, nutmeg; season with salt and pepper and mix. Add to the egg mixture and whisk until well combined.

In a nonstick sauté pan, melt 1 tablespoon of butter over high heat. Place 4 pieces of bread in the egg mixture. Let soak for 5 seconds, flip over and soak a few more seconds. Hold the pieces over the bowl to drain excess. When the butter starts to turn brown and coats the bottom of the pan, about 2 minutes, place bread slices in the pan and turn the heat down to medium high. Cook for 1 to 1½ minutes on each side, until golden brown and heated through.

Remove the French toast from the pan and place in a warm area. Wipe the pan with a paper towel and cook the next batch of slices; repeat until all the bread has been cooked. Dust with confectioners' sugar and serve immediately with syrup, molasses, or honey butter.

Serves 8

⌣ Tory McPhail ⌣

COMMANDER'S PALACE (NEW ORLEANS, LA)

Chef Tory McPhail doesn't rest on the laurels of one of America's most popular and venerated restaurants. Gayot considers it one of the forty best restaurants in the United States while under McPhail's reign.

What was your favorite food as a kid?
Corndogs.

What three adjectives describe your cuisine?
Fresh, fun, and exciting.

What book most influences your food, cookbook or otherwise?
All of chef John Folse's books.

What chef do you most admire?
Mario Batali.

What is your favorite ingredient?
The "Holy Trinity" (onions, celery, and green bell peppers), and garlic—they are the backbone of all our Creole recipes.

What music do you like to hear when you cook?
I listen to reggae on Sunday afternoons with an ice-cold Red Stripe.

What is your favorite hangover meal?
Definitely a bacon cheeseburger with a loaded baked potato from Port of Call down on Esplanade Avenue in New Orleans.

What is your favorite midnight snack?
Triscuits or pretzels.

What restaurant in the world are you most dying to try?
El Bulli in Spain.

What kitchen utensil is most indispensable to you?
A Vita-Prep blender.

Who do you most like to cook for?
The Brennan family.

If you could do one other job, what would it be?
I'd be a professional fishing guide in the Florida Keys.

What do you most value in a sous chef?
Commitment to excellence in every detail.

What food trend would you most like to erase from the annals of history?
Foam, foam, foam. Foam sucks!

What one food would you take with you to a desert island?
Citrus.

What is your favorite guilty-pleasure treat?
Coconut rum.

What most satisfies your sweet tooth?
Butterfinger candy bars.

What would you eat at your last meal, if you could plan such a thing?
Dude . . . seriously? That's depressing.

Cheeseburger or foie gras?
Cheeseburger.

What's your favorite place (and what is your favorite thing to order) for:

Happy hour?
A Caribbean Painkiller at Foxy's on Jost Van Dyke, British Virgin Islands.

A splurge meal?
Per Se in the Time Warner Building in New York City. I eat everything.

Breakfast?
Bananas Foster French Toast at Another Broken Egg Cafe in Destin, Florida.

A greasy-spoon meal?
Dot's Diner on Jefferson Highway, in Jefferson, Louisiana.

Groceries?
Rouse's—our friendly neighborhood supermarket.

Kitchen equipment?
Caire Hotel and Restaurant Supply in New Orleans.

Comme Ça

Comme Ça may have the coolest dining room in Los Angeles. The designer, Chris Barrett, has taken chef and owner David Myers's French bistro and reflected it through the looking glass. Chef Myers's food is less fanciful than fantastic and more bistro than tea party; but the combination of design and degustation works harmoniously.

Part of the elevation of the classic bistro look is the main hallway, which has a chalkboard, like any old brasserie, but stretched out to take over a wall. Instead of being limited to the specials of the day, it is smattered with quotes about relishing the carnal pleasures of the plate and a diagram of a pig and all its parts and other reifications of the bistro.

Our dinner of fried chicken, mashed potatoes, greens, and brownies was a treat beyond the obvious—I was operating under the misapprehension that people in LA don't eat. The plates were scraped clean, which was reassuring. It is a comfort to know that even servers/actresses are powerless against buttermilk-soaked, deep-fried chicken thighs. With a meal like this, there is the narrative arc of the feast: anticipation, consummation, lull of digestion. In the dark-walled back dining room, we lingered a moment too long with greasy lips and crumb-covered laps.

David Myers has an enviable French culinary resume, from Les Crayères, a three-Michelin-star restaurant in Reims, France, to Daniel in New York. Comme Ça, which has another location in Las Vegas, could just be a blown-up version of the French standard, but it relies more on the spirit than the template. Buying locally raised produce and conscientiously farmed protein, Myers translates the importance of ingredients, as well as technique, of the French plate. Great ingredients are something that were long ignored in American fine dining. Though we all hear about the farmers' market approach of many chefs now, it is still a relative rarity and a harder row to hoe for restaurants—it deserves accolades and appreciation.

If, like me, you grew up in a home that never deep-fried anything, this will be a Pandora's Box for you. If you are an old hand at this Southern classic, then you will appreciate Myers's version. It is as good as it gets in flavor and texture, well-spiced and moist with a perfect crunch on the exterior. The mashed potatoes are simple—add a big salad with a tart dressing and call it a picnic.

OFF THE MENU

Buttermilk Fried Chicken

Mashed Potatoes

Brownies

Suggested wine:
Porter-Bass Estate
Chardonnay 2008

Buttermilk Fried Chicken

This is a moist and piquant version of one of the most classic American recipe. You are well served to let the chicken soak up the buttermilk and spice mix overnight. Fried preparations like this are best enjoyed right out of the fryer, but this holds up well chopped in a salad or cold later in the day.

2 whole chickens, or 16 pieces chicken: drums, thighs, wings, and/or breasts

Kosher salt

¼ cup smoked paprika

2 tablespoons garlic powder

2 teaspoons cayenne

4 cups buttermilk

Flour for dredging

Peanut or canola oil for frying

Cut each whole chicken into 8 pieces. (Reserve the backbone to make chicken stock for another use.) Evenly salt the chicken with a light layer of kosher salt and let sit for 20 minutes. In a small bowl, combine the smoked paprika, garlic powder, and cayenne; evenly distribute this mixture over the chicken. Next, place the chicken in a large sealable container, pour the buttermilk over it, and use your hands to gently mix until the chicken is fully coated. Seal the container and let it sit in the refrigerator for 24 to 36 hours.

The next day, drain off the excess buttermilk. Set up two sheet pans with wire racks and put some flour for dredging in a large bowl. Completely coat each piece of chicken with flour and set on the wire racks. Let the chicken sit for 20 minutes, until the seasoned buttermilk coating has absorbed most of the flour. Coat each piece of chicken once more with the flour and set back on the wire racks.

Fill a deep fryer or large cast-iron pot with oil—the oil must be deep enough so that you can completely submerge the chicken pieces being fried. Heat the oil over medium-high heat to 325°F. Place the chicken in the oil in batches, being careful not to overcrowd. Fry each batch for about 7 minutes until golden, and drain on clean wire racks over sheet pans lined with paper towels. Once all the chicken has been fried, heat the oil to 355°F and fry in batches once more for 2½ minutes per batch, until golden brown. (Interior of chicken should read 165°F on a meat thermometer.) Place the chicken on the wire racks again to drain.

Serves 6 to 8

Mashed Potatoes

These are classic mashed potatoes, which set the scene for main dishes that are spicy and rich in proteins. If you want to make them more of a centerpiece by adding cheese or herbs, do so at the end, right after the cream and butter and before the salt and pepper.

6 Yukon gold potatoes
1 cup heavy cream
1 stick butter, room temperature
Salt and freshly ground black pepper

Peel and medium dice the potatoes. Submerge diced potatoes in a pot of salted water. Bring to a boil and reduce heat to simmer; cook until a knife can easily pierce the potato, about 15 to 20 minutes. Drain the potatoes and mash using a food mill, a potato ricer, or by hand. Once mashed, place them back in the pot over low heat. Add the cream, butter, salt, and pepper and combine. Serve immediately.

Serves 6 to 8 as a side

Brownies

Perfectly balanced betwixt cake and fudge, the brownie is after-school in edible form—a sense memory of the freest moment of a kid's day. You can ratchet up the complexity of these with your favorite chocolate, though good old Toll House does the trick, too.

3 eggs

1⅓ cups brown sugar, tightly packed

1 tablespoon vanilla extract

1¾ sticks European butter

10 ounces dark chocolate (at least 70 percent), or about 1½ cups chocolate chips, divided

¾ cup all-purpose flour

1½ teaspoons baking powder

¼ teaspoon salt

Whisk the eggs, sugar, and vanilla extract in a stand mixer on medium speed until pale in color (about 5 minutes). Melt the butter and half of the chocolate in the top of a double boiler. Sift the dry ingredients together and fold into the egg/sugar mixture. Fold in melted chocolate and butter. Last, fold the remaining chopped chocolate into the batter. Bake in an 8 x 10-inch pan lined with foil and greased for 18 to 25 minutes at 325°F. Brownies are done when the batter holds its shape and a shiny layer has formed on top. Cool and cut into squares

Makes about 2 dozen brownies

∾ David Myers ∾

COMME ÇA (LOS ANGELES, CA)

Chef David Myers's food is enjoyed globally, from Costa Mesa to Tokyo. At Comme Ça, Comme Ça Las Vegas, Pizzeria Ortica Costa Mesa, Sona, David Myers Café, and Sola, Myers has international renown. He has earned his reach working for Charlie Trotter and Daniel Boulud as well as at Les Crayères, a manor with a three-Michelin-star restaurant in Reims, France.

What was your favorite food as a kid?
Fresh corn from the garden and grilled steak.

What was the first meal you made that you were proud of?
Roasted chicken.

What three adjectives describe your cuisine?
Californian, Asian-inspired, and pure.

What book most influences your food, cookbook or otherwise?
Washoku: Recipes from the Japanese Home Kitchen by Elizabeth Andoh.

What chef do you most admire?
I have had many great chefs that I admire. Charlie Trotter was one of the first.

What is your favorite ingredient?
Sudachi.

What music do you like to hear when you cook?
Dexter Gordon.

What is your favorite hangover meal?
Ramen and another beer.

What is your favorite midnight snack?
Cold soba.

What restaurant in the world are you most dying to try?
Koju in Tokyo.

What kitchen utensil is most indispensable to you?
Japanese knives.

Who do you most like to cook for?
My friends.

If you could do one other job, what would it be?
Architect.

What do you most value in a sous chef?
Willingness to make things happen.

What one food would you take with you to a desert island?
Sushi or soba.

What most satisfies your sweet tooth?
Gummy bears.

Cheeseburger or foie gras?
Both—that's the beauty of it.

What's your favorite place (and what is your favorite thing to order) for:

Happy hour?
Beer at the Otheroom in Venice, California.

A splurge meal?
Urasawa in Beverly Hills. Just let the chef cook for you.

Breakfast?
Eggs with arugula and crispy prosciutto at Gjelina in Venice, California.

A late-night/after-work meal?
Sushi Nozawa in Los Angeles—my favorite thing to order is the Trust Me.

A cup of coffee?
Espresso at Intelligentsia's Coffeebar in Venice, California.

A greasy-spoon meal?
A burger at the Apple Pan in West Los Angeles.

Groceries?
Organic Japanese vegetables at Nijiya Market in West Los Angeles.

Ice cream?
Il Laboratorio del Gelato in New York City.

Chocolate?
Chocolat BEL AMER from Tokyo.

Corton

NEW YORK, NY

Paul Liebrandt's path to Corton is gilded in genius and hotheaded, bridge-burning departures. There is an elusiveness to him that is narcotic. He is an artist. Much of this glamour derives from the repeated narrative of Liebrandt cooking glorious, rarified food at places with Michelin stars totaling eleven, but leaving with the slamming of a door. Corton is a partnership with Drew Nieporent, a restaurateur with an astonishing stable, holding thoroughbreds like Nobu, Tribeca Grill, Rubicon, and Montrachet. Doors regularly close here without a crash, in what seems, finally, to be a happy home for Liebrandt.

This staff meal stands alone. It is much more laborious than the other dishes in the book but it is impeccable. The shepherd's pie and potato purée are made in stages that are not all passive. Some stages are of the put-in-a-pot-and-go-in-the-other-room nature; but many are focused detail work, like ricing and peeling and being the agent that changes the food. I suspect most people would begin to incorporate shortcuts into the recipe after the first rendition because home cooking is often about creating the least distance between ingredients and dinner. But, please, for yourself, make

> **OFF THE MENU**
>
> ~
>
> Shepherd's Pie
>
> Cauliflower Gratin
>
> Caesar Salad
>
> Oatmeal Cookies
>
> *Suggested wine:*
> Kunin Wines Syrah 2006

it the way Chef Liebrandt would make it, at least once. It will give you an insight into why haute cuisine is so complex and rich. Ah, these mashed potatoes are without lumps, are practically creamed because you don't just throw them in a bowl and smash them. There is a process. It is chemistry. And butter. Learn Liebrandt's science and then go forth in your own way—if you still want to.

Corton is a heads-down type of kitchen with a large staff. They eat in the kitchen, *in medias res.* But the smallish dining room is so lovely, I wanted to take some photos of the crisp cooks eating in front of the elegant whiteness of the decor, which is both pristine and gentle, lit on the oblique. The staff was ruffled by the procession into the dining room. They were polite but irritated to be taken from their work. It is a truth that most anywhere, people are not irritated to be taken away from work in order to sit and eat a splendid meal of shepherd's pie, cauliflower gratin, and oatmeal cookies. Liebrandt is yoked to an idea of perfection that is unique. And at this meal, his staff's dedication and his adroit attention to my queries are all refractions of that artistic exactitude.

TOP RIGHT: Chef Paul Liebrandt in his *cuisine magnifique.*

Shepherd's Pie

Corton's shepherd's pie pays homage to the country dish, with its complexity of three meats and crown of potato purée. You may, of course, use your favorite mashed-potato recipe to top the dish, but for potato connoisseurs or the potato curious, it is worth visiting the farmers' market to find La Ratte potatoes.

4 tablespoons grapeseed oil

½ pound short ribs

¾ cup beef stock

½ pound ground veal

½ pound ground pork

4 tablespoons unsalted butter

½ onion, diced

3 cloves garlic, diced

½ carrot, diced

3 star anise

½ fresh jalapeño, seeds removed, diced

2 red bell peppers, roasted or confit, diced

¾ tablespoon chili powder

1½ tablespoons tomato purée

½ cup Jack Daniel's whiskey

½ cup milk

Potato Purée (page 90)

2 tablespoons minced chives

This can be done the day before or morning of. Preheat the oven to 250°F. Heat 2 tablespoons of the oil in a medium Dutch oven or heavy-bottomed pot over medium-high heat and brown the short ribs. Remove the meat and place in a pot with the stock. Cover and cook the short ribs in the oven for 8 to 9 hours, until falling apart. Allow the meat to cool, then remove from the pot, reserving the cooking liquid. Shred the meat.

Heat the remaining 2 tablespoons of the oil in the Dutch oven. Brown the veal and pork over high heat; remove the meat and set aside. In butter, lightly brown the onions, garlic, carrot, star anise, jalapeño, red bell pepper, and chili powder over medium heat, about 3 minutes. Add the veal, pork, short ribs, tomato purée, whiskey, milk, and ½ cup of the reserved short-rib cooking liquid. Cover, but leave a small vent, and cook for about 4 hours over low heat, until tender.

Spoon or pipe about 3 to 4 cups of Potato Purée over the meat, covering completely. Place under a broiler for 2 minutes, until browned. Top with a sprinkling of minced chives.

Serves 6 to 8

Potato Purée

2½ pounds La Ratte or
    other fingerling potatoes
1 to 1½ cups milk
2 to 3 sticks unsalted
    butter, room temperature
Salt and freshly ground
    black pepper

Scrub the potatoes, peel, and slice evenly. Place the potatoes in a hot-water bath at 158°F (this is under a simmer) for 30 minutes. Then, refresh the potatoes in an ice-water bath, put them back in the pan, and boil until fully cooked. This method preserves the starch granules in the potatoes and prevents a gummy purée. Drain the potatoes as soon as they are cooked. Dry in pan for 5 minutes to remove any residual water.

Meanwhile, in a large saucepan, bring the milk just to a boil over high heat and set aside.

Once the potatoes are cool enough to handle, pass them though the finest grind of a food mill into a large, heavy-bottomed pot. Place the pot over low heat, and with a wooden spatula, stir the potatoes vigorously for 4 to 5 minutes to dry them.

Now begin adding about three quarters of the butter, little by little, stirring vigorously until each batch of butter is thoroughly incorporated and the mixture becomes fluffy and light. Slowly add about three quarters of the hot milk in a thin stream, stirring vigorously, until the milk is thoroughly incorporated. For an extra-fine purée, pass the mixture though a fine drum sieve into another heavy-bottomed pot (optional).

Place over low heat and stir vigorously. If the mixture seems a bit heavy and stiff, add additional butter and milk, whisking all the while. Adjust seasoning to taste.

Makes about 5 cups

Cauliflower Gratin

Gratin is rich and creamy and gives a vegetable a state of grace. My family serves this at Thanksgiving in lieu of mashed potatoes, and no one complains.

2 small heads cauliflower, cut into florets
4 tablespoons unsalted butter
¼ onion, chopped
2 cloves garlic, chopped
1 tablespoon all-purpose flour
1 cup milk
1 cup grated Parmesan cheese
Juice of ½ lemon
Tabasco, to taste
Salt and freshly ground black pepper
½ cup bread crumbs
2 tablespoons chopped parsley

Bring a pot of salted water to a rolling boil. Blanch cauliflower for 2 minutes and remove to an ice-water bath until cool; drain and pat dry. In a large pan, melt the butter and sauté the onion and garlic over medium-high heat until softened. Add the cauliflower and cook over low heat until tender. Add the flour and cook 2 minutes, stirring occasionally. Add the milk, bring to a simmer, and then add the Parmesan, lemon juice, and Tabasco. Season with salt and pepper. Pour the mixture into a baking dish and top with bread crumbs. Place under a broiler for 3 minutes. Top with chopped parsley to serve.

Serves 6 to 8 as a side

Caesar Salad

While the exoticism of Caesar salad has diminished, its excellence has not. This recipe is perfect and it will become instinct in only a few attempts.

2 small egg yolks
3 anchovy fillets
½ tablespoon Dijon mustard
1 clove garlic
1 cup grapeseed oil
Juice of ½ lemon
1 cup grated Parmesan cheese
Salt and freshly ground black pepper
2 heads romaine lettuce, chopped
2 cups croutons

In a food processor, blend egg yolks, anchovies, mustard, and garlic. With the processer still running, drizzle in the oil in a thin stream. Add the lemon juice and half of the Parmesan, and season with salt and pepper. Toss the romaine with the dressing and top with croutons and the remaining ½ cup of Parmesan.

Serves 6 as a side

Oatmeal Cookies

There is a wide spectrum of oatmeal cookie. Even in such a narrow category, the texture can vary wildly. This recipe hits just the right chewy, comforting, and not cakey chord.

1¾ cups all-purpose flour

1 teaspoon baking soda

½ teaspoon salt

1½ teaspoons cinnamon

3 sticks unsalted butter, cubed, at room temperature

2 cups brown sugar, packed

½ cup granulated sugar

3 large eggs

4 cups oatmeal

8 ounces raisins

Preheat the oven to 350°F. In a small bowl, sift together the flour, baking soda, salt, and cinnamon. Set aside.

Cream together the softened butter and sugars. Slowly add the eggs, one by one. Add the mixed dry ingredients in stages. Once incorporated, fold in the oats and raisins with a spatula. Line your baking sheets with parchment paper. Using a tablespoon, measure the dough in spoonfuls and drop about 1½ inches apart. Bake for 8 to 10 minutes, until lightly browned. Transfer the cookies to wire racks and let them cool.

Makes about 4 dozen cookies

THE ESCOFFIER QUESTIONNAIRE

✦ Paul Liebrandt ✦

CORTON (NEW YORK, NY)

Paul Liebrandt spent his culinary formative years in kitchens like Le Manoir Aux Quat'Saisons in Oxford, England. Now well formed, he is garlanded in laurels: Among many Michelin stars and gobsmacked reviews, he was the youngest chef ever awarded three stars by the *New York Times*.

What was your favorite food as a kid?
Chinese.

What was the first meal you made that you were proud of?
Shepherd's pie! I was nine years old.

What three adjectives describe your cuisine?
Simple, graphic, and feminine.

What book most influences your food, cookbook or otherwise?
Cooking for Kings: The Life of Antonin Careme by Ian Kelly, *White Heat* by Marco Pierre White, *Modernist Cuisine: The Art and Science of Cooking* by Nathan Myhrvold.

What chef do you most admire?
Pierre Gagnaire.

What is your favorite ingredient?
Fleur de sel.

What music do you like to hear when you cook?
The "music of the kitchen." I don't really play any music while I cook.

What is your favorite hangover meal?
Vanilla ice cream.

What is your favorite midnight snack?
Carr's water crackers with Saint-Marcellin cheese.

What restaurant in the world are you most dying to try?
Koju in Ginza, Tokyo.

What kitchen utensil is most indispensable to you?
My tasting spoon.

What is your favorite pot?
My CookTek induction wok.

Who do you most like to cook for?
Young, aspiring cooks. They have saved their money to come in here and you can just see the excitement on their faces.

If you could do one other job, what would it be?
Cinematographer.

What do you most value in a sous chef?
Passion, commitment, tenacity, and humility.

What food trend would you erase from the annals of history?
Macrobiotic food.

What one food would you take with you to a desert island?
Pad Thai noodles.

What is your favorite guilty-pleasure treat?
Kettle New York Cheddar potato chips.

What most satisfies your sweet tooth?
Pierre Hermé, Paris.

What would you eat at your last meal, if you could plan such a thing?
A full royal Thai banquet.

Cheeseburger or foie gras?
Foie gras.

What's your favorite place for:

Happy hour?
The Violet Hour, Chicago.

Splurge meal?
Masa, New York City.

Late-night/after-work meal?
Blue Ribbon Sushi, New York City.

A cup of coffee?
La Colombe, New York City.

A greasy-spoon meal?
Lure Fishbar, New York City.

Bread desire?
Le Pain Quotidien, New York City and everywhere.

Groceries?
Union Square Greenmarket in New York City.

Crook's Corner

Crook's Corner is deeply Southern. The *New York Times* calls it "the sacred ground for southern foodies." From Hoppin John to Celery Root Remoulade with Country Ham, the food is slow, in all the best ways: Slow-cooked, as so much of the regional cuisine is, like pork butt barbecued for hours; slowly developed over generations, in a community that fuels tradition with food; and in the Slow Food way of using not just the time-tested techniques but also the ingredients of the local food shed.

Award-winning author of *Seasoned in the South*, Bill Smith is the executive chef. He keeps the pot boiling day in and out in Crook's Corner's busy dining room. His shrimp and grits are at least as worthy of a side trip as Civil War sites. His staff meal risotto is as simple as it looks but it yields dividends in richness. A small bowl with lots of ground black pepper is a meal.

OFF THE MENU

~

Southern Risotto

Suggested wine:
Steele Wines
Steele Viognier 2010

Southern Risotto

The creaminess of this risotto comes not just from cream, though there's plenty of that, but from the choice of rice and the stirring. Like polenta, you need a vigilant hand at the pot.

2 tablespoons unsalted butter
2 stalks celery, finely diced
1 small onion, finely diced
2 cups Carolina Gold rice
2 cups heavy cream
About 3 cups chicken broth
1 teaspoon salt
Freshly ground black pepper
1 cup grated Parmesan cheese

In a heavy-bottomed, steep-sided pan, heat the butter over medium-high heat. When the butter starts to foam, add the celery and onion and stir until softened, about 5 minutes. Add the rice and stir for a few minutes to brown a little. Begin adding the liquids in small amounts, alternating the cream with the broth, and cook at a gentle simmer. Continue adding liquid until it is absorbed, stirring all the while. You may not need all of the broth. Add the salt. Cook until the rice is softened and creamy but not mushy, about 20 minutes, stirring occasionally. Stir in the Parmesan, adjust seasoning, and serve immediately.

Serves 6

Delfina

Delfina is an anchor in one of my favorite food lagoons in the world. In the Mission neighborhood of San Francisco, there is a walkable nook that is a culinary Siren—ice-cream shops, cafés, bakeries and even lawn-sloped Dolores Park in which to loll and digest. Delfina is two restaurants that sit cozied up next door to each another. Pizzeria Delfina serves shareable snacks and Neapolitan pizza, with an extra-thin crust and few toppings, so that every bite lets you appreciate each element both separately and as one unified taste. You can also sit outside and watch the hipster parade go by. Restaurant Delfina, where I had staff meal, is more of a trattoria, with a daily-shifting menu that focuses on seasonal ingredients. This is where I come in the first days of crab season because I know they will be celebrating the moment with reverence.

As Delfina is a hub in the neighborhood, staff meal is a hub for the pre-shift bustle of the restaurant. We ate together, in a manner. Some people continued working—chopping and peeling, polishing and straightening—while others sat in small groups, at different tables around the restaurant. Toward the end of the meal, chef and co-owner Craig Stoll

> ## OFF THE MENU
> —
> Duck and Lettuce Wraps
>
> *Suggested wine:*
> Unti Vineyards Rosé 2010

gathered everyone to go over an Italian wine dinner taking place that evening. With a map of Italy, broken down by DOC (*Denominazione di Origine Controllata*, or the mandated wine regions), and the furiously notating and nodding crew, one could imagine a coup d'etat being plotted instead of a tasting menu.

Our meal had little to do with Italy but was expertly dispatched, nonetheless. We shared roasted duck salad in lettuce cups. I am a sucker for a vegetal, cold meat salad. Beyond taste, and beyond being a reviver of leftover meat, glowering in a Tupperware, it is filling and energizing at once. This recipe has the holy triumvirate of Asian cooking—ginger, garlic, and soy sauce. You can meddle endlessly with this flavor combination, though you don't have to here.

Anne and Craig Stoll, co-owners, are both of East Coast origins, Philadelphia and New York, respectively, and Delfina has the benefit of that depth. Though the restaurant and pizzeria fit in perfectly in the bastion of ingredient-focused California cuisine, the naturalness of it is all old world. They're not reinventing the wheel, they're slowly turning it.

Duck and Lettuce Wraps

These wraps call for a whole roasted duck. Your best bet for sourcing this is at a Chinese market, where duck is a protein staple. A lovely meal, simultaneously light and rich.

Sauce

1½ cups soy sauce

½ cup sherry vinegar

3 tablespoons finely grated ginger

2 bunches scallions, sliced

1 clove garlic, germ removed and finely grated

1 teaspoon chili flakes

2 tablespoons sesame oil

2 tablespoons canola oil

2 tablespoons olive oil

3 red onions, diced

3 fennel bulbs, diced

Fronds from 1 fennel, sliced

6 ribs celery, diced

6 carrots, diced

2 bunches chard stems

2-inch piece of ginger, julienned

3 cloves garlic, smashed

1 quart chicken stock

½ cup soy sauce

1 tablespoon chili flakes

Salt

2 pounds roasted duck meat, diced into
   ½-inch cubes

4 heads Little Gem lettuce or similar romaine variety

Combine the sauce ingredients in a bowl. Cover and refrigerate at least 1 hour.

Heat the oil in a large sauté pan over medium-high heat. Add the vegetables, ginger, and garlic, and cook until tender, about 5 to 8 minutes, stirring occasionally. Add the chicken stock and soy sauce and reduce the liquid to glaze the vegetables, about 10 minutes. Add the chili flakes and season with salt. Add the cubed duck at the last minute, just to warm through.

To serve, separate the leaves of the lettuce and trim any large leaves. Spoon duck and vegetable mixture into lettuce cups and top with the soy-sherry sauce.

Serves 6 to 8

~ Craig Stoll ~

DELFINA (SAN FRANCISCO, CA)

Craig Stoll is the chef and owner of San Francisco's Delfina, Delfina Pizzeria Mission, and Pacific Heights. The three locations are named in honor of Da Delfina, the Michelin-starred Tuscan restaurant where Stoll derived the inspiration and knowledge to propel his success in California.

What was your favorite food as a kid?
I liked everything, but I guess I would say Chinese food. My parents were cooking Szechuan food before anyone else.

What was the first meal you made that you were proud of?
I was a sophomore or junior in high school, and I was cooking for a girl. I made chicken with raspberry vinegar sauce.

What three adjectives describe your cuisine?
Delicious, clean, and honest.

What book most influences your food, cookbook or otherwise?
Probably Paul Bertolli's cookbooks or Julia Child's *Art of French Cooking.* I've always encouraged the people who work with me to read Waverly Root's *The Food of Italy.*

What chef do you most admire?
Thomas Keller.

What is your favorite ingredient?
Olive oil.

What music do you like to hear when you cook?
I am my own best DJ. So I mainly listen to my iPod on shuffle. It's full of angst-ridden post-punk rock 'n' roll.

What is your favorite hangover meal?
Dim sum.

What is your favorite midnight snack?
Spaghetti *aglio e olio,* topped with bread crumbs or Parmesan.

What restaurant in the world are you most dying to try?
Arzak in San Sebastián, Spain.

If you could do one other job, what would it be?
Something related to urban planning, design, or architecture.

What do you most value in a sous chef?
Attention to detail, speed, leadership, honesty, and directness.

What food trend would you most like to erase from the annals of history?
Fear of fat.

What one food would you take with you to a desert island?
A year's supply of BLTs.

What is your favorite guilty-pleasure treat?
I don't feel guilty about anything I eat.

What most satisfies your sweet tooth?
Ben & Jerry's New York Super Fudge Chunk.

What would you eat at your last meal, if you could plan such a thing?
I'd grill a bunch of meat, drink a bunch of red wine, and then die in my sleep.

Cheeseburger or foie gras?
Cheeseburger.

What's your favorite place (and what is your favorite thing to order) for:

Happy hour?
Zuni Café in San Francisco. I generally go for oysters, shoestring fries, and margaritas.

A splurge meal?
Chez Panisse in Berkeley, California.

Breakfast?
Balompie Café in San Francisco.

Pastry?
Tartine in San Francisco.

A late-night/after-work meal?
Yuet Lee in San Francisco, for salt-and-pepper anything.

A cup of coffee?
Four Barrel Coffee in San Francisco—the beans from Gibraltar.

Groceries?
Bi-Rite Market in San Francisco.

Ice cream?
Bi-Rite Creamery in San Francisco for black-and-white soft serve.

Chocolate?
Recchiuti Confections in San Francisco.

Dirt Candy

Dirt Candy is a wee vegetarian (dirt candy = vegetables) restaurant in New York City's East Village. So wee that the entire dining room is used for prep by the kitchen staff during the day because the actual kitchen would make a navy cook claustrophobic. I love it when there is just enough room for things: it seems more ethical to me, a spatial form of living within your means. The chef and owner, Amanda Cohen, is unapologetic about the tiny quarters and well she should be, for the restaurant is very successful.

Amanda Cohen is unapologetic about nearly everything, at least the subjects we covered. "Staff meal is kind of a test. Though they may not know it's a test. When new people come in, we throw staff meal at them and if it isn't done in thirty minutes, they are done." Staff meal is a tool for demonstrating basic cooking chops: extract the most flavor and nutrition, spending as little time and money as possible. So it makes sense that if you can't pull together staff meal, then your hopes of executing complicated menu items consistently are meager.

> ### OFF THE MENU
>
> Stone-Ground Grits and Corn Cream
>
> *Suggested wine:*
> Shinn Estate Vineyards Rosé

Cohen recognizes the window that staff meal can provide into the restaurant's undressed state. Dirt Candy's website is a blog where Cohen ran a year-long family meal photography project, where she shared images of what the crew eats. Unlike many restaurants where the staff splinters off into subgroups, there is no room for splinters here. So the staff eats as an entity—perhaps while still de-stemming parsley or making dough—but as one entity nonetheless.

Putting honesty above preserving a beautiful façade is an ethos for Cohen. Which makes it all the more charming that her family-meal blog doesn't gloss over the recurrence of dishes again and again. Mushroom hearts appear frequently because mushrooms are the umami in a vegetarian meal, but the stalk, or heart as Cohen calls it, doesn't usually end up on a customer's plate. And that is all right. A few simple additions can make the old new again, some herbs, a sauce, different vegetables grilled as an accompaniment. Staff meals are delicious, always delicious, but unvarnished. Unapologetically so.

Stone-Ground Grits and Corn Cream

Dirt Candy staff meals are grounded in fueling up for a long night of work. Like a weeknight at home, there's often little time to prepare and less time to enjoy. Mostly, this equates to serving leftovers: perhaps their famous grits or an easy pasta, accompanied by grilled vegetables and a smoothie from ingredients on hand. It's not very romantic or glamorous, but it's honest.

4 cups corn kernels
1 tablespoon extra-virgin olive oil
½ cup diced onions
1 tablespoon minced garlic
4 cups stone-ground yellow grits
¼ cup white wine
6 cups corn stock
Salt

Put 2 cups of corn kernels in a blender and barely cover them with water. Blend until smooth. Strain the corn cream through a sieve a few times to remove chunky bits. Set aside.

In a large sauté pan, heat olive oil over low heat. Add the onions and cook until translucent, about 5 minutes. Add the garlic and sauté until soft. Add grits, and mix to coat the onion and garlic and toast the grits about 5 to 7 minutes.

Add the wine and keep stirring until all the liquid has been absorbed by the grits. Incorporate the stock into the grits, stirring in 1 cup at a time. Let the grits absorb each cup of stock before adding the next, about 10 to 15 minutes total. Add the corn cream and stir. Stir in remaining 2 cups of corn kernels. Season with salt. Serve with grilled vegetables.

Serves 8

❧ Amanda Cohen ❧

DIRT CANDY (NEW YORK, NY)

Amanda Cohen has been an influential cook or consultant in many of New York's top vegetarian enclaves, including Teany, Blossom Café, Broadway East, and Pure Food and Wine. But none are as well-regarded as her little spot. Dirt Candy has even been recommended for a Michelin star, which is a coup.

What was your favorite food as a kid?
Coffee Crisps and dim sum.

What was the first meal you made that you were proud of?
In fifth grade, I spent a summer making hamburgers and peach pies for my family. It was the first time I'd cooked a meal and it was great. Until I made it for the twelfth time, at which point the reviews got bad.

What three adjectives describe your cuisine?
Meatless, disreputable, and crazed.

What chef do you most admire?
I admire any chef who actually works every night in their own kitchen.

What is your favorite ingredient?
Something I've never used before.

What is your favorite hangover meal?
A Canadian cracker. Unfortunately the one place that made them went out of business.

What kitchen utensil is most indispensable to you?
My sous chef.

What is your favorite pot?
Whatever's being offered.

Who do you most like to cook for?
My regulars.

If you could do one other job, what would it be?
Trophy wife.

What do you most value in a sous chef?
The ability to ignore most of what I say.

What food trend would you erase from the annals of history?
Vegetables are the new meat.

What one food would you take with you to a desert island?
Something really gross so I'm compelled to get off the island faster.

What is your favorite guilty-pleasure treat?
Sleep and *Jersey Shore*, but I don't actually feel guilty about *Jersey Shore*.

What most satisfies your sweet tooth?
Any deli selling Canadian chocolate bars.

What would you eat at your last meal, if you could plan such a thing?
An all-you-can-eat buffet. That way my meal never ends and I would never die.

Cheeseburger or foie gras?
Neither, sorry.

What's your favorite place (and what is your favorite thing to order) for:

Happy hour?
Any happy hour that starts before 3 P.M.

A splurge meal?
Dragon Well Manor in Hangzhou, China.

Bread desire?
Panya Bakery in New York City.

Groceries?
Fresh Direct.

Distrito

Sometimes a staff meal is the score of leftovers from an event. I liken this to getting my parents' doggie bag after one of their grown-ups-only nights out when I was a kid. Distrito had just such a staff meal the day I came, a trove of goodies from a tony catering gig, which fit perfectly with the restaurant's playfulness and adult kiddish enthusiasm. In the dining room, you could sit in a Distrito Federal taxicab tricked out with a table, or in a booth with extravagantly tall enclosures, within eyeshot of a wall of hundreds of Mexican wrestling masks, or you could have a drink in the lounge while swaying in a swing. "They don't swing too high," I was assured when I questioned the possible outcome of several margaritas and an indoor swing.

Distrito is Chef Jose Garces' ode to Mexico City—it is mad and vibrating and sprawling. The dish of coconut chicken enchiladas was rich and filled out with beans and rice and lovely salsas, made by the kitchen staff. Leftovers do not have to be microwaved as lesser versions of themselves. Like coming to a city that can be entered from a thousand portals, taking a different tack with your food on the second day

---

OFF THE MENU

Chicken Enchiladas
with Salsa Ranchera

Charros Frijoles

Suggested wine:
Willamette Valley Vineyards
Pinot Noir 2008

---

can yield entirely new and equally special results. The tamales can be revived with fresh salsas and a little salad with pickled onions. The beans and rice can enter a new pact and become El Salvadoran *casamiento* or be divorced entirely into separate meals.

Garces is an Iron Chef and the owner of seven restaurants. The restaurants culinarily cover the Latin diaspora, focusing on the food traditions of Catalonia, Basque country, and Mexico, and serving classic Spanish tapas. There is also Chifa, a Spanish/Asian fusion restaurant and a bar and retail spots. This kind of ferocious success is a result of ambition and excellence and also of a talent for delegation and leadership. Maria Schmidt, Distrito's chef de cuisine, is one of Garces' trusted generals, and she executed the family meal with grace. The large staff gathered to eat in the lounge, a few of the cooks eating their enchiladas on plates resting on their laps while they slowly rocked trepidatiously in the swing. There was a sweet incongruity to the crew, already in serious work mode, eating quickly in this lounge built for lackadaisical pleasure, low lit and luxuriant. "This is good," Garces said approvingly.

BOTTOM LEFT: Chef Jose Garces in Distrito's swinging lounge.

Chicken Enchiladas
with Salsa Ranchera

This is a decadent stretch for chicken with cream and coconut milk. After making this, I was poaching chicken in all kinds of creamy concoctions, rescuing everyone from my go-to roast chicken. Big trays of enchiladas are often a dish for parties, and this recipe is impressive enough for that but easy enough for a night at home as well.

1 quart heavy cream

¾ cup coconut milk

1 habenero, cut in half

¼ bunch oregano

1 sprig epazote

Salsa Ranchera (page 108)

2 tablespoons olive oil

5 onions, julienned

5 poblanos, roasted and julienned

2 pounds chicken thighs, poached
  and shredded

2 pounds chicken breasts, poached
  and sliced thin

½ bunch parsley, minced

½ bunch basil, minced

Salt

Sixteen 6-inch corn tortillas

1 cup grated Cotija cheese

Thinly sliced and julienned radish,
  optional

In a medium saucepan, combine heavy cream, coconut milk, habenero, oregano, and epazote. Simmer over low heat and reduce the sauce by half, about 30 minutes. Strain and set aside. While the cream sauce is simmering, make the salsa ranchera.

Heat 2 tablespoons oil in a large skillet over medium heat and lightly sweat or cook the onions, about 5 minutes. Add the poblanos and cream sauce and reduce over medium heat until the liquid is thick and creamy, about 30 minutes. Fold in chicken, parsley, and basil, and season with salt. Spread mixture out on a sheet pan to cool.

Preheat the oven to 350°F. Coat the bottoms of two 13 x 9-inch pans with a ladle of salsa ranchera. Rub a bit of oil on the tortillas to make them more pliable. Fill tortillas with chicken cream mixture, roll, and place 8 filled enchiladas in each pan, seam side down. Top enchiladas with remaining salsa ranchera and bake for 15 minutes. Top with grated Cotija cheese, garnish with radish if desired.

Serves 6 to 8

Salsa Ranchera

1 onion, coarse diced

10 plum tomatoes

2 to 3 jalapeños

2 cloves garlic

2 cups roasted red peppers

2 tablespoons extra-virgin olive oil

Salt

Bring a large pot of water to a boil and add onion, tomatoes, and jalapeños. Blanch until the skins start to break on the tomatoes; remove from water. In a blender, purée all the ingredients except half the jalapeños until smooth, working in batches if needed. Taste and adjust the seasoning. Purée in the remaining jalapeño, if desired, for spiciness.

Makes about 6 cups

Charros Frijoles

Beans are a long-simmering food and their rise to glory lies in seasoning them well and then letting them be. Distrito's pinto beans are both a salve and a celebration.

1 pound dry pinto beans

½ pound smoked bacon, small diced

2 onions, small diced

3 cloves garlic, minced

1 jalapeño, small diced

1 can diced tomatoes

1 cup chicken stock

1 bottle Dos Equis beer

½ bunch epazote

½ bunch parsley

½ bunch cilantro

Wash and soak beans in water overnight. Drain.

In a large pot, combine the beans with enough salted water to cover. Bring to a boil. Reduce heat and simmer for one hour.

Heat a skillet over medium-low heat and cook the bacon until the fat is rendered. Add the onions, garlic, and jalapeño and cook for 10 minutes. Add the tomatoes and cook for 5 minutes. Add the chicken stock and bacon-and-vegetable mixture to the beans and simmer another 1½ to 2 hours, until beans are tender. Add the beer and simmer about 45 minutes longer, or until desired consistency, stirring occasionally. Fold in the epazote, parsley, and cilantro; adjust seasoning and serve.

Serves 6 to 8 as a side

THE ESCOFFIER QUESTIONNAIRE

ᴖ Jose Garces ᴖ

DISTRITO (PHILADELPHIA, PA)

Jose Garces is—there's no other way of saying it—a king. He is an Iron Chef America, the owner of seven restaurants, and the author of the cookbook *Latin Evolution*. He opened his first restaurant, Amada, in 2005, so it has taken him just six years to accumulate his empire so far. Garces the Great.

What was your favorite food as a kid?
Classics that my grandmother Mamita Amada taught me to make, such as empanadas and arepas. She brought the recipes with her from Ecuador when she came to visit.

What was the first meal you made that you were proud of?
When I was in culinary school: Herb-roasted chicken with baby carrots and Cipollini onions, dauphinoise potatoes, and chocolate crème brûlée with raspberries for dessert.

What three adjectives describe your cuisine?
Flavorful, thoughtful, and globe-trotting.

What book most influences your food, cookbook or otherwise?
Douglas Rodriguez's *Nuevo Latino* is a big one for me, and I've always loved *The French Laundry Cookbook*. Right now, I've been reaching for *Thai Street Food* and Heston Blumenthal's *Further Adventures in Search of Perfection*.

What chef do you most admire?
Ferran Adrià—he is an innovator, an icon.

What is your favorite hangover meal?
There's nothing better after a night out than Chinese dumplings, wings, and noodles.

What is your favorite midnight snack?
A bowl of Kashi Strawberry Fields cereal with almond milk.

What restaurant in the world are you most dying to try?
I'd love to try Noma in Copenhagen, especially since I've been reading René Redzepi's *Noma* cookbook so much lately.

What kitchen utensil is most indispensable to you?
I love my Japanese blades. I have a perfectly balanced Yo-deba that allows me to break down any fish with precision, and an eleven-inch Yanagi with a thin single-edge blade, allowing for clean slices and quick preparation for ceviches.

If you could do one other job, what would it be?
I'd like to live and work near the sea as a marine biologist.

What food trend would you most like to erase from the annals of history?
I'm not big on processed vegetarian "proteins" such as seitan.

What one food would you take with you to a desert island?
As long as it had plenty of veggies, I could survive on arroz con pollo.

What is your favorite guilty-pleasure treat?
Bourbon. We purchased a barrel of Four Roses for Village Whiskey, and I've been known to stop by after a long night for a quick nip on the rocks.

Cheeseburger or foie gras?
Can't I have both?

What's your favorite place (and what is your favorite thing to order) for:

A splurge meal?
The sushi bar at Hotel Okura in Tokyo, and I'd leave myself in the hands of the chef.

Breakfast?
The Fountain at the Four Seasons in Philadelphia, for an à la carte brunch that is perfectly executed. I usually order a bagel with smoked salmon and cream cheese.

Pastry?
Guava and cream cheese Cuban pasteles from the take-out window at La Carreta Restaurant in Miami.

Kitchen equipment?
Korin in New York City for knives, Fante's and Previn here in Philadelphia for everything else.

Chocolate?
Éclat Chocolate in West Chester, PA.

Flour + Water

Chef Thomas McNaughton has a precocity and sense of his style that seems beyond his age. Not yet thirty, he is the instigator of a restaurant culture within Flour + Water that is both efficient and free. Most young people don't have the confidence to lead and allow others to be leaders.

Flour + Water has the feel of a workshop. Upstairs, next door to where McNaughton and his pet pig, Kalua, live, is the dough room, which doubles as the private dining room. The restaurant is known for their handmade pastas, which are rolled, extruded, and cut daily in this sunny room, with its one large central worktable. I thought we might have pasta for staff meal but was met with a pause and a head scratch. According to McNaughton, "We never have pasta for staff meal. I guess because it is so valuable here and so expensive—it takes a large amount of labor." So in a paradox of value, a roasted leg of lamb with salsa verde is foisted upon the workers, while noodles remain the highest culinary currency. Of course, not a complaint was uttered.

Flour + Water is located smack in San Francisco's Mission District, a quarter that has had a long gentrification arc. It has mostly been the domain of dicey (and occasionally divine) Mexican restaurants and dive bars. But with Flour + Water newly in its folds, suddenly the Mission is the home of the next, next wave of California cuisine, which is not just ingredient driven but source specific, and more likely based on regional cuisine than haute cuisine. Their pasta, and also the brick-oven-baked pizza, has been called out by *Sunset Magazine*, the *New York Times*, *Travel + Leisure*, and the James Beard Foundation, among many others.

In a city long known as a harbor of culinary greatness and innovation, it is a salve to see so much freshness. There's a golden-haired young man in the neighborhood, and he is quotidianly creating modern food. And by "modern food," I mean food that has a long memory.

OFF THE MENU

Roasted Leg of Lamb
with Salsa Verde

Potato Confit

Spring Vegetable Salad
with Bagna Cauda

Suggested wine:
Skylark's Rodgers Creek
Syrah 2007

BOTTOM RIGHT: Chef Tom McNaughton (far left) waits for his helping of lamb.

Roasted Leg of Lamb
with Salsa Verde

This is a spring feast, fit for the Easter, Passover, or Equinox table. Though lamb is available all year in most parts of the country, it is at its peak in spring. This is the time when lambs are just ready for harvesting and have all the freshness of the protein-rich grasses and forbs of the season. This dish would also be fitting in the winter, with earthy greens.

2 to 3 pounds lamb top sirloin

1½ tablespoons sea salt

1 tablespoon cracked black pepper

1 cup white wine

2 bunches summer savory or rosemary

½ cup salt-packed anchovy fillets

½ cup olive oil

Salsa Verde

1 bunch parsley

1 bunch tarragon

½ bunch spearmint

1 cup olive oil

4 anchovy fillets

2 tablespoons capers

½ clove garlic

1 tablespoon Meyer lemon zest

Juice of ½ Meyer lemon

Salt and freshly ground black pepper

Truss the meat for even cooking and season with salt and pepper. In a blender, combine and purée the wine, herbs, anchovies, and olive oil, and generously rub the meat with the marinade mixture. Cover and refrigerate for at least 24 hours.

For the salsa verde, pick all herbs from stems and thinly slice leaves. Grind the herbs in a mortar until a paste is formed. With a rubber spatula, transfer the paste to a plastic container and cover with olive oil. Pound the anchovies, capers, and garlic in the mortar to form a paste. Combine all ingredients and add lemon zest and juice. Season with salt and pepper. Set aside.

Preheat the oven to 400°F. Remove lamb from the refrigerator and allow to come to room temperature. Brush off excess marinade from the meat and set it on a roasting rack in a large, deep roasting pan. Roast the meat until caramelized, about 10 minutes, and lower the heat to 325°F. Roast about 20 minutes to an internal temperature of 140°F on a meat thermometer. Let the roast rest at room temperature for 15 minutes. Thinly slice meat against the grain and serve with the salsa verde.

Serves 6

Potato Confit

This potato confit is a decadent accompaniment to the bright flavors of the salsa verde in the lamb and bagna cauda in the salsa. What's a little duck fat once in a while?

2 pounds fingerling potatoes
2 quarts duck fat
3 sprigs of rosemary
12 cloves garlic, peeled
¼ cup chopped fresh parsley
¼ cup chopped green garlic
¼ cup chopped fresh mint
Sea salt

Preheat the oven to 325°F.

Rinse the potatoes in 2 or 3 changes of cold water until water runs clear. Drain and pat very dry. Heat the duck fat in a large saucepan over medium heat until melted.

Place the potatoes, rosemary, and garlic in a 3-inch-deep baking pan. Cover potatoes with melted duck fat and cook in the oven until potatoes are fork tender, about 20 minutes. Let potatoes cool in the fat to room temperature, remove, and set aside. Save the duck fat.

Heat the fat in a large skillet over medium heat until it reaches a temperature of 350°F. Add a small batch of potatoes and cook until crisp and golden brown, about 5 minutes. Transfer to a plate lined with paper towels. Repeat with remaining potatoes. Toss the potatoes with parsley, green garlic, and mint, sprinkle with sea salt, and serve immediately.

Serves 6 as a side

Spring Vegetable Salad
with Bagna Cauda

Salsa verde and bagna cauda are kissing cousins, the former more herbaceous and pickled and the latter more focused on citrus and anchovy. Both recipes are worth doubling because you will want to slather them on almost everything.

1 cup olive oil

4 cloves garlic, sliced

7 anchovy fillets

Juice of 3 Meyer lemons

2 tablespoons Meyer lemon zest

1 bunch asparagus, shaved

2 cups baby carrots, peeled

2 cups radishes, shaved

1 cup peas, blanched

1 cup fava beans, blanched

½ cup fresh mint, thinly sliced

Salt and freshly ground black pepper

To make the bagna cauda, combine the olive oil, garlic, and anchovies in a small saucepan over low heat. Cook until a paste forms, about 1 hour. Take the pan off the heat and allow the mixture to cool to room temperature. Add the lemon juice and zest and stir.

In a large bowl, combine all the vegetables with the bagna cauda. Season with salt and pepper.

Serves 6 as a side

THE ESCOFFIER QUESTIONNAIRE

~ Thomas McNaughton ~

FLOUR + WATER (SAN FRANCISCO, CA)

CIA-trained Thomas McNaughton has collected enviable knowledge in his young life. La Folie, Gary Danko, and Quince were his training grounds, along with work/travel in Europe, including time at a pasta factory in Bologna. It all comes to fruition at Flour + Water, where he is chef and partner.

What was your favorite food as a kid?
Pork roll from any bodega in South Jersey. They served it fried with egg and cheese on a Kaiser roll.

What was the first meal you made that you were proud of?
Seared pork loin and apple mostarda for my family.

What three adjectives describe your cuisine?
Focused, local, and fun.

What book most influences your food, cookbook or otherwise?
Culinaria: European Specialties, because it breaks down all the food regionally.

What chef do you most admire?
There are a broad range of them, from classic cookbook authors that I used to read such as Michel Bras and Hugh Fearnley-Whittingstall, to a lot of young Bay Area chefs cooking good food.

What is your favorite ingredient?
Something that is in season. As soon as a new season begins, we immerse ourselves in the produce available at the time. Cooking with seasonal ingredients keeps things fun and exciting and does not allow for complacency.

What is your favorite hangover meal?
Pho from Turtle Tower in San Francisco.

What is your favorite midnight snack?
Toast, right out of the wood oven and paired with good cheese.

What kitchen utensil is most indispensable to you?
A long utility knife.

If you could do one other job, what would it be?
Woodworker.

What do you most value in a sous chef?
An intellectual understanding of food and a willingness to immerse oneself in what he or she does.

What food trend would you most like to erase from the annals of history?
Micro greens—the bad ones.

What one food would you take with you to a desert island?
A six-pack—maybe more if I was going to be there for a while.

What is your favorite guilty-pleasure treat?
Philly cheesesteak.

What most satisfies your sweet tooth?
Strawberries and lemon curd.

What would you eat at your last meal, if you could plan such a thing?
A simple wood-roasted game bird and a good bottle of wine.

Cheeseburger or foie gras?
Foie gras.

What's your favorite place (and what is your favorite thing to order) for:

Happy hour?
The Brazen Head in San Francisco, for good bourbon.

A splurge meal?
David Kinch's Manresa in Los Gatos, California.

Breakfast?
The back patio of Zazie in San Francisco.

Pastry?
Tartine Bakery and Cafe in San Francisco.

A late-night/after-work meal?
Nopa in San Francisco.

A cup of coffee?
Four Barrel Coffee in San Francisco.

A greasy-spoon meal?
Golden Coffee Shop on Sutter and Leavenworth in San Francisco. There's an old man flipping eggs behind the counter.

Groceries?
Bi-Rite Market in San Francisco.

Ice cream?
Humphry Slocombe Ice Cream in San Francisco.

4th & Swift

The restaurant 4th & Swift sits in the Old Fourth Ward, a neighborhood that is in transition. In a few years, the blocks surrounding it will house a development focused on food and food media and a new park with paths and water features. But for now, the edges are still worn and space lies unused. The birthplace of Martin Luther King, Jr., the quarter is festooned with plaque-worthy Atlanta history, however, and Jay Swift is setting a place for its future.

Swift invested in the neighborhood, buying up a large restaurant space and gambling that people would cut a new path in their routines and reconsider the Old Fourth Ward. They did. Swift cooks Southern fine-dining food. He describes his food as comfort food redefined with a modern sensibility. I describe his menu as ingredient-focused, seasonal, and drawing on Southern flavors and French technique. I have thought long on the term *comfort food*, as many of my favorite restaurants use it self-referentially. Comfort food is about scratching an emotional itch. It is heavy enough to physically sedate you and it generally means eating too much of just one thing. Servings from great restaurants are almost always none of those things. And yet I

OFF THE MENU

Baby Back Ribs
with Barbecue Sauce

Three-Cheese
Mac and Cheese

Suggested wine:
Robert Sinskey
Pinot Noir 2009

understand the meaning. Jay Swift makes food from ingredients you know and prepares them in a way that is understood to you. Pan-fried trout, ragout of pheasant leg, brisket smoked for two days. There is a comfort in eating the bounty of your own domain and recognizing it as such.

I arrived in Atlanta and headed straight to 4th & Swift. It was a charming welcome. Staff meal at 4th & Swift I would categorize as unmitigated comfort food—baby back ribs and mac and cheese. If I were not forced to share out of a sense of decorum, I would have eaten enough to be physically sedated.

"Man, are you even working tonight?" Jay Swift asks a server who is not scheduled for dinner service but has shown up for staff meal. "This guy's got great rib-dar." I can tell Swift is just warming up. He is at ease with his staff. He likes to teach them about ingredients as well as cooking. Every inch of un-cemented ground surrounding the restaurant is garden. A narrow strip of dirt that runs along the perimeter is for peppers, and raised beds in the outdoor eating area will grow greens and onions and beans and tomatoes. Someday this place will be the old institution in a new Old Fourth Ward neighborhood.

TOP LEFT: Bar manager James Ives gets down on some ribs. TOP RIGHT: Sous chef Jeb Aldrich babysits the greens.

Baby Back Ribs
with Barbecue Sauce

Chef Jay Swift feels everyone should have a barbecue sauce of their own devising. Grocery-store shelves are full of them, but I never find one that hits just the right spot for me. In my estimation, they are often too sweet. If you need a starting point for your recipe, let this be it. Swift's sauce— with its complexity, and its balance of sweet, spice, tart, and heat—stands up to any barbecue cut.

1 onion, sliced

1 to 2 jalapeños

2 tablespoons olive oil

¼ cup blackstrap molasses

¼ cup apple cider vinegar

4 tablespoons brown sugar

2 cloves garlic

3 tablespoons capers with brine

2 tablespoons chili paste

¼ teaspoon allspice

¼ teaspoon ground cardamom

¼ teaspoon ground coriander seed

¼ teaspoon ground cumin seed

¼ teaspoon ground ginger

¼ teaspoon mustard seed, toasted
   and ground

¼ teaspoon dried oregano

¼ teaspoon paprika

¼ teaspoon black pepper

28-ounce can whole tomatoes with
   juice, chopped

6-ounce can tomato paste

4 racks of pork baby back ribs, about
   4 to 5 pounds

Toss sliced onion and jalapeños in olive oil and cook under the broiler until charred. In a large saucepan, cook down the molasses over medium-low heat for about 10 minutes and add the vinegar, scraping the sides of the pan. Add the rest of the ingredients except the ribs to the pan, bring to a boil, and lower the heat to simmer. Cook about 20 minutes or to desired consistency. In a food processor, blend the sauce and chill in the refrigerator for 12 hours.

Preheat the oven to 325°F. Pour the sauce over the ribs and spread evenly. Cover with foil and bake for 1½ hours. To crisp, cook for about 15 minutes on medium-hot grill, or run it under the broiler for a few minutes. Cut into individual portions. Serve immediately.

Serves 6 to 8

Three-Cheese Mac and Cheese

This mac and cheese does not sacrifice taste for ease. The key is, of course, the excellent cheese combination, which creates a thicker sauce than most milk or cream sauces. This supposedly serves six to eight with the ribs, but you may decide to eat it all yourself.

¼ cup half-and-half
8 ounces Quicke's or favorite cheddar
¼ cup crumbled Sweet Grass or
  favorite chèvre
3 ounces Grana Padano, grated
Dash of Tabasco
Dash of Worcestershire sauce
Salt and freshly ground black pepper
1 pound large elbow macaroni,
  cooked al dente

In a large saucepan over low heat, combine half-and-half and all other ingredients except the pasta. Melt the cheese and stir occasionally until smooth. Once cheese sauce is hot, add the pasta and stir over low heat until hot throughout. Serve immediately.

Serves 6 to 8 as a side

⌒ Jay Swift ⌒

4TH & SWIFT (ATLANTA, GA)

Jay Swift gathered experience in top-tier restaurants in his native Baltimore, Washington, D.C., and Manhattan, culminating in his own restaurant in Atlanta, where his well-rounded education in eastern seaboard food culture really shines.

What was your favorite food as a kid?
Peanut butter and jelly on white bread with Utz potato chips and milk.

What three adjectives describe your cuisine?
Tasty, tasty, and tasty.

What book most influences your food, cookbook or otherwise?
The Omnivore's Dilemma by Michael Pollan.

What chef do you most admire?
The "soup nazi" from Seinfeld.

What is your favorite ingredient?
Pork, alliums, herbs, and citrus.

What music do you like to hear when you cook?
Blues.

What is your favorite hangover meal?
Bacon, eggs, toast, and coffee.

What is your favorite midnight snack?
Peanut butter and jelly and a glass of milk.

Who do you most like to cook for?
Food geeks.

What restaurant in the world are you most dying to try?
Momofuku in New York.

What kitchen utensil is most indispensable to you?
Mixing bowl.

If you could do one other job, what would it be?
Venture capitalist.

What do you most value in a sous chef?
Commitment.

What food trend would you most like to erase from the annals of history?
Crappy, fake Mexican food.

What is your favorite guilty-pleasure treat?
Cinnamon buns.

What would you eat at your last meal, if you could plan such a thing?
A large cake with a loaded automatic weapon baked into it.

Cheeseburger or foie gras?
Both—in no particular order.

What's your favorite place (and what is your favorite thing to order) for:

Happy hour?
Local Three Kitchen and Bar in Atlanta for a beer.

A splurge meal?
Bacchanalia in Atlanta for anything.

Breakfast?
The Silver Skillet Restaurant in Atlanta for Southern breakfast.

Pastry?
Sugar-Coated Radical in Atlanta.

A late-night/after-work meal?
Atkins Park Restaurant in Atlanta.

Groceries?
Whole Foods.

Frances

In December of 2009, Frances opened its doors. In 2010, Frances received a Michelin star. A prodigious beginning, even among the froth of praise that laps up to Frances daily. It is endearing to see such a familial welcome for a neighborhood bistro; named after chef and owner Melissa Perrello's grandmother and opened with the crafting and constructing skills of her parents. There is no press page on Frances' website, no publicity contact, and no overly poetic descriptions of food or ambiance. It quiets me to be there and to know the chef seeks to be good, more than to appear good.

Perrello is a pedigreed white-tablecloth chef. She was executive chef at both Fifth Floor and Charles Nob Hill, where she started at only 25 years old. These are serious jobs. Frances is small—small, but serious. It is like a neighborhood restaurant but culinarily elevated, a little more expensive and way harder to get a reservation. In places like Fifth Floor and the now defunct Charles Nob Hill, you can feel like an audience member or an acolyte, but at Frances the dining experience is more personal. The scale and scope of the restaurant has humility to it. The food has earned its Michelin star in less than a year, which is the sort of precociousness we expect from Perrello, but it is not a three-ring circus. Her food is homage to ingredients and season.

Perrello sits, momentarily, to eat with her staff and jokes in a low-key way. Sous chef Michaela, who prepared the empanadas, doesn't take the moment to sit. She is rushing through her paces. I imagine Perrello would normally be eating on her feet, but as the face of Frances, she is also obliged to sit and graciously humor people like me.

We all eat one empanada and then do the mathematics of politesse, figuring if it is fair to have another. And maybe another. The recipe for the meat filling, as well as the pastry, feels ancient. An early course at a Moorish wedding. The cilantro sauce is very modern, though. The idea is to balance the raisins and warm spices with the brightness of fresh aromatics.

Perrello is a different kind of wunderkind than we normally see in culinary stardom. She doesn't have the teenage audacity of attempting to uproot what came before. She is earnestly talented and she has the big gold star to prove it.

OFF THE MENU

Michaela's Empanadas

Suggested wine:
Paul Hobbs Napa Valley
Cabernet Sauvignon 2008

Michaela's Empanadas

These are delicate empanadas, the dough more like pastry than bread. The winter seasonings and raisins feel almost medieval in their unabashed union of sweet and savory. Frances serves them with a sauce of grilled scallions, blanched cilantro, and minced onions blended with garlic and olive oil.

3 eggs

2 tablespoons white vinegar

4½ cups all-purpose flour

3 teaspoons salt

2 sticks cold unsalted butter

1 teaspoon cumin seed

1 tablespoon dried chili flakes or powder (espelette, cayenne, etc.)

1 teaspoon ground coriander

2 tablespoons olive oil

1½ pounds ground beef

Salt and freshly ground pepper

½ onion, minced

3 cloves garlic, minced

1 pound Yukon gold potatoes, peeled, cooked, and diced

3 eggs, hard-boiled, peeled, and coarsely chopped

3 tablespoons golden raisins, soaked in hot water, drained, and chopped

¼ bunch cilantro, washed, picked, and chopped

¼ bunch parsley, washed, picked, and chopped

In a bowl, beat together ⅔ cup ice water, 2 of the eggs, and the vinegar. In a separate bowl, mix together the flour and salt. Cut and work the butter into the flour until pea-sized pieces form. Make a well in the dough and pour the egg mixture into the center. Mix the dough with a fork until stiff, turn onto a lightly floured surface, and knead until just mixed and smooth. Gather the dough into a ball, wrap in plastic, and refrigerate for 1 hour.

Toast the cumin seed and combine with chili powder and coriander in a spice mill; grind to a fine consistency. Heat the oil in a large skillet over medium-high heat. Sauté the beef for a few minutes, until it is no longer pink, and season with salt and pepper. Remove the meat from the pan, drain off excess fat, and sauté the onion and garlic until translucent, about 5 minutes. Add the beef and the spice blend, lower the heat and simmer for 5 minutes. Let cool slightly and combine the beef mixture with the potatoes, eggs, raisins, and fresh herbs. Adjust seasoning. Spread the mixture out on a tray to cool to room temperature before stuffing the empanadas.

Preheat the oven to 400°F. Divide the dough into 16 balls and roll each piece to a square shape about ⅜-inch thick and roughly 6 inches square. In a small bowl, lightly beat the remaining egg with 2 tablespoons of water. Brush the inside of the square with a little egg wash and spoon on roughly ¼ cup of the meat filling. Fold the dough over, corner to corner, and use a fork to crimp the edges. Brush each triangle with egg wash and bake for 15 to 20 minutes until golden and cooked through. Let cool slightly on wire racks and serve warm.

Makes 16 empanadas

~ Melissa Perello ~

FRANCES (SAN FRANCISCO, CA)

Melissa Perello is chef and owner of Frances. She earned her chops at Charles Nob Hill and then the famous Fifth Floor, where she earned her first Michelin star. Her second star was earned at her very own Frances in its first year.

What was your favorite food as a kid?
I have always been a big fan of bread; as a child, any kind of sandwich was a treat.

What was the first meal you made that you were proud of?
My first cookbook was Jill Krementz's *The Fun of Cooking.* I think I cooked every recipe out of the book, but I think I was quite proud once I tackled the Teddy-bear-shaped bread loaves with raisins for the eyes and belly button.

What three adjectives describe your cuisine?
Feminine, approachable, and fun.

What chef do you most admire?
My boyfriend, who is a chef.

What is your favorite ingredient?
Chicken.

What music do you like to hear when you cook?
A lot of Gomez, Iron and Wine, Black Keys, and Bon Iver.

What is your favorite hangover meal?
Anything fried.

What is your favorite midnight snack?
Grilled-cheese sandwich.

What restaurant in the world are you most dying to try?
El Celler de Can Roca in Spain.

What kitchen utensil is most indispensable to you?
My palette knife—it has sentimental value to me.

Who do you most like to cook for?
My family and friends. My favorite evenings off are spent cooking at home.

If you could do one other job, what would it be?
Dog walker, but only on non-rainy days.

What do you most value in a sous chef?
Determination, eagerness, humility, a good spirit, and a good sense of humor!

What food trend would you most like to erase from the annals of history?
Anything being plated with tweezers.

What is your favorite guilty-pleasure treat?
Doughnuts.

What most satisfies your sweet tooth?
Ice cream.

Cheeseburger or foie gras?
Cheeseburger, for sure.

What's your favorite place (and what is your favorite thing to order) for:

Happy hour?
Tommy's Mexican Restaurant in San Francisco, for margaritas.

A splurge meal?
Manresa in Los Gatos, California.

A late-night/after-work meal?
Nopa in San Francisco.

A cup of coffee?
Blue Bottle Coffee in San Francisco.

Groceries?
Bi-Rite Market in San Francisco.

Kitchen equipment?
Sur La Table.

Ice cream?
Humphry Slocombe Ice Cream in San Francisco.

Franny's

BROOKLYN, NY

Franny's has been described to me as the Chez Panisse of Brooklyn. Falling short as any comparison like this would, it still reverberates with a chord of truth. Food prepared as simply as possible, with a mandate to allow the ingredients to speak in their purest voice. Cooking at home can get bogged down in "the dish." It is a different kind of cook that looks in the refrigerator for the makings of a meal, notices the asparagus, and thinks, *Oh, asparagus, first green thing of the year, tonight is your night.*

The family meal at Franny's is unfussy and delicious in the way their menu items are. Chef John Adler wrangled the kitchen together for this meal. "We like to braise meat because we can put it in on very low heat in the oven when we leave for the night and it's ready the next day. That way we don't have to give up the oven for prep." This chilaquiles dish, which I put in both the homey and hangover-cure categories, is beer-braised pork. "We had some beer left that wasn't getting used, so I put that in, and it was so good."

The eggs and pickles are another lesson in readiness. If you have some jars of things always in your cupboard and refrigerator, then you don't need to

---

OFF THE MENU

~

Pork Chilaquiles

Hard-boiled Eggs
with Spicy Pickles

S'mores

Suggested wine:
Channing Daughters
Vino Bianco 2008

---

do much other than cook something to doneness. A boiled egg is not a meal, but with some pickled radishes and a few olives, on a little salad of chopped greens, it becomes one.

I ate the s'more right out of the wood oven but the cook who made the marshmallow fluff from scratch assured me that a gas stove burner does the trick just fine, as it does in his girlfriend's apartment. I left Franny's feeling sure that no dessert would ever go without a dollop of fluff again, not on my watch.

Chef John Adler's sister is a friend of mine and she told me with sibling pride that a diner had come to Franny's once and the server noticed he hadn't ordered anything. The man said he had been battling a serious illness and it had restricted his diet to nearly nothing. He was used to it, he assured the server, and he would just eat something at home. The server insisted on getting his short list of "cans" and long list of "can'ts" and took them to John. Despite a fever pitch in the kitchen, he stopped to make a meal of simple ingredients so the man could eat with his family. It is the kind of kitchen that can look in the walk-in and give some special ingredient its night.

Pork Chilaquiles

Chilaquiles is fit for a hangover breakfast or a solid midday meal, spicy and rich. The chipotles en adobo might be too spicy for some people, so if you are concerned about heat, try using just half of the can.

1 cup dried red beans

2 pounds pork shoulder, belly, or other trimmings

Salt and freshly ground black pepper

1 medium onion, sliced

6 cloves garlic, smashed

32-ounce can diced tomatoes

8-ounce can chipotle en adobo

22 ounces Budweiser or similar beer

Canola oil for frying

Twenty 6-inch corn tortillas, quartered or torn into strips

2 cups sour cream

1 bunch cilantro, chopped

Soak the beans overnight and drain. Preheat the oven to 475°F. Season the pork with salt and pepper and place it in a roasting pan with the onion, garlic, tomatoes, chipotle en adobo, and beer. Cover with parchment paper (make sure to tuck parchment into the roasting pan) and then aluminum foil. Roast in the oven for 20 minutes and then lower the heat to 200°F. Slow-cook for 8 hours. Cook beans according to package directions and set aside, reserving the cooking liquid.

Heat about 2 inches of canola oil in a frying pan over medium-high heat. When the oil begins to smoke, fry the tortillas in batches until crisp and golden, about 30 seconds per side. Remove fried tortillas to a rack to drain. Set aside.

Set the oven to 375°F. Remove the pan from the oven and uncover. Let the meat cool a bit in the liquid, remove, and set aside. Put the vegetables and some of the liquid into a food processor and purée. Adjust sauce consistency with more or all of the liquid until the sauce coats the back of a spoon. Add a bit of water if it is too thick.

Mix pork, cooked beans, sauce, and tortillas in a baking dish. Work aggressively with your hands to insure even distribution and sufficient moistening of the tortillas. Add the reserved bean-cooking liquid if needed or if you like a soupier consistency. Adjust the seasoning. Bake, covered, in the oven until completely warmed through, about 20 to 30 minutes. Serve with sour cream and cilantro.

Serves 6 to 8

Hard-boiled Eggs with Spicy Pickles

This is like a grown-up egg salad, reliant on the quick pickling recipe to bring what a relish might add in a more traditional version. If you prepare extra pickled veggies, they will happily accompany meals for weeks to come.

12 eggs

12 jalapeños, thinly sliced

6 carrots, peeled and thinly sliced
   into rounds

2 medium Spanish onions, thinly sliced

1 quart white wine vinegar

1 cup granulated sugar

¼ cup salt

Juice of 4 lemons

Sea salt

1 cup chopped fresh parsley

¾ cup full-bodied extra-virgin olive oil

Salt and freshly ground black pepper

Toast optional

Bring a large pot of water to a boil. Add the eggs and cook at medium boil for 10 minutes. Remove the eggs and shock in an ice bath. Peel and set aside.

In a nonreactive container, combine peppers, carrots, and onions; set aside. In a medium saucepan, bring the vinegar, salt, sugar, and 2 cups water to a boil. Pour over the vegetables and let cool completely.

Quarter the eggs or break them up roughly with your hands. Halve one of the lemons and squeeze the juice over the eggs. Sprinkle with sea salt.

In a large mixing bowl, combine 2 cups of the spicy pickle mix, parsley, juice of the remaining 3 lemons, and olive oil. Adjust seasoning with salt and pepper. Spoon pickle salad over eggs and sprinkle again with sea salt. Delicious when served with plenty of toast.

Serves 6 to 8 as a side

S'mores

You can make marshmallow fluff at home. Doesn't that just expand the boundaries of the universe? At the very least, it makes s'mores a constant possibility. Or homemade versions of Ho Hos or any of those other mysterious and wonderful convenience-store snacks that can survive nuclear fallout.

3 egg whites
2 cups light corn syrup
½ teaspoon salt
2 cups confectioners' sugar
½ to 1 tablespoon vanilla extract *
16 graham crackers
Two 3.5-ounce chocolate bars or 1 cup
    chocolate chips (milk or semisweet)

*To make strawberry fluff, substitute strawberry flavoring for the vanilla and add one or two drops of red food coloring.

In a large bowl, combine the egg whites, corn syrup, and salt. Beat with mixer on high speed for 10 minutes, or until thick and opaque. Add the confectioners' sugar and beat on low speed until well blended. Add the vanilla and mix well, adjusting flavoring. It's now ready to use, store, or freeze for later use. (Fluff can be refrigerated for up to one week. If refrigerated or frozen, stir well with a spoon before serving.)

Preheat the oven to 450°F. Line the bottom of a 9 x 13-inch pan with foil (for easier cleanup). Then line the pan with half of the graham crackers, each broken in half. Spoon a tablespoon of fluff onto each cracker half. Place a piece of chocolate on each, or if using chocolate chips, evenly sprinkle the chips across the crackers. Top each s'more off with another graham cracker half. Bake until golden, for 5 minutes, checking to make sure the fluff and graham crackers don't brown too much. Serve warm.

Serves 8

~ Andrew Feinberg ~

FRANNY'S (BROOKLYN, NY)

Andrew Feinberg and his wife, Francine (AKA Franny) Stephens, co-own Franny's and BKLYN Larder. Franny's is a chefs' restaurant, the excellence of its ingredients and preparations widely acknowledged by professional cooks. BKLYN Larder has the same credence in retail, selling cheeses and other provisions of exquisiteness.

What was your favorite food as a kid?
Lamb chops.

What was the first meal you made that you were proud of?
I made a fresh tagliatelle and Bolognese sauce for my grandparents.

What three adjectives describe your cuisine?
Flavorful, fresh, and satisfying.

What book most influences your food, cookbook or otherwise?
The River Café cookbooks.

What chef do you most admire?
Paul Bertolli.

What is your favorite ingredient?
Artichokes.

What music do you like to hear when you cook?
Dizzy Gillespie.

What is your favorite hangover meal?
Bacon, egg, and cheese sandwich.

What restaurant in the world are you most dying to try?
Asador Etxebarri in Spain.

What kitchen utensil is most indispensable to you?
My MAC chef's knife.

What is your favorite pot?
Le Creuset rondeau.

Who do you most like to cook for?
My family.

If you could do one other job, what would it be?
Major-league baseball player.

What do you most value in a sous chef?
Loyalty.

What food trend would you erase from the annals of history?
Bacon-flavored anything.

What one food would you take with you to a desert island?
Salami.

What is your favorite guilty-pleasure treat?
Drinking an entire Fantôme beer myself.

What most satisfies your sweet tooth?
BKLYN Larder in Brooklyn.

What would you eat at your last meal, if you could plan such a thing?
Prosciutto di Parma, kale *fettunta*, spaghetti with garlic and oil, *bistecca alla Fiorentina*, roasted potatoes, and tiramisu.

Cheeseburger or foie gras?
Cheeseburger.

What's your favorite place (and what is your favorite thing to order) for:

A splurge meal?
Lincoln in New York.

A cup of coffee?
Southside Coffee in Brooklyn.

A greasy-spoon meal?
M. Wells Diner in Long Island City, New York.

Hamburger craving?
Diner in Williamsburg, Brooklyn.

Bread desire?
St. John Bread in London.

Frasca Food and Wine

The menu at Frasca is a tribute to the wines and cuisine of the Friuli-Venezia Giulia region, a little nook that sits where Slovenia and Austria border on northeastern Italy. Since Friuli-Venezia Giulia is both mountainous and coastal, it reflects both the reality and fantasies of a Colorado kitchen.

Chef Lachlan Mackinnon and master sommelier Bobby Stuckey are the collaborative forces behind Frasca. They began as a local secret in the mountains, but these French Laundry alums quickly outshone their humble start. They have been featured and praised by *tutti*, from the *Today Show* to *Food & Wine* and *Bon Appétit*.

> ## OFF THE MENU
>
> ~
>
> Shrimp Curry
>
> *Suggested wine:*
> Copain "Tous Ensemble"
> Mendocino County
> Viognier 2009

The shrimp curry they serve at staff meal is a Thai dish, but it also provides the comfort needed in both wintry climes and the marine haul of a fishing town. The versatile curry base would graciously accommodate chicken or tofu just as well, or simply more of the vegetables already called for. It is a luscious stew—spicy, creamy, and very rich. With a bowl of steaming rice and some dark, earthy greens, a restrained scoop of this makes a meal. Although an eight-year old at my table declared adamantly before dinner that she did not like shrimp, coconut milk, or curry, she did manage to empty three bowls without a pause.

Shrimp Curry

All the vegetal detritus of preparation for this curry (ends of carrots, fennel, scallions, onion, and skins of potato, carrot, ginger, etc.) can be used to make a stock while the curry simmers. The stock can then be used to cook the rice, which adds a finishing layer of flavor and also makes an excellent fried rice the next day.

2 tablespoons grapeseed oil

1 tablespoon chopped fresh ginger

1 tablespoon chopped fresh garlic

½ cup each medium-diced carrot, fennel, and onion

1 teaspoon salt

⅓ cup fish sauce

⅓ cup soy sauce

½ cup rice vinegar

Three 14-ounce cans coconut milk

2 tablespoons curry paste

2 teaspoons madras curry powder

½ cup medium-diced potato

1 pound shrimp, peeled and deveined

1 bunch cilantro, coarsely chopped

2 scallions, sliced thin

¼ cup peanuts, toasted and crushed

2 limes, cut into wedges

Steamed rice

In a large pan over medium heat, heat grapeseed oil until it shimmers, add the ginger and garlic, and let it cook for 2 minutes. Add the carrot, fennel, onion, and salt, and cook for 10 minutes or until the onions are translucent, stirring occasionally.

Add the fish sauce and reduce by one third over medium-high heat, about 5 minutes. Add the soy sauce and rice vinegar and reduce by one third over medium-high heat, about 8 minutes. Add the coconut milk, curries, and potatoes; stir and adjust the seasoning. Simmer until the mixture has reduced the coconut milk by half, about 1 hour. Add the shrimp and keep simmering until they are pink and cooked through, about 5 minutes. Add the cilantro, scallions, and peanuts, and serve with lime wedges and steamed rice.

Serves 6

Galatoire's

New Orleans has an old-world style of service. Waiters—a word that feels anachronistic everywhere but here—keep their jobs a long time and staff turnaround is often in eras rather than seasons. Nowhere is this more true than at Galatoire's. Though many tourists will recognize the name, Galatoire's business remains about eighty percent locals. The dining room is dollhouse perfect, with intricate wallpaper, mirrors, and sconces.

Service here is not based on the American norm. Instead of sections, waiters are given tables when they are requested. Since the diners are mostly regulars, and most of the servers have been at Galatoire's for twenty-five to forty years, there are relationships that evolve over time. The dining room is long and so a communication technique has developed wherein a front maitre d' signals to a back maitre d' which server has been asked for. The signal is a gesture like a catcher in baseball might throw. The pretend firing of a machine gun indicates a waiter who served in combat, a flapping hand indicates another server who is notoriously chatty.

The staff meal had the languorous air of a European midday meal. There was no information to share: these men know the menu, they know the customers, they know their work. There was only a spell of time to share. Some read the paper but most conversed. Before lunch there was talk of a run down to the sandwich shop, but word got out that Yakamein would be served and the talk died down.

Yakamein is a NOLA hangover cure. You would have to imagine that this city would have a hangover cure in its collective repertoire. It is pho that has been hanging out in Louisiana for a few generations. Like pho or noodle soup from many Asian cuisines, it is simple and nourishing, cheap to prepare, and finished at the table with condiments. Yakamein is served in a pot with accoutrements like yellow mustard, ketchup, hot sauce, and scallions. It is a simple dish, but one that fortifies. It is a favorite at Galatoire's, and the line in the kitchen stayed long all through lunch, with the staff returning multiple times to refill their bowls.

After we ate, we sat a good long time in the empty dining room and I heard stories from the new guy by a decade, a waiter who had been there about eight years. He was going to see a concert and was sharing names of singers now past their era of cool, proving his credentials to the senior servers. In this dining room, the old man is king.

OFF THE MENU

Yakamein Soup

Suggested wine:
Anne Amie Vineyards
Pinot Gris 2009

Yakamein Soup
(aka Old Sober)

Yakamein soup has earned the alias "Old Sober" in New Orleans because of its reputation as an elixir to cure the French Quarter hangover. It is a favorite of the Galatoire's staff. Now sold in corner stores all over the city, it is generally believed to have originated with the Chinese immigrants of the 1800s who were brought to the area to work on railroads and sugar plantations. The dish has taken on the character of the city over the years.

5 quarts beef stock or low-sodium beef broth

1 tablespoon creole seasoning

3 to 4 tablespoons soy sauce

3 to 4 tablespoons Worcestershire sauce

3 to 4 tablespoons ketchup

2½ to 3 pounds chuck roast

1½ pounds spaghetti, cooked

3 or 4 hard-boiled eggs, peeled and halved

2 bunches scallions, chopped

Optional:

Soy sauce

Ketchup

Sriracha or hot sauce

Worcestershire sauce

Yellow mustard

In a stockpot, combine the stock, creole seasoning, soy sauce, Worcestershire, and ketchup. Add the chuck roast and simmer over medium-low heat for 1½ to 2 hours, until fork tender. Set the roast aside to cool, reserving the broth and skimming off most of the fat that accumulates at the top. Shred or chop the meat. Divide the spaghetti into individual soup bowls and add meat, eggs, scallions, and hot broth. Serve with optional condiments on the side.

Serves 6 to 8

~ Brian Landry ~

GALATOIRE'S (NEW ORLEANS, LA)

As executive chef of both Galatoire's in New Orleans and Galatoire's Bistro in Baton Rouge, Brian Landry is charged with upholding the standards of diners with long memories. In 2008, he was voted "King of Louisiana Seafood" by the Louisiana Seafood Promotion and Marketing Board.

What was your favorite food as a kid?
Shrimp.

What was the first meal you made that you were proud of?
Sautéed speckled trout with toasted pecans.

What three adjectives describe your cuisine?
Fresh, local, and simple.

What book most influences your food, cookbook or otherwise?
Larousse Gastronomique.

What chef do you most admire?
Eric Ripert.

What is your favorite ingredient?
Fish that I caught myself.

What music do you like to hear when you cook?
New Orleans jazz.

What is your favorite midnight snack?
A scrambled-egg sandwich with white truffle oil.

What is your favorite hangover meal?
A cheeseburger with sauce from Bud's Broiler in New Orleans.

What restaurant in the world are you most dying to try?
The Fat Duck in Berkshire, England.

What kitchen utensil is most indispensable to you?
Fish spatula.

If you could do one other job, what would it be?
Musician.

What do you most value in a sous chef?
Being able to read my mind.

What food trend would you most like to erase from the annals of history?
Canned vegetables.

What one food would you take with you to a desert island?
Bacon.

Cheeseburger or foie gras?
Cheeseburger.

What's your favorite place (and what is your favorite thing to order) for:

Happy hour?
A Dark and Stormy at any beach on the Gulf Coast of Florida.

Pastry?
La Boulangerie, New Orleans.

A late-night/after-work meal?
La Peniche, New Orleans.

A cup of coffee?
Rue de la Course, New Orleans.

A greasy-spoon meal?
Camellia Grill, New Orleans.

Ice cream?
Chocolate and peanut-butter ice cream from Creole Creamery, New Orleans.

Chocolate?
Southern Candy Makers, New Orleans.

Hatfield's

When Hatfield's re-opened in their current location, there were hefty expectations. Quinn Hatfield had been making highly praised food already that seemed to herald a renaissance of fine dining. And Karen and Quinn were moving to Melrose Avenue, into the former Citrus space (Michel Richard's Hollywood hobnobbery closed in 2001, but every successive tenant is compared, unfavorably, to the restaurant that made it "Real Estate"). Los Angeles loves the latest thing, and so the press coverage was vast.

I had eaten at Hatfield's, so I have my own ideas about the excellence of the food and the glamorous starkness of the dining room. I was curious, though, what Angeleno food writers had wrung from their first meal at Hatfield's on Melrose. I learned as much about food writers as I did about Hatfield's. Everyone mentioned the same dishes, like Chef Hatfield's Croque Madame, which has yellowtail sashimi and prosciutto in a brioche with a quail egg over the top (instead of the traditional grilled ham-and-gruyère sandwich with a fried egg on top). The Croque Madame was an unqualified hit, but almost every other dish was starkly disagreed upon. One writer's "creative" was another

> ## OFF THE MENU
>
> ~
>
> Pork Meatballs
>
> Salsa Cruda
>
> Endive, Almond, Apple, and Manchego Salad
>
> Rosemary and Goat Cheese Potato Gratin
>
> Apple-Huckleberry Cobbler
>
> *Suggested wine:*
> Frei Brothers Dry Creek Valley Zinfandel 2009

writer's "fussy." This is my plea to taste for yourself. Sometimes a bad meal isn't a failure but a mismatch between the diner and the chef. And discovering what you don't like can be just as important as knowing what you do like. All that said, I am certain you would like Hatfield's.

Our staff meal was in the back room, where a very long table was full of employees. Karen Hatfield was in the final throes of pregnancy, which made her even more the mother of the table, teasing and reminiscing. The kitchen is behind a glass wall, so that diners can see their meal being prepared and experience the juxtaposition of the linen-crisp serenity in the dining room and the clamor of the kitchen. So sitting in the dining room, unobserved, is a time of silliness and camaraderie.

Besides goofing off, the meal had the pleasures of being tasty. It has one of my favorite qualities in a dinner: variety—variety of texture, of richness, of flavors and of temperatures. I like that I could have had a healthy dinner of salad and a few meatballs and just the tiniest sliver of gratin. Or, I could have done just what I did and divided my plate equally among greens, meat, and dairy.

BOTTOM: Chef Quinn Hatfield at the helm of the table.

Pork Meatballs

These meatballs are tender on the inside and slightly crisp on the outside. They are elegantly paired with a fresh salsa and a creamy potato gratin. For the meatballs, Hatfield uses the trim from pork loin and belly, which yields a good mixture of lean meat and firm fat. You can also substitute ground pork and a bit of lard for the mixture.

2½ pounds lean pork, cut into 1-inch dice
¾ pound pork fat, cut into 1-inch dice
1 egg
2 egg yolks
½ cup grated Parmesan cheese
¼ cup chopped fresh parsley
Salt and freshly ground black pepper
3 cups fresh bread crumbs
¾ cup milk
Canola oil or lard for frying

To get a nice grind and produce a tender meatball, remove the silver skin, connective tissue, and any stringy fat from the trimmed pork. Put the prepared meat and fat on a tray in a single layer and place in the freezer until very cold, about 15 minutes. Set up a meat grinder with a large bowl in an ice bath underneath to catch the ground meat and keep it cold. Grind all of the meat and fat.

Preheat the oven to 325°F. Add the eggs, Parmesan, parsley, and salt and pepper to the meat; thoroughly mix these ingredients by hand to insure a homogenous blend. Toss the bread crumbs with the milk to evenly moisten them, add to the meat, and mix well. Form the meat mixture into large balls, about 2 inches in diameter.

Heat about 1 inch of oil or lard in a large skillet and fry the meatballs in batches until golden brown all over. Transfer each batch of meatballs to a rack placed on top of a sheet pan. After frying, put the pan in the oven and cook meatballs until internal temperature reaches 160°F on a meat thermometer, about 10 more minutes. Serve immediately with Salsa Cruda.

Serves 6

Salsa Cruda

In high summer, when tomatoes are ubiquitous, make this. Make it until you begin to add your own ideas. It could end there, with a slap of salsa cruda on your plate. Or it could be the beginning of soup, pasta, meatloaf, eggs poached in tomatoes . . .

½ cup vegetable oil
3 cloves garlic, thinly sliced
2 shallots, thinly sliced
1 tablespoon oregano leaves
¼ cup fresh basil leaves
¼ cup fresh parsley leaves
3 cups diced fresh Roma tomatoes
1 tablespoon extra-virgin olive oil
Salt and freshly ground black pepper

Combine the vegetable oil, garlic, and shallots in a small saucepan and heat gently over medium temperature. The garlic and shallots should cook slowly and become tender without picking up any color, about 8 minutes. Once they are tender, add the herbs and fry them for one minute. Immediately combine the garlic mixture with the tomatoes; purée it in a blender or food processor. Season the sauce with the olive oil, salt, and pepper, and blend to combine. Serve immediately or keep at room temperature until ready to serve within a couple of hours.

Makes about 4 cups

Endive, Almond, Apple, and Manchego Salad

A Hollywood salad, glamorous and chic. The nuttiness and warmth of the Manchego and almonds set it apart from the standard.

½ cup sliced blanched almonds

6 ounces manchego cheese

1 large Pink Lady apple

1 teaspoon lemon juice

½ cup balsamic vinegar

2 teaspoons Dijon mustard

1 teaspoon honey

¾ cup vegetable oil

3 heads Belgian endive

12 fresh basil leaves

6 cups lollo rosso lettuce

6 cups tango lettuce

Zest of 1 lemon

Salt and freshly ground black pepper

Preheat the oven to 350°F. Put the almonds on a sheet pan in a single layer and toast in the oven until golden brown, about 8 to 10 minutes. Set aside to cool at room temperature. Cut the manchego into very thin slices. Quarter, core, and thinly slice the apple. Toss in a bowl with the lemon juice.

Place the vinegar, mustard, and honey in a bowl and whisk well to combine. Slowly drizzle in the oil while whisking, until the dressing is emulsified.

Cut off the stem ends of the endive heads and separate the leaves. Tear each leaf into 1-inch pieces. Tear the basil into ¼-inch pieces. Wash the lettuces well and dry in a salad spinner.

Place the greens, endive, and basil in a large mixing bowl. Add the almonds, apple, and lemon zest. Spoon some vinaigrette around the inside of the bowl and season with salt and pepper. Toss the salad well and taste; add more vinaigrette, salt, or pepper if needed. Transfer the salad, alternating with layers of manchego slices, to a serving platter or individual plates; a little salad, a slice of cheese, and so on. Serve immediately.

Serves 6 as a side

Rosemary and Goat Cheese Potato Gratin

In college, I spent a year in Grenoble, France, where I first encountered an excellent gratin and its creamy decadence. Hatfield's version expands on the classic by adding the woodiness of rosemary and the tang of goat cheese.

9 medium russet potatoes, peeled
1½ sticks unsalted butter
¾ cup all-purpose flour
5 cups milk, room temperature
4 ounces fresh goat cheese
Salt and freshly ground black pepper
½ cup grated Parmesan cheese
¼ cup chopped fresh parsley

Preheat the oven to 340°F. For the potatoes, fill a large stockpot halfway with water and bring to a boil; lightly salt the water.

Meanwhile, melt the butter in a large saucepan. Add the flour and whisk over medium-low heat to create a roux; continue to cook gently for a few minutes, until it begins to turn a blond color. While whisking, gradually add the milk, being sure to beat smooth any lumps. Continue whisking until the béchamel sauce comes to a gentle simmer and begins to thicken. Simmer very gently, stirring frequently, for about 10 minutes. Turn off the heat, add the goat cheese and rosemary, and whisk until smooth. Season well with salt and pepper. Keep the sauce in a warm place; if it gets too thick, add some milk to achieve a pourable consistency.

Use a mandoline to slice the potatoes into disks about ⅓-inch thick. Add the potatoes to the pot of boiling water and allow it to return to a simmer. Lower the heat and simmer until the potatoes are still a bit firm in the center, about 5 minutes; drain in a large colander.

Place a layer of potatoes in the bottom of 3½- to 4-quart pan or rondeau and spoon some béchamel over just to cover. Repeat this layering process until all the potatoes and béchamel are used, topping the final layer of potatoes with enough béchamel to cover completely. Sprinkle the Parmesan cheese over the gratin and bake for 1 to 1½ hours, until the top is a nice golden brown and the potatoes are very tender. Allow the gratin to cool for 10 minutes. Sprinkle with chopped parsley and serve.

Serves 6 to 8 as a side

Apple-Huckleberry Cobbler

Cobbler is the perennial dessert of summer, a vehicle for all those backyard fruit harvests. The shortcake gives this version a buttery richness that hums in harmony with the brightness of berries.

Filling

8 or 9 Granny Smith apples, peeled, cored
   and sliced
½ cup granulated sugar
1 cup huckleberries, or substitute blueberries
Zest and juice of ½ lemon
1½ teaspoons apple pectin

Shortcake

1⅔ cups all-purpose flour
3½ tablespoons granulated sugar
⅛ teaspoon salt
1½ tablespoons baking powder
6 tablespoons unsalted butter, cold,
   cut into ½-inch cubes
⅔ cup plus 1 tablespoon heavy cream
3 tablespoons raw sugar

In a bowl, toss the apples in the sugar and let sit for an hour.

Meanwhile, make the shortcake: put all dry ingredients except raw sugar in a mixing bowl. Add butter cubes and mix on medium-low speed until the pieces of butter are pea-sized. Slowly pour in ⅔ cup cream until just combined. Do not overmix. Pat dough into a circle and chill for 15 minutes. Then roll dough out with a rolling pin to a ¾–inch thickness and punch out 2½-inch circles with a cutter or the rim of a glass (or any other desired shape with a cookie cutter). Brush with the remaining 1 tablespoon cream and sprinkle raw sugar on top. Chill until needed.

Add the lemon zest, lemon juice, and pectin to the apples. In a buttered 3-quart casserole dish, layer a third of the apples and sprinkle a third of the huckleberries over them. Repeat two more times, saving a few apples to cover the top.

Bake at 375°F for 10 minutes. Then remove from oven and arrange shortbread circles evenly over the top, covering about 50 percent of the fruit. Lower the heat to 350°F and bake for an additional 15 to 20 minutes, or until shortcake is golden and fruit is bubbly.

Serves 12

~ Karen Hatfield and Quinn Hatfield ~

HATFIELD'S (LOS ANGELES, CA)

Chef Quinn Hatfield co-owns and manages this eponymous establishment with his wife, Karen. Hatfield's Restaurant was one of *Bon Appétit* magazine's Best New Restaurants in 2010 and has earned a Michelin star.

What was your favorite food as a kid?
KH & QH: When we were really young, we both loved fettuccini Alfredo.

What was the first meal you made that you were proud of?
QH: Both of us started cooking at a young age (under ten years old). For Karen, it was sausage with peppers and onions; for me, it was fried-egg-and-cheese sandwiches.

What three adjectives describe your cuisine?
KH & QH: California/French, modern, and seasonal.

What book most influences your food, cookbook or otherwise?
KH & QH: Andrew Dornenburg and Karen Page's *Culinary Artistry*.

What chef do you most admire?
KH & QH: Jean Georges Vongerichten.

What is your favorite ingredient?
KH: Persian mulberries, and celery root.
QH: Kabocha squash.

What music do you like to hear when you cook?
KH & QH: We never cook with music in the restaurant, but at home, we went through a phase where we always played Mose Allison.

What is your favorite midnight snack?
KH & QH: Greasy deli food; we sometimes go for a Reuben.

What restaurant in the world are you most dying to try?
KH & QH: L'Espérance in Vézelay, France.

If you could do one other job, what would it be?
KH: Photographer. QH: Professional cyclist.

What food trend would you most like to erase from the annals of history?
KH: Cupcakes. QH: Food trucks.

What one food would you take with you to a desert island?
KH: Pasta. QH: Hamburgers.

What is your favorite guilty-pleasure treat?
KH: Hamburgers and pie from Apple Pan in Los Angeles. QH: Shoyu noodle soup from Rai Rai Ken in New York City.

What most satisfies your sweet tooth?
KH: Ice cream satisfies my sweet tooth.
QH: Definitely doughnuts.

What would you eat at your last meal, if you could plan such a thing?
KH: Blue Ribbon in New York City.
QH: Really good Chinese food.

Cheeseburger or foie gras?
KH: Foie gras. QH: Cheeseburger.

What's your favorite place (and what is your favorite thing to order) for:

A splurge meal?
KH: Urasawa in Los Angeles, for omakase.

Breakfast?
KH: BLD in Los Angeles, for the ricotta pancakes.

Pastry?
KH: Joan's on Third in Los Angeles, for the morning buns.

A late-night/after-work meal?
KH: Canters Deli or Damiano's Mr. Pizza in Los Angeles, for anything on the menu.

A cup of coffee?
KH: An espresso from Stumptown in Portland or New York.

Groceries?
KH: The farmers' market in Hollywood.

Kitchen equipment?
KH: Sur La Table.

Chocolate?
KH: See's Candies.

Herbsaint

Herbsaint is the grande dame in Donald Link's coterie of restaurants, the most haute—three restaurants, an event space, and a butcher shop being the other gals. Even among his peers, the famous chef-restaurateurs of New Orleans, Link is in the top tier. He is also profoundly Louisianian: his family was influential in the rice industry of the region and his food continues to add dimension to the area's cuisine. Link has this place in his blood. Where a non-native chef's politely constrained attempts to honor the region's food traditions might fall short, Link suffers from no such rigidity. He uses the ingredients and techniques like a language, freely speaking in his native tongue.

Staff meal at Herbsaint was a NOLA tradition of red beans and rice on the Monday I visited. The first day of the week being a time set aside for chores and work, this meal is something you put on the stove and don't fuss with again until supper, except to occasionally stir or smash a bean against the side of the pot to check the tenderness. The beans are tender and spicy hot and completed by the starchiness of rice. Rice and beans are also, of course, a complete protein and one of the least expensive ways to meet this nutritional need. Link's version brings some bounty to a meal based on scarcity of time and resources. The ham bone, smoked ham, and sausage add decadence, even in smaller amounts. You should always be able to provide for yourself and your family; the richness and storied past of this combination elevates it from making do.

Link's staff is young and nomadic, unlike many of the other restaurants I have visited in New Orleans with staffs that remain for decades and sometimes for generations. The other staff meals I had in the city tended to move at the pace of the elders at the table and were punctuated by polished anecdotes. This was more like the kiddy table. New Orleans is an American anomaly, identified very deeply with roots in a land of churning earth. But it is also a young culture, and kids drive in to learn and play music and eat and stay up very, very late. Herbsaint is also the name of an anise-flavored liqueur that originated in New Orleans and was engineered as a post-Prohibition answer to absinthe. The name evokes those two rivulets of influence here, both the staid glory of a gilded era and a willingness toward madness that lives outside of eras.

OFF THE MENU

New Orleans
Red Beans and Rice

Suggested wine:
Hanzell Vineyards Estate
Pinot Noir 2008

BOTTOM LEFT: Chef Donald Link in the Herbsaint kitchen. BOTTOM RIGHT: Brian Fuller, a server, eating in the dining room.

New Orleans Red Beans and Rice

A Louisiana staple, red beans and rice are there in times of scarcity as well as times of bounty. The most critical element is to give the beans enough time and liquid to really cook through. There's nothing worse than a pot of beans that came off the heat too soon and nothing so good as a perfectly prepared red bean.

1 pound dry red beans

Ham bone

6 bay leaves

8 ounces sausage, ½-inch dice

8 ounces smoked ham,
   ½-inch dice

1 medium onion, small diced

1 small tomato, small diced

2 jalapeños, finely chopped

1 teaspoon cayenne or other
   dried pepper, optional

6 cloves garlic, finely chopped

2 tablespoons whole-grain
   mustard

¼ cup red wine vinegar

2 teaspoons dried thyme

1 tablespoon salt

½ tablespoon freshly ground
   black pepper

4 cups cooked rice

Soak the beans overnight; drain.

In a large stockpot, combine 1 gallon of water, beans, ham bone, and bay leaves over high heat and bring to a simmer.

In a separate pan, brown sausage and ham for 4 to 5 minutes. Add onion and brown for 5 minutes more. Add tomato, jalapeños, cayenne, garlic, mustard, vinegar, thyme, salt, and pepper, and continue to sauté for an additional 5 to 8 minutes.

Transfer the sausage mixture to the pot of beans and simmer slowly, uncovered, for 2½ to 3 hours. Stir occasionally.

Approximately 10 minutes before beans are done, use a wooden spoon or spatula to mash and cream the beans along the inside of the pot. If beans are too firm, add a bit more water and cook until beans are soft. Serve over individual bowls of hot rice.

Serves 8

～ Donald Link ～

HERBSAINT (NEW ORLEANS, LA)

Donald Link is executive chef and owner at not only Herbsaint, but also Calcasieu, Cochon, and Cochon Butcher, a butcher shop and eatery. Author of the award-winning *Real Cajun: Rustic Home Cooking from Donald Link's Louisiana*, Link was the recipient of the James Beard Award for Best New Chef of the South in 2007.

What was your favorite food as a kid?
My granddad's creamed corn.

What was the first meal you made that you were proud of?
Gumbo.

What three adjectives describe your cuisine?
Focused, fresh, and flavorful.

What book most influences your food, cookbook or otherwise?
Paul Prudhomme, Fernand Point, and Elizabeth David's *Italian Food*.

What chef do you most admire?
Fernand Point.

What is your favorite ingredient?
Salt.

What music do you like to hear when you cook?
Rock.

What is your favorite hangover meal?
Fried eggs, grits, and sausage.

What is your favorite midnight snack?
Left-over fried rice.

What restaurant in the world are you most dying to try?
Cal Pep in Barcelona, which I am going to this year.

If you could do one other job, what would it be?
Astrophysicist.

What do you most value in a sous chef?
A great palate and a great leader.

What one food would you take with you to a desert island?
Boudin sausage.

What is your favorite guilty-pleasure treat?
Fried rice with fried eggs for breakfast.

What most satisfies your sweet tooth?
Chocolate.

What would you eat at your last meal, if you could plan such a thing?
Boiled crawfish étouffée from Hawk's Crawfish Restaurant in Rayne, Louisiana.

Cheeseburger or foie gras?
Cheeseburger.

What's your favorite place (and what is your favorite thing to order) for:

A splurge meal?
La Tour d'Argent in Paris for the Burgundy, the duck, and the view.

Breakfast?
Bacon, grits, biscuits, and eggs at my dad's fishing camp.

Pastry?
La Boulangerie in New Orleans for croissants and the French king cake during Mardi Gras.

A late-night/after-work meal?
Bouligny Tavern in New Orleans for the *fritto misto* and short ribs.

A cup of coffee?
Chicory blend from Community Coffee's in New Orleans.

A greasy-spoon meal?
Louie's Café in Baton Rouge for the omelets.

Chocolate?
Jean-Paul Hévin Chocolatier in Paris.

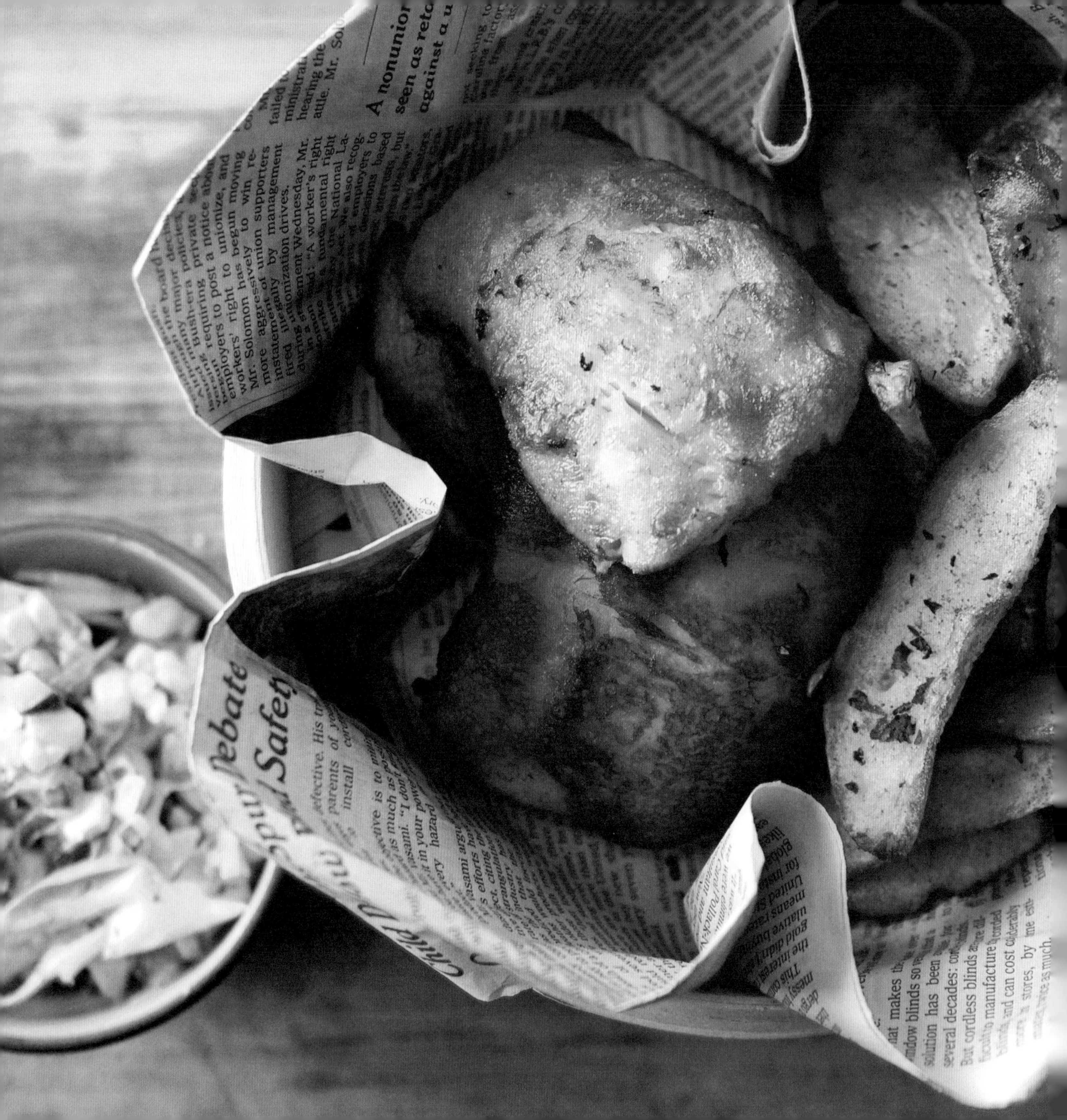

La Condesa

La Condesa is named for a neighborhood in Mexico City, which was the Hollywood of the capital in the 1950s. The restaurant resonates that glamour, in spirit more than stylistic reference. It is vital and buoyant and serves Saturday night cocktails, with a massive selection of tequilas.

Chef Rene Ortiz's menu rises from Mexican street food, but prepared with pasture-fed and heritage meats. He staunchly suggests indulging in all five of his versions of ceviche and locals endorse his crickets and the *torta de queso de cabra*. When diners rave about insects and goat dishes, you know the chef can cook.

At La Condesa, their regional Mexican cooking generates a healthy amount of fish trimmings, which inevitably wind up in the staff meal coffers. It takes creativity and commitment to make cod appealing to the staff every day but this version of fish and chips is eternally popular. It may be more Saturday afternoon than Saturday night but that doesn't diminish its excellence. The frying is fast and the fish wants to be eaten straight away. Make extra of the slaw dressing. Dipping the potatoes in it is like grown-up fries and ranch dressing.

OFF THE MENU

Fish and Chips

Cabbage and Corn Slaw

Fried Paprika Potatoes

Suggested wine:
Preston Vineyards
Madam Preston 2009

Fried Paprika Potatoes

**It always strikes me as a form of magic to make fried potatoes at home.
The paprika is the lingering note, so play with that, if you play with anything.**

Canola oil for frying
4 pounds Idaho potatoes, peeled and cut
    into wedges
1½ tablespoons dried Mexican oregano
½ tablespoon smoked paprika
3 cloves garlic, thinly sliced
1 jalapeño, thinly sliced

Par-fry the potatoes at 250°F until tender. Take out and drain on paper towels. Raise oil temperature to 375°F and fry the potatoes again until golden brown. Remove and drain on paper towels. Mix together all the other ingredients. Season fries with the spice mixture and salt and pepper. Hold until ready to eat.

Serves 6 to 8

Fish and Chips

This recipe calls for one Tecate in the batter but you will want many more than that. This is a meal for hammocks and sunlight and having just one more bite, all day long.

2 cups all-purpose flour

2 teaspoons salt

2 teaspoons baking powder

12-ounce can Tecate beer

1 cup whole milk

4 eggs

3 pounds cod or fish trimmings, cut into bite-size pieces

Canola oil for frying

Salt and freshly ground black pepper

Small white corn tortillas

Lime wedges, for garnish

Chopped fresh cilantro, for topping

White vinegar, for sprinkling

Mix the flour, salt, and baking powder in a bowl. Mix beer, milk, and eggs in a large bowl. Add the flour to the beer mixture and mix just enough. Do not overmix, to keep the carbonation. Working in batches, add the fish to the batter and let it stand a few minutes. Remove and fry at 375°F until golden brown, about 1 to 2 minutes. Transfer to a wire rack over a sheet pan lined with paper towels to drain. Season with salt and pepper and hold in a warm place until all the fish is fried. Serve with warmed corn tortillas, lime wedges, cilantro, and vinegar.

Serves 6 to 8

Cabbage and Corn Slaw

As an alternative to tartar sauce, I make extra slaw dressing to use as a dipping sauce for the fish and the potatoes, but then I'm decadent.

1 head green cabbage, shredded

1 red onion, thinly sliced

Kernels from 4 ears of corn

1 bunch cilantro, coarsely chopped

1¼ cups mayonnaise

1 teaspoon granulated sugar

Juice of 1 lime

Salt and freshly ground black pepper

Mix all the ingredients together and season with salt and pepper.

Serves 6 to 8 as a side

◦ Rene Ortiz ◦

LA CONDESA (AUSTIN, TX)

Chef Rene Ortiz has an impeccable resume. He has traveled extensively as a cook and toughed it out under famous, demanding chefs, like Boulud and Ducasse. After becoming chef de cuisine at Patria, New York, he moved to La Esquina, New York, and finally, La Condesa.

What was your favorite food as a kid?
Boiled shrimp that my mother would make about once every month.

What was the first meal you made that you were proud of?
Pasta with arrabbiata sauce when I was fifteen. It was a special at Antibes Restaurant in San Antonio.

What three adjectives describe your cuisine?
Sensual, complex, and rustic.

What book most influences your food, cookbook or otherwise?
Joy of Cooking, for its simplicity.

What chef do you most admire?
Peter Gordon.

What is your favorite ingredient?
Chilies.

What music do you like to hear when you cook?
Right now, CSS [Brazilian band] or anything electronic and good to dance to.

What is your favorite hangover meal?
Huevos rancheros.

What is your favorite midnight snack?
A peanut-butter-and-jelly sandwich.

What restaurant in the world are you most dying to try?
Noma in Copenhagen.

What kitchen utensil is most indispensable to you?
My Gray Kunz sauce spoon.

Who do you most like to cook for?
My family; I would most like to cook for Rick Bayless.

If you could do one other job, what would it be?
Designing denim jeans.

What do you most value in a sous chef?
Dedication to the craft and honesty.

What food trend would you most like to erase from the annals of history?
Cooking food with lasers.

What one food would you take with you to a desert island?
A whole pig.

What is your favorite guilty-pleasure treat?
Jamón ibérico.

What would you eat at your last meal, if you could plan such a thing?
Crispy fontina bread from Avec in Chicago.

What's your favorite place (and what is your favorite thing to order) for:

A splurge meal?
Anything at Uchiko in Austin.

Breakfast?
Continental breakfast at Balthazar Restaurant in New York City.

A late-night/after-work meal?
The chicken "Karaage" from Uchiko's executive chef Paul Qui's food truck East Side King in Austin.

A cup of coffee?
A single-cup brew from Stumptown in Portland, Oregon.

A greasy-spoon meal?
A burger at the Corner Bistro in New York City.

Kitchen equipment?
J. B. Prince Company on East 31st Street in New York City.

Ice cream?
Mexican vanilla with Nutter Butter crushed into it at Amy's Ice Creams in Austin.

Chocolate?
Caffe Falai on Lafayette St. in New York City.

La Provence

As its name suggests, a visit to La Provence resembles an escape to the French countryside. From New Orleans, over Lake Pontchartrain and through some woods, you arrive at John Besh's restaurant, not grand but proper and timeless. It is the sort of place you come to propose marriage (and if a young man makes a reservation with this intention, the couple will be seated at either Table 11 or Table 63, both romantically nookish spots).

I arrived early to spend a few hours with the staff before the meal, time in which the restaurant's chronology tiled into place. La Provence was opened forty years ago by Mr. Chris (Chris Kerageorgiou). Ms. Joyce was hired thirty-seven years ago. She shared these numbers and facts with me as she stoked the fireplace near the bar, known as Ms. Joyce's Fire. Her current incarnation is bartender and, I rapidly surmised, ambassador of local history. We sat together by the fire briefly, and watched the birds outside in the courtyard, flitting to and from the houses she had built for them. And Ms. Joyce flitted to and from the fire, bringing me fresh herbs from the garden, sheets of her poetry, and well-masticated helpings of information.

I learned that chef John Besh worked at La

OFF THE MENU

Mangalitsa Jambalaya

Gumbo z'Herbes

King Cake

Suggested wine:
Merry Edwards
Sonoma Coast
Pinot Noir 2008

Provence as a young cook and that Mr. Kerageorgiou was his hot-tempered mentor. Besh bought the restaurant intending to let his teacher continue running it but Mr. Kerageorgiou died just a few days later. Chef Besh continues, according to Ms. Joyce, with the same level of excellence and fiery intensity. Under Besh's tenure, there has been a renovation. There are also hogs being raised outside and a garden, both ingredient providers for the kitchen.

This place is obviously a touchstone for John Besh, who has entered the world of celebrity-chef. Like any brand of fame, star chefs fall into a whoosh of disorienting exposure. On television, Besh is an articulate, and sophisticated chef. At La Provence, he is all those things, but he is also the young cook who was temporarily fired by Chef Kerageorgiou via Ms. Joyce. "She was one of only two people to fire me. And I had little boys to feed!" John clearly takes a devious pleasure in ribbing Ms. Joyce.

Ms. Joyce is tough on Besh, as if she is still taking stock of him after all these years. "He is a good man. He works very hard," she confides just before I leave. I almost tear up. It has the heft of parental approval, of being loved in the place where you are from.

TOP RIGHT: Chef John Besh reminisces with Ms. Joyce Bates.

155

Mangalitsa Jambalaya

The Hungarian Mangalitsa pig was imported to America in 2007 by Heath Putnam. Mangalitsa was first featured at the French Laundry and quickly gained popularity among chefs for its fat. Most American pigs have been bred for large amounts of lean meat. This is a lard-type pig and chefs love the juicy meat and the thick backfat for curing. La Provence gets their pigs from Heath Putnam Farms and fattens them to control the quality of meat and fat.* Jambalaya is often thought of as a Creole paella. The rice is fortified with slow-cooked pork and piles of seasonings. The addition of tomatoes is typical of New Orleans cookery.

1 pound Mangalitsa or regular bacon, diced

4 cups diced onions

3 cups diced bell peppers

3 cups diced celery

⅓ cup minced garlic

1½ tablespoons pimentón de la vera

1 tablespoon celery salt

1 teaspoon dried thyme

1 dried bay leaf

1 teaspoon cayenne

1 teaspoon salt

1 teaspoon freshly ground black pepper

3½ cups converted Louisiana white rice

3½ cups or 28-ounce can crushed tomatoes

3 cups rich chicken broth

Braised Mangalitsa Boar (page 157)

1 bunch green onions, chopped

Heat a large cast-iron pot over high heat until hot; reduce the heat to medium-high. Add the bacon and cook, stirring occasionally, until crisp, about 5 to 8 minutes. Leave the fat in the pot and add the onions, bell pepper, celery, and garlic. Continue to stir, allowing the ingredients to brown, about 5 minutes. Stir in all the dry seasonings, then add the rice. Cook the rice for 5 to 7 minutes over medium heat. Add the crushed tomatoes, broth, and braised pork to the pot and raise the heat to high until the liquids boil, then simmer, covered, for an additional 15 minutes, until the rice is cooked. Remove the pot from the heat and add the green onions. Adjust salt and pepper and serve.

Serves 8 to 10

* For more information on Mangalitsa pigs, see woolypigs.com and mosefund.com. Mangalitsa pork is available nationwide from DeBragga.com.

Braised Mangalitsa Boar

3 tablespoons olive oil

4 pounds Mangalitsa shoulder, bone out, or substitute pork butt

1 teaspoon salt

1 teaspoon freshly ground black pepper

4 cups diced onions

2 cups diced carrots

2 cups diced celery

2 cups rehydrated porcini mushrooms cut into 1-inch pieces (about 2 ounces dried mushrooms)

½ cup finely chopped garlic

¼ cup chopped fresh thyme

½ cup tomato paste

4 cups diced fresh tomatoes

1 orange peel

1 large sachet of rosemary

8 cups veal remouillage, or substitute veal or chicken stock

Heat a large heavy-bottomed rondeau or cast-iron pot over high heat and add the olive oil. Season the meat with salt and pepper and sear it until dark, rich brown, about 4 to 5 minutes per side. Remove the meat and set it aside in a large ovenproof pot with a lid.

Add the onions to the hot pot, lower the heat to medium, and cook until caramelized, about 5 minutes. Add the carrots, celery, mushrooms, garlic, and thyme, and cook for 2 minutes. Add the tomato paste and diced tomato; cook down for an additional 5 minutes. Add the orange peel, rosemary sachet, and stock, and simmer uncovered about 1 hour. Add this sauce to the pot with the meat, cover, and braise at 325°F for about 5 hours, until tender. Let the meat cool slightly and cut into cubes for Mangalista Jambalaya. (You can also slice and simply serve with the sauce over polenta or pasta.)

Gumbo z'Herbes

This is a brothy, herbacious gumbo, unlike the super-rich, roux-thickened version from Restaurant Eugene. Chef Besh reminds us to use "whatever greens you have on hand, such as mustard, turnip, collard, kale, arugula, spinach, cress, sorrel or whatever." He also sends along a few New Orleans "gumbo-stitions": for every green you use, you will get a new friend in the new year; and for better luck, use an odd number of herbs.

3 onions, medium diced

1 tablespoon rendered bacon fat

1 stalk celery, medium diced

4 cloves garlic, minced

4 smoked ham hocks

3 pounds greens, washed and coarsely chopped

1 pound okra, chopped

1 bay leaf

3 sprigs thyme, picked

1 clove, crushed

¼ teaspoon allspice

¼ teaspoon cayenne

Salt and freshly ground black pepper

4 eggs, hard-boiled, chopped

2 cups cooked white rice

2 green onions, chopped

In a large stockpot over high heat, cook and stir the onions in the rendered bacon fat until they become translucent; then add the celery and garlic. Cook until the celery and garlic soften, then add the ham hocks, greens, and 5 quarts of water. Cover the pot and bring the liquid to a boil. Once it is boiling, lower heat to a slight simmer; add the okra, bay leaf, thyme, clove, allspice, cayenne, and a pinch of salt. Cover the pot again and allow the mixture to cook slowly for at least 2 hours.

Remove the pot from the heat and correct the seasoning with additional salt and pepper. Carefully remove the ham hocks from the soup and separate the meat from the bones. Discard the bones and chop the meat, adding it back to the soup. Serve the soup garnished with a tablespoon of chopped egg, a couple spoonfuls of rice, and chopped green onions.

Serves 8

King Cake

This is a Mardi Gras tradition, which shows in its celebratory frosting of many colors. A plastic baby (or fava bean or other trinket) is hidden in the cake. The recipient of the baby bakes the cake for the next Mardi Gras. Chef Besh reminds you to watch for the dough to begin to pull away from the sides of the mixing bowl as you knead. If that doesn't happen (because the moisture content in flour fluctuates with the humidity), add a spoonful or two more flour.

Cake

1 cup lukewarm milk, about 110° F

½ cup granulated sugar

2 tablespoons dry yeast

3¾ cups all-purpose flour

2 sticks unsalted butter, melted

5 egg yolks, beaten

1 teaspoon vanilla extract

1 teaspoon grated fresh lemon zest

3 teaspoons cinnamon

Several gratings of fresh nutmeg

Icing

2 cups confectioners' sugar

¼ cup condensed milk

1 teaspoon fresh lemon juice

Purple, green, and gold decorative sugars

1 fève (fava bean) or plastic baby to hide in the cake after baking

For the cake: pour the warm milk into a large bowl. Whisk in the granulated sugar, yeast, and a heaping tablespoon of the flour, mixing until both the sugar and the yeast have dissolved. Once bubbles have developed on the surface of the milk and it begins to foam, whisk in the butter, eggs, vanilla, and lemon zest. Add the remaining flour, cinnamon, and nutmeg, and fold the dry ingredients into the wet ingredients with a large rubber spatula. After the dough comes together, pulling away from the sides of the bowl, shape it into a large ball. Knead the dough on a floured surface until it is smooth and elastic, about 15 minutes. Put the dough back into the bowl, cover with plastic wrap, and set aside in a draft-free place to let it proof, or rise, for 1½ hours, or until the dough has doubled in volume.

Preheat the oven to 375° F. Once the dough has risen, punch it down and divide it into three equal pieces. Roll each piece of dough between your palms into a long strip, making three ropes of equal length. Braid the ropes around one another and then form the braided loaf into a ring, pinching the ends together to seal. Gently lay the braided dough on a nonstick sheet pan and let it rise until it doubles in size, about 30 minutes.

continued on page 160

continued from page 159

Once the dough has risen, place the sheet pan in the oven and bake until the braid is golden brown, about 30 minutes. Remove the cake from the oven, place on a wire rack, and cool for 30 minutes.

For the icing: while the cake cools, whisk together the confectioners' sugar, condensed milk, and lemon juice in a bowl until the icing is smooth and very spreadable. If it's too thick, add a bit more condensed milk; if it's a touch too thin, add a little more confectioners' sugar.

Once the cake has cooled, spread the icing over the top and sprinkle with purple, green, and gold decorative sugars while the icing is still wet. Tuck the fève or plastic baby into the underside of the cake and, using a spatula, slide the cake onto a platter.

Serves 10 to 12

⌒ John Besh ⌒

LA PROVENCE (LACOMBE, LA)

Chef John Besh's restaurant group includes August, Besh Steak, Lüke, Lüke San Antonio, Domenica, American Sector and, of course, La Provence. His accolades are as numbered as the publications and organizations that give them. He is also the author of the personal and beautiful *My New Orleans: The Cookbook* and a guest and host of multiple TV shows.

What was your favorite food as a kid?
Trout Amandine.

What was the first meal you made that you were proud of?
Shrimp Creole.

What best describes your cuisine?
Regional and local celebration of cultures that influenced New Orleans.

What book most influences your food, cookbook or otherwise?
Ma Gastronomie by Fernand Point.

What chef do you most admire?
Alain Chapel.

What is your favorite ingredient?
Lake Pontchartrain [Louisiana] blue crabs.

What music do you like to hear when you cook?
In the restaurants, no music. At home, I listen to anything from Dave Matthews to Branford Marsalis.

What is your favorite hangover meal?
Cheeseburger with a fried egg on top from the Camellia Grill in New Orleans.

What is your favorite midnight snack?
Any kind of wrap!

What restaurant in the world are you most dying to try?
Noma in Copenhagen.

If you could do one other job, what would it be?
A mercenary or clergyman.

What do you most value in a sous chef?
Passion for food.

What one food would you take with you to a desert island?
Well, I'll have all that seafood—so some great white wines.

What is your favorite guilty-pleasure treat?
Fried chicken from Willie Mae's Scotch House in New Orleans.

What most satisfies your sweet tooth?
Cannoli.

Cheeseburger or foie gras?
Depends on my mood.

What's your favorite place (and what is your favorite thing to order) for:

A splurge meal?
Blackbird in Chicago or Vetri in Philadelphia.

Pastry?
Pasticceria Bruno in Greenwich Village in New York City, for a cannoli.

A late-night/after-work meal?
When in New York, after cooking for an event, there's nothing better than to be at that last seating at Momofuku Ssäm Bar.

A cup of coffee?
Angelo Brocato's has the best cappuccino in New Orleans.

A greasy-spoon meal?
Willie Mae's fried chicken in New Orleans.

Groceries?
Langenstein's in New Orleans.

Ice cream?
La Divina Gelateria in New Orleans.

Chocolate?
Theo Chocolate from Seattle.

Lark

The menu at Lark is meant for sharing and experimentation. There are five savory sections: Cheese, Vegetables/Grains, Charcuterie, Fish, and Meat. It forces the mind to think about a meal as elements, to take care with the balance you create. It also burrows you into the farm- and artisan-sourced brainwaves of Chef and Owner Johnathan Sundstrom.

Lark is directly across the street from my alma mater in Seattle, so I know the neighborhood well. When I was a college student in the late 1990s, Lark's corner of the Capital Hill neighborhood seemed seedy and forgotten. This street, once full of pre-condemned houses, now showcases a Ferrari dealership and several excellent restaurants. This exaltation of real estate has made the area a setting for Seattle's new food scene.

Seattle has struggled to find its food identity. There was the rainy climate, grunge (garage rock, if you actually listened to it), REI, and Microsoft, but food remained unidentifiable as something from Seattle. Sundstrom is part of the awakening of Seattle's

---

OFF THE MENU

Adobo-Style
Pork and Chicken

Pineapple Tarte Tatin
with Crème Fraîche Sorbet

Suggested wine:
Syncline Wine Cellars
Subduction Red
Columbia Valley 2008

---

culinary scene, the de-stodgification of its cuisine.

Lark serves ingredients, set in preparations like precious stones on share plates. Staff meal is more like an awesome rock you find at the beach. The adobo is a dish that can be stretched in any direction: quantity or ingredients can be added at will. The pineapple upside down cake is served because it was left over from dinner service the evening before. No matter it's a day old, it is decadent, irresistible, and sweet in an old-fashioned way.

There is a tub of transition in which staff meal floats, bobbing up when there is a moment. Tonight, a server's pants split and she good-naturedly finds a longer shirt to borrow; and the "linen guy" showed up with red napkins instead of white. Apparently, there was a city-wide napkin shortage. And though service begins fifteen minutes from now, there are already three tables full of diners. The adobo is wafting into the dining room but staff meal is always the first thing to get pushed aside. Lucky for you, you can sit and enjoy with any color napkin you like.

Adobo-Style Pork and Chicken

Chef John Sundstrom learned this preparation from his former sous chef, Joseph Margate, whose Filipino heritage inspired this recipe. It is a soupier version than traditional adobo, so it stretches accommodatingly for several meals. A pot to start with little fanfare on a Saturday morning and eat lazily throughout the day, over rice or greens stewed in coconut milk.

2 pounds boneless pork shoulder or butt,
   cut into 2-inch cubes
1 whole chicken, cut into 12 pieces,
   bone included
2 onions, diced
20 cloves garlic, smashed
8 bay leaves
1 tablespoon black peppercorns
1 cup coconut vinegar
2 quarts chicken or pork stock
2 tablespoons kosher salt
½ cup soy sauce

In a large stockpot, combine all the ingredients and bring to a boil. Cover and gently simmer for 3 to 3 ½ hours, until the pork is very tender and the chicken is just beginning to fall off the bone. (You can instead place the entire covered pan in a 325°F oven for the same amount of time.) Adjust seasoning with salt or soy sauce and serve over rice.

Serves 8

Pineapple Tarte Tatin with Crème Fraîche Sorbet

A tarte tatin is usually prepared with apples but gets an even sweeter treatment with pineapple in Chef Sundstrom's version. The crème fraîche balances the buttery confection with gentle tanginess.

Sorbet

1 cup heavy cream

1 cup crème fraîche

2 cups simple syrup*

1 tablespoon lemon juice

½ teaspoon salt

Caramel Sauce

1 cup granulated sugar

¼ cup light corn syrup

3 tablespoons unsalted butter, cubed

½ cup heavy cream

2 tablespoons grappa or rum

Pinch of salt

Tarte Tatin

1 frozen puff pastry, thawed slightly
   and cut into 8 squares

1 ripe pineapple, peeled, cored and
   cut into ¼-inch-thick rounds

1 large egg, beaten

Confectioners' sugar

To make the sorbet: whisk ingredients together until smooth, chill about 30 minutes then pour into ice-cream maker and freeze according to instructions.

To make the caramel sauce: cook the sugar and syrup with ¼ cup water on high heat until the color is an amber brown. Remove from heat and whisk in the butter one cube at a time; then slowly whisk in cream until incorporated. Add alcohol and salt and whisk smooth. Let the sauce cool to room temperature before placing it in Tupperware or other plastic tub. Chill in refrigerator.

Place Silpat (or other nonstick ovenproof liner) on a half sheet pan, dot with 1 teaspoon caramel for each of the 8 tatins, then place pineapple slice on top of each caramel dot. Top each pineapple slice with a square of pastry, and brush with egg wash. Bake at 350°F for 12 to13 minutes, or until the pastry has puffed up and is golden brown. Tatins can be cooled on the pan until ready to use. When you are ready to serve, just reheat for 1 minute; then, using a spatula, carefully lift each tatin and turn over onto a serving plate. Drizzle with warm caramel, sprinkle with confectioners' sugar, and top with a scoop of the sorbet.

Serves 8

* To make simple syrup: combine 1½ cups water with 1½ cups granulated sugar in a saucepan and bring to a boil. Stir for about 30 seconds, until sugar has completely dissolved. Cool completely before using.

THE ESCOFFIER QUESTIONNAIRE

~ Johnathan Sundstrom ~

LARK (SEATTLE, WA)

Chef and co-owner at Lark and Licorous in Seattle's Capital Hill neighborhood, Johnathan Sundstrom cooked at many of Seattle's best restaurants, including Campagne, Café Sport, Carmelita, and Dahlia Lounge, before opening Lark and earning the James Beard Award for Best New Chef Northwest in 2007.

What was your favorite food as a kid?
My grandmother Estrid's Swiss steak with gravy and mashed potatoes.

What was the first meal you made that you were proud of?
It wasn't a full meal, but scalloped potatoes with bacon when I was about twelve.

What three adjectives describe your cuisine?
Honest, grounded, and balanced.

What book most influences your food, cookbook or otherwise?
Fergus Henderson's *The Whole Beast: Nose to Tail Eating.*

What chef do you most admire?
Martin Picard of Au Pied de Cochon in Montreal—he cooks what he wants!

What is your favorite ingredient?
It would have to be butter.

What music do you like to hear when you cook?
The Black Angels, Fitz and The Tantrums, Destroyer, and LCD Soundsystem come to mind.

What is your favorite midnight snack?
Rosemary Triscuits with a little of my home-brewed Pilsner!

What restaurant in the world are you most dying to try?
Noma in Copenhagen, and Mugaritz in Errenteria, Spain.

If you could do one other job, what would it be?
Architect.

What do you most value in a sous chef?
Honesty.

What food trend would you most like to erase from the annals of history?
Americanized sushi with cream cheese.

What one food would you take with you to a desert island?
Coffee.

What is your favorite guilty-pleasure treat?
Beard Papa's cream puffs.

What would you eat at your last meal, if you could plan such a thing?
Butter-poached spot prawns with a little lemon and salt, and a bottle of Bandol rosé.

What's your favorite place (and what is your favorite thing to order) for:

Happy hour?
Anchovy and Olives in Seattle, for a Stella and a couple dozen Shigoku oysters.

A splurge meal?
Café Juanita in Seattle for the sweetbreads. Or Chez Panisse in Berkeley. And, of course, Joël Robuchon anywhere!

Breakfast?
Revel in Seattle for delicious Korean street-food-inspired brunch.

Pastry?
Cafe Besalu in Seattle, for their cardamom twist or ham-and-cheese croissant.

A late-night/after-work meal?
Café Presse in Seattle, right across the street for croque-madame and some frites.

A cup of coffee?
Stumptown. Or when at home, I use an old-school La Pavoni espresso maker.

Groceries?
Madison Market in Seattle—it's my neighborhood co-op.

Kitchen equipment?
Sur La Table.

Ice cream?
Old School Frozen Custard in Seattle, for Meyer lemon or chocolate malt.

Chocolate?
Theo Chocolate in Seattle, for a hazelnut brittle bar.

Le Comptoir

Located in South Williamsburg in Brooklyn, Le Comptoir is a neighborhood restaurant in a neighborhood that is growing up fast. It was a young hipster quarter a few years ago, and like many areas of Brooklyn, it was something else not long before that. The gentrification is reaching its apex now, with be-strollered, sexy moms and tattooed, box-framed dads. Le Comptoir is just the place to feed them. It is hip but relaxed in atmosphere and palate.

Chef and owner Sebastien Chamaret has run the gamut of New York's French kitchens. From La Goulue to Daniel, Chamaret has worked in serious restaurants with huge staffs. Now he is ready to be more ensconced in a neighborhood than on a hot line. The closet-sized open kitchen of Le Comptoir is within chatting distance of the long counter, where locals come for French toast crème brûlée and tartines with braised short ribs and a poached egg. This is just where we situated ourselves as Chamaret prepared staff meal.

"At Daniel, it was the rule to sit down for thirty minutes to staff meal. Once you sat down, you had to stay the whole half hour without working." Chamaret likes this ritual of spending enough time to talk with your coworkers and acknowledge the food before you. Today we are having pork tacos with guacamole. The pork is marinated, seared, and then finished off in the oven. The preparation is easy enough to be consistently good. The tacos are an excellent meal but you could also serve the delicious roast pork sliced with greens and mashed butternut squash or on a sandwich of crusty bread.

The Daniel rule is applied at Le Comptoir, though with more relaxed enforcement. The bartender got up to fuss with the lights, and Chameret's partner, Adrien Angelvy, who runs the front of the house, looked through his clipboard of to-dos. The restaurant remained open during staff meal and before too long a regular named Ellen came in for a cocktail. She was rushing home to make dinner for friends, but after a drink and the house-made potato chips that were set out for her, the rush dwindled to a dawdle. There was so much to catch up on with the bartender, and maybe she would have her friends meet her at Le Comptoir instead.

OFF THE MENU

Pork Tacos
with Valentina
Mayonnaise

Suggested beer/wine:
Brooklyn Brewery's Lokal 1
Belgian Strong Pale Ale
or Raphael First Label
Merlot 2005

TOP RIGHT: Chef Sebastien Chamaret in his kitchen. BOTTOM: Edouard Netter, waiter, helps himself to tacos *a la francaise.*

Pork Tacos
with Valentina Mayonnaise

This is Chef Chamaret's iteration of the pork taco, frenchified with Valentina mayonnaise. The pork tenderloin is more elegant than the simple preparation would intimate; and accompanied by the spicy mayonnaise, mushroom-onion mixture, and a simple salad, it would make a rounded meal, even sans tortillas.

Marinade

4 tablespoons honey

3 sprigs thyme, chopped

2 cloves garlic, chopped

2 tablespoons soy sauce

2 tablespoons olive oil

2 pinches toasted cumin

Salt and freshly ground black pepper

2 pork tenderloins, about 3 pounds

2 tablespoons vegetable oil

2 tablespoons Valentina Mexican hot sauce

½ cup mayonnaise

1 spanish onion, chopped

1 red onion, chopped

10 ounces shitake mushrooms, sliced

Corn tortillas

Guacamole

2 cups chopped lettuce

½ cup chopped fresh cilantro

2 limes, cut in wedges

½ to 1 cup crème fraîche

1 cup queso fresco, crumbled

Dash of Tabasco

Combine the marinade ingredients and spread over the pork. Cover and refrigerate overnight for best results.

Preheat the oven to 400°F. Heat a large skillet over medium-high heat and add the oil. When the oil is hot, sear the pork on all sides until brown and then cook in the oven for 10 to 12 minutes until just done or internal temperature reads 155°F on an instant-read thermometer. Remove the pork and let it rest. Leave the cooking juices in the skillet.

While the pork is in the oven, prepare the Valentina mayonnaise. Mix the hot sauce with the mayonnaise in a small bowl and set aside.

In the skillet with pork juices (remove some of the juices if you prefer a lighter sauce), cook the onions and mushrooms. Sauté the onions on medium-high heat until soft, about 3 minutes. Add the mushrooms, reduce the heat to medium, and sauté the mushrooms until the vegetables are caramelized, about 5 to 8 minutes.

Chop the pork into bite-size pieces and place in a bowl. Warm the tortillas in a skillet for about a minute on each side to make them pliable. Build individual tacos with the tortillas, pork, guacamole, sauces, and the rest of the ingredients.

Serves 6 to 8

THE ESCOFFIER QUESTIONNAIRE

⁓ Sebastien Chamaret ⁓

LE COMPTOIR (BROOKLYN, NY)

Sebastien Chamaret holds a culinary and pastry degree from France and has been cooking in New York since 1996. He was chef de cuisine at the legendary La Goulue on Madison Avenue. He opened Le Comptoir in 2010 in the Williamsburg neighborhood of Brooklyn.

What was your favorite food as a kid?
Crepes.

What was the first meal/dish you made that you were proud of?
Béarnaise sauce. I made it by myself for the first time when I was fourteen for my parents.

What three adjectives describe your cuisine?
Delicious, timeless, and accurate.

What book most influences your food, cookbook or otherwise?
The Escoffier Cookbook.

What chef do you most admire?
For his talent, Alain Raye. For his personality, Daniel Boulud or Jacques Pépin.

What is your favorite ingredient?
Salt.

What music do you like to hear when you cook?
Reggae.

What is your favorite hangover meal?
I don't drink anymore, but lobster eggs Benedict would be it.

What is your favorite midnight snack?
Brioche and Nutella.

What restaurant in the world are you most dying to try?
Alain Senderens in Paris.

What kitchen utensil is most indispensable to you?
My knife.

What is your favorite pot?
Le Creuset.

If you could do one other job, what would it be?
Professional soccer player.

What do you most value in a sous chef?
Skills and personality.

What food trend would you erase from the annals of history?
Liberty fries.

What one food would you take with you to a desert island?
Salt.

What is your favorite guilty-pleasure treat?
Chocolate.

What most satisfies your sweet tooth?
Macarons from anywhere.

What would you eat at your last meal, if you could plan such a thing?
Seafood platter, foie gras terrine, steak and fries béarnaise, and cheese plate.

Cheeseburger or foie gras?
Foie gras *bien sûr*.

What's your favorite place (and what is your favorite thing to order) for:

A splurge meal?
The Modern at the Museum of Modern Art, New York City.

Late-night/after-work meal?
Cercle Rouge in Tribeca, New York City.

A cup of coffee?
La Colombe Café, New York City.

Bread desire?
Pain d'Avignon at the Essex Street Market in New York City is delicious.

Groceries?
Natural Food Market on Austin Street, Forest Hills, New York.

Locanda Verde

Locanda Verde is a spacious Tribeca restaurant serving chef Andrew Carmellini's personal, regional and colloquial Italian food. But staff meal today is a Moroccan spread, and AC, as Carmellini is called by the staff, is dining happily with his crew on the couscous, chicken tagine, onion-and-raisin jam, and jalapeño vinaigrette.

Most staff meals are like meals at home, tried-and-true recipes. Cooks, like home cooks, go back to what is comfortable and within arm's reach when there is so much other work to be done. But there are those meals that become touchstones for a staff, like siblings remembering a father's Sunday breakfasts. Bouche is a cook at Locanda Verde, and he and his wife prepare traditional Moroccan dishes for the occasional family meal.

As we sit in the dining room, crowded on black leather banquettes, and enjoy the sweet-hot-sour balance that Moroccan cooks navigate so well, it is clear the staff is proud of Bouche and his meal, as if they had stewed, chopped, soaked, and steamed it themselves.

The tagine is one of my favorite dishes because it is flexible and forgiving, but also because its long cook time, which yields such fully realized flavors, makes it very rewarding to prepare. There are hundreds of tagine recipes, but Bouche's chicken-and-vegetable version is among the best I've had. I'd recommend making the onion condiment in a larger quantity than you need, so you can use it to improve other simple things you prepare, like a whole fish, a bowl of rice or a pork sandwich. And couscous is handy to be expert at because, on account of its tiny granules, it is a quick pasta to prepare, and because it has a fluffiness unmatched by other common starches. Together, these elements are a perfect dinner, and apart, they are all delicious pieces of other meals.

Carmellini has been at the top of the heap at Le Cirque and Café Boulud, has been Governor Mario Cuomo's chef, and is in the constellation of Michelin stars. It always makes me chuckle that I am traveling the country to sit in an exquisite dining room and hork down staff meal. But the truth is, that whether it is staff meal or dinner service, it is the same kitchen, with the same chefs. Carmellini has said he cooks most of all to make people happy. The staff is certainly happy this afternoon.

OFF THE MENU

Chicken and Winter Vegetable Tagine

Couscous

Sweet Onions and Raisins

Suggested wine:
Dierberg Chardonnay
Santa Maria Valley 2008

TOP RIGHT: Cook Bouche Jehhar with chef Andrew Carmellini.

Chicken and Winter Vegetable Tagine

Tagine is the word for a Moroccan stew and also the special clay dish it is prepared in, which has a round or square bottom with a tall, cone-shaped top. This recipe is a suggestion, as well as a finite thing—make this recipe once, as is, and then experiment or use it as a culmination for all the stewable vegetables skulking in your produce drawer.

2 tablespoons olive oil

2 pounds onions, chopped

2 pounds chicken legs, cut in half

½ pound tomatoes, diced

1 tablespoon salt

1 tablespoon freshly ground black pepper

1 tablespoon ground cumin seed

1 tablespoon ground coriander seed

1 tablespoon cinnamon

1 tablespoon dried ground ginger

1 to 1½ cups chicken broth

½ pound carrots, peeled and cut into
1-inch pieces

½ pound turnips, peeled and cut into
1-inch pieces

½ pound butternut squash, peeled and
cut into 1-inch pieces

½ pound sweet potatoes, peeled and cut
into 1-inch pieces

½ pound zucchini, cut into 1-inch pieces

Heat the olive oil over medium heat in a tagine or other heavy ovenproof stew pot or Dutch oven. Sauté the onions until golden, about 5 minutes. Add the chicken, tomatoes, salt, spices, and 1 cup of the broth. Bring to a simmer, then cover and cook over medium-low heat for 30 minutes.

Uncover the pot and stir in all of the vegetables except the zucchini. Add the remaining ½ cup of broth if needed. Reduce the heat to low and cover. Add the zucchini after 10 minutes and adjust seasoning. Cover again and cook until vegetables are tender and chicken is just starting to fall off the bone, about 30 minutes longer.

Serves 6 to 8

Couscous

Understand how to prepare couscous perfectly and it will serve you well. A quick-cooking pasta that stands up to hearty stews like the tagine, it can round out a meal or bind together bits of leftovers.

6 cups chicken broth
  or water
1 teaspoon salt
4 cups dry couscous

In a medium saucepan, add the broth and salt and bring to a rolling boil. Stir in the couscous. Make sure to stir thoroughly so there are fewer clumps. Cover the pot, turn off the heat, and let stand for 15 minutes. Fluff the couscous with a fork to lighten it before serving.

Serves 6 to 8 as a side dish

Sweet Onions and Raisins

This is the Moroccan *Tfaya*, which here is a condiment to enrich the tagine and couscous. If you add beef, it can also be a dead-of-winter stew, heaped on couscous, warmed with ghee.

1 cup golden raisins
2 tablespoons unsalted butter
2 large onions, thinly sliced
2 tablespoons granulated sugar
1 tablespoon cinnamon
½ tablespoon salt
½ to ¾ cup chicken broth

Soak the raisins in water for 15 minutes, drain, and set aside.

In a medium saucepan, melt the butter and add the onion, sugar, cinnamon, and salt. Cook over medium-low heat, stirring, for about 10 minutes. Add the raisins and broth, bring to a simmer, cover, and cook over low heat for 30 to 40 minutes, stirring occasionally, until the onions are very soft and golden. Add more broth if the liquid evaporates before the onions are cooked.

Once the onions are cooked and richly colored, uncover and reduce the liquid over medium-low heat to a thick syrup. Turn off the heat and set the caramelized onions aside. Reheat the onions prior to serving.

Makes about 1 cup

◡ Andrew Carmellini ◠

LOCANDA VERDE (NEW YORK, NY)

Andrew Carmellini came up through Lespinasse and Café Boulud, as well as kitchens in Italy, France, and England. He has earned four stars from the New York Times and Michelin, and Best New Chef recognition from *Food & Wine*. AC is enjoying the gifts of success now: a big beautiful restaurant, and business partners like Robert DeNiro.

What was the first meal you made that you were proud of?
I made Melba toast from Jacque Pépin's cookbook *La Methode.*

What three adjectives describe your cuisine?
Flavorful, rustic, and soulful.

What book most influences your food, cookbook or otherwise?'
Jacques Pépin's *La Methode* and *La Technique.*

What chef do you most admire?
Jacques Pépin.

What is your favorite ingredient?
Most importantly, quality is the number one ingredient. Whatever it is, from fresh basil to oysters, I'm looking for the best.

What music do you like to hear when you cook?
We don't have music in my professional kitchens, but when I'm cooking at home I listen to all kinds of music, but if I have to choose I'd say hip hop—early Al Green to Marc Ronson to Mos Def.

What is your favorite hangover meal?
Baked eggs with tomato sauce and chorizo at The Breslin in New York.

What is your favorite midnight snack?
Whatever is coming up at 3 A.M. family meal at my new restaurant, The Dutch.

What restaurant in the world are you most dying to try?
René Redzepi's Noma, in Copenhagen.

What kitchen utensil is most indispensable to you?
A good cast iron skillet and really high heat.

Who do you most like to cook for?
Between the two restaurants I feed over 1500 strangers a day and I love it, but what's really fun is when I get fellow chefs in and I get to play.

If you could do one other job, what would it be?
Musician.

What do you most value in a sous chef?
A passion for working hard and the ability to bang it out and make it happen.

What is your favorite guilty-pleasure treat?
Really good caviar or really fantastic Neapolitan pizza.

What most satisfies your sweet tooth?
Coconut cream pie.

What's your favorite place (and what is your favorite thing to order) for:

Happy hour?
Margaritas or some place with exceptional bourbon.

A splurge meal?
Daniel in New York for the tasting menu.

Breakfast?
Abraco Espresso in New York for an almond milk cappuccino and black olive cookies.

Pastry?
Standing at the café counter at Locanda Verde eating a zuccherino freshly prepared by Pastry Chef Karen DeMasco.

A late-night/after-work meal?
Once in a while I take my staff out to Kyochon for Korean fried chicken.

A cup of coffee?
La Colombe on Lafayette Street..

Groceries?
The Union Square Green Market for whatever looks fresh and tasty that day.

Kitchen equipment?
Our smoker from Southern Pride.

Chocolate?
Kee's chocolate in New York City.

Marea

I arrived at Marea four minutes late. Depending on the circumstances, four minutes can have a wide spectrum of importance. Generally for a staff meal, four minutes is a negligible length of time. Especially in New York, where you don't consider someone late until they've missed at least two cocktails. At Marea, four minutes is not negligible. I arrived to a perfect tableau: the entire staff, both front and back of house, in their pressed whites and service attire, plates in hand and standing in line ready to devour the steaming Korean buffet. There was a one-second pause, one second outside of time where everyone stared and I blushed, and then time suddenly caught up by moving extra fast.

Staff meal can be a time for cooks to share something about their cooking past or their cooking aspirations. This meal was about four Korean line cooks, all female, who had prepared dishes very familiar to them and completely outside the Italian seafood-focused menu of the dining room. Everyone scraped the steam trays empty of the tripe stew and three accompanying

---

OFF THE MENU

~

Slow-Roasted Pork

Spicy Tripe Stew

Jicama Salad

Kimchee Pancakes

Korean Dipping Sauces

Suggested wine:
Wind Gap
Trousseau Gris 2010

---

kimchis made in-house.

The staff is large enough to accommodate many subcultures: male cooks in their twenties sat at a long able and compared new cookbooks they had seen; managers ate at a round table with legal pads of notes in front of them; bussers at another table, laughing loudly. And the four young cooks who had prepared the meal sat together, hushing up when I approached. "Smile for a photo, I want you to get the credit you deserve," chef Jared Gadbaw said. "Yes, Chef." "Put one of those roses in your teeth," Gadbaw teased one of the cooks, and the table bubbled with laughter. She gave me the best smile.

Owner and executive chef Michael White recently split his partnership with restaurateur Chris Cannon, each of them taking custody of a few restaurants, seven between them. While Cannon suddenly closed two of his charges, Marea continues to be exquisite and successful. There's some golden equation to the place that fosters all those different voices and also knows the value of every last minute.

TOP RIGHT: Chef Jared Gadbaw in the sleek Marea dining room.
BOTTOM RIGHT: Three of the cooks responsible for the Korean feast.

Marea's Korean Feast

Tripe is often the least-expensive meat in the butcher case, so it is a wonderful trick to be able to transform it into such a soulful stew. The play of eggplant, tomato, and oyster sauce, and the cascade of chili heat, have a cumulative effect that almost makes me food-drunk. The pork is silky and fall-apart and makes you sneak into the kitchen and take little bites and spoil your appetite. The kimchee pancakes and dipping sauces are what elevate this from dinner to celebration. This meal qualifies, in any estimation, as a feast. The parade of tastes, textures, and temperatures will hold you fast to the table for hours.

Slow-Roasted Pork

2 tablespoons ground coriander seed
2 tablespoons ground fennel seed
2 tablespoons ground Szechuan pepper
2 teaspoons ground cumin seed
1 teaspoon cayenne
3 tablespoons kosher salt
2 tablespoons brown sugar
2 pounds pork shoulder or butt

Toast the spices in a pan just to bring forth some aroma. Combine in a large bowl with the salt and sugar, and rub the mix liberally into the pork. Refrigerate overnight.

To slow-roast the pork, preheat the oven to 250°F. Place the meat in a large pan or roasting dish and add a cup of water to the pan. Cover with foil and bake for about 7 to 8 hours, until it is fork tender. Toward the end of the cooking process, remove the foil and turn the oven up to 350°F to allow an outer crust to form. Remove the roast from the oven and allow it to rest for 30 minutes before serving.

Serves 4 to 6

Spicy Tripe Stew

2 pounds honeycomb tripe

2 tablespoons olive oil

1 onion, sliced

1 bulb fennel, sliced

1 red bell pepper, seeded and sliced

2 or 3 serrano chilies, seeded and sliced, plus a few extra for garnish, optional

½ head garlic, sliced

2 tablespoons chopped fresh ginger

28-ounce can tomatoes, crushed

½ cup oyster sauce

2 bay leaves

½ tablespoon ground cumin seed

1 tablespoon ground coriander seed

1 teaspoon cayenne

2 chinese eggplants, cut into 1-inch pieces, optional

½ cup chopped fresh cilantro

3 limes

Place tripe in cold salted water and bring to a boil; drain. Repeat this process two more times in order to clean the tripe. Once cool, cut the tripe into thumb-size pieces.

Heat the oil in a stewing pot over medium heat. Add the onion, fennel, red pepper, chilies, garlic, and ginger, and sweat for about 5 minutes. Add the tomatoes and juices, oyster sauce, bay leaves, and dried spices. Allow mixture to come to a simmer and add the tripe. Simmer over medium-low heat until the tripe is slightly chewy and almost tender, about 45 minutes to 1 hour, adding stock or water if the stew becomes too dry.

Sauté or fry the eggplant until tender, and add to the stew before serving. Garnish the dish with cilantro and fresh lime juice—and perhaps some more fresh chilies. Serve as is, or with rice, tortillas, or lettuce wraps.

Serves 4 to 6

Jicama Salad

1 small jicama, peeled and julienned

1 carrot, peeled and julienned

½ bunch cilantro, roughly chopped

2 limes

1 tablespoon sesame oil

Pinch of salt

In a medium bowl, mix together the jicamas, carrots, and cilantro. In a small bowl mix juice from 2 limes with the oil. Season with salt and more lime juice as necessary. Toss the vegetables with the dressing and serve immediately.

Serves 4 to 6 as a side

Kimchee Pancakes

2 cups chopped kimchee
3 tablespoons kimchee juice
1 cup all-purpose flour
½ cup water
2 scallions, chopped
2 tablespoon granulated sugar
1 teaspoon salt
4 tablespoons canola oil
Korean Dipping Sauces (recipe below)

To make the batter, mix together all ingredients except the oil in a medium bowl. Heat 2 tablespoons oil in a 12-inch skillet over medium heat. Pour half the batter into the pan and spread it evenly with a spoon. Cook for 1 to 2 minutes, until the bottom is golden brown. Flip the pancake and brown the other side. Transfer to a serving plate and repeat for the second pancake. Cut pancakes into bite-size pieces. Serve with Korean Dipping Sauces on the side.

Makes two 10-inch pancakes

Korean Dipping Sauces

Orange Ginger Sauce
2 pieces ginger, finely chopped
1 cup grapeseed oil
¼ cup orange juice
3 tablespoons fish sauce or oyster sauce
3 tablespoons low-sodium soy sauce
Pinch of salt

Korean Chili Sauce
1 cup Korean chili paste
½ cup water
2 tablespoons soy sauce
2 tablespoons rice vinegar
¼ cup sesame oil

Soy Scallion Sauce
¼ cup soy sauce
¼ cup rice vinegar
2 tablespoons honey
¼ cup water
¼ cup sesame oil
2 teaspoons red-pepper flakes
2 tablespoons sesame seeds, toasted and crushed
2 scallions, chopped
Pinch of salt

Mix the ingredients of each sauce in its own separate bowl. Serve the three sauces as condiments for dipping kimchee pancakes or slathering over rice.

~ Michael White and Jared Gadbaw ~

MAREA (NEW YORK, NY)

Chef Michael White is the executive chef and owner of Marea, Osteria Morini, and Ai Fiori, three of Manhattan's finest restaurants. Marea is the star of the crown, with its seafood-based menu hauling in two stars from *The Michelin Guide*. Jared Gadbaw is chef de cuisine at Marea.

What was your favorite food as a kid?
MW: Pasta. JG: Escargot.

What was the first meal you made that you were proud of?
JG: Lobster and mussel tagliatelle for Valentine's Day.

What three adjectives describe your cuisine?
MW: Fresh, flavorful, and delicious.
JG: Bold, balanced, and straightforward.

What book most influences your food, cookbook or otherwise?
MW: *Grand Livre de Cuisine: Alain Ducasse's Culinary Encyclopedia*, by Alain Ducasse.
JG: *The Flavor Bible* by Andrew Dornenberg and Karen Page.

What chef do you most admire?
MW & JG: Alain Ducasse.

What is your favorite ingredient?
MW: Mortadella, sriracha, and mollica (Italian bread crumbs). JG: Anchovies.

What is your favorite hangover meal?
JG: Pho (Vietnamese soup).

What is your favorite midnight snack?
JG: Dumplings.

What restaurant in the world are you most dying to try?
JG: Au Pied de Cochon in Montreal.

What kitchen utensil is most indispensable to you?
MW: Truffle slicer and my hands.
JG: Kuntz spoon.

Who do you most like to cook for?
MW & JG: Family.

What do you most value in a sous chef?
MW & JG: Self-motivation.

What is your favorite guilty-pleasure treat?
MW: I love to whip up Jamie Oliver's bread-and-butter pudding on holidays.
JG: Häagen-Dazs coffee ice cream.

What would you eat at your last meal, if you could plan such a thing?
JG: Dry-aged sirloin, creamed spinach, and pommes Anna.

Cheeseburger or foie gras?
MW: My White Label Burger at Ai Fiori with white American cheese, Florida black tomatoes, thick-cut Nueske's bacon, and bibb lettuce. JG: Foie, only if it is seared. No torchon.

What's your favorite place (and what is your favorite thing to order) for:

A splurge meal?
JG: Kyo Ya in New York City.

Breakfast?
JG: Corned beef hash at the Stage Restaurant on 2nd Avenue in New York City. Hole in the wall with counter service.

Pastry?
JG: Don't often have the pleasure, but the pastry at Le Bernardin is incredible.

A late-night/after-work meal?
JG: Baby pig at Great NY Noodletown in New York City.

A cup of coffee?
JG: Black with a touch of half-and-half at Atlas Cafe on Clinton Street in New York City.

A greasy-spoon meal?
MW: Hill Country BBQ in New York City.
JG: Fried chicken, charred spring onions, and potatoes with sausage gravy at Mama's Fried Chicken in New York.

Ice cream?
JG: Il Laboratorio del Gelato

Marlow & Sons

— BROOKLYN, NY —

Marlow & Sons is part of a restaurant group. Not a restaurant group in the corporate, monotonous way, but a restaurant group in the chummy, cooperative way. There are three restaurants and a butcher shop, all within a few blocks of one another. There is also *Diner Journal*, a quarterly magazine about the food culture through Marlow's lens. This lens imposes narratives on carrots and makes metaphors of meat.

Staff meal at Marlow & Sons starts downstairs, where the cooking happens. A barely human-sized stairwell leads the meal to a long table in the dining room, a table under the handwritten sign listing the day's oyster offerings and just south of the bar. The platters are full of kale salad, fried rice with scallions, and empanadas, and they land on the table like a gavel announcing a call to order. Staff meal is an important time for Marlow & Sons, a time used to both share a meal and dispatch information to the crew.

There were some in-jokes and teasing, but throughout the lineup, the staff was completely engaged and penetratingly tuned in. If you imagine someone taking close-up photos in the middle of a board meeting, zooming in on faces and file folders, you can imagine the level of focus it takes to ignore

---

OFF THE MENU

—

Chorizo Empanadas

Tuscan Kale Salad

Suggested wine:
Huber's Orchard, Winery &
Vineyards Chardonel
Barrel-Fermented 2008

---

me. Chef Sean Rembold changes the menu daily, and servers have to understand the nuances of a dish well enough to explain it to diners, to rattle off the particular offerings of the night over and over. In a source-conscious restaurant, this also means knowing farms and breeds and growing seasons. It isn't rote, it is a constant evolution of understanding.

Besides the kale salad, the food served at staff meal is not particular to the style of Marlow & Sons but it is of the same quality: it came from their kitchen. Some staff meals feel like a lull; this is a working lunch. Every server has their pen aloft and is jotting down new cheeses, wines, and menu items as Sean reads from his massive clipboard of notes. "Is the pork shoulder chop braised?"—a server foresees the question that will be asked of her throughout the evening, or just follows her own curiosity. She knows that pork shoulder is a braising meat, but wonders if it being served as a chop changes the preparation.

"We are not the only restaurant in the world that does farm to table food," says restaurant manager Jason Schwartz. "People come here for the warmth." As any good host knows, having the capacity to focus on your guests requires careful preparation.

TOP: Chef Sean Rembold (left), lead cook Jose Santiago, and sous chef Kenneth Wiss.

Chorizo Empanadas

Empanadas are party food. You keep making them until a platter stays populated with them for more than a few minutes. You can make other versions as well: black beans and cheese, roasted vegetables, shredded chicken adobo. Chef Rembold's recipe is lush with cheese and chorizo, and a few of the half moons next to a green salad are a meal.

Canola oil for frying

½ pound chorizo or other sausage

½ onion, diced

½ fennel bulb, diced

1 jalapeño, seeded and diced

1 cup tomato sauce

Salt and freshly ground
    black pepper

2 to 3 ounces fontina cheese,
    grated

2 to 3 ounces cheddar cheese,
    grated

2 to 3 ounces gruyère cheese,
    grated

2 tablespoons granulated sugar

½ tablespoon yeast

2 tablespoons salt

2 tablespoons oil

3½ cups all-purpose flour

Heat 1 tablespoon of canola oil in a medium skillet over medium-low heat. Remove the sausage meat from its casing and sauté it until brown, breaking it apart with a spatula as you cook. Remove meat with a slotted spoon. Place the onion, fennel, and jalapeño in the pan and let the mixture cook in the remaining sausage fat over low heat until soft, about 5 to 10 minutes, stirring occasionally. Return the sausage to the pan and add the tomato sauce; season with salt and pepper and simmer for about 30 minutes. Add the grated cheeses to the mixture and set aside.

In a large mixing bowl, combine 1½ cups warm water, sugar, and yeast. Let the mixture sit for 10 minutes. Add the salt and oil, and then add the flour. Form the dough into a ball and let it rest in a warm spot for 20 minutes. Roll the dough into a cylinder and cut into 8 or 16 slices. Form each slice into a ball and roll flat into 3- or 6-inch circles about ⅛ inch thick. Lightly brush the edge of each circle with water. Place about 2 or 4 tablespoons of filling in the middle and fold the dough over the filling, making a half circle. Press the edges with a fork to seal. (At this point, the empanadas can be stored frozen for up to a month.)

Heat an inch of oil in a large skillet to about 360°F and fry empanadas in batches until golden brown, about 2 to 3 minutes on each side. Remove each batch of empanadas to paper towels; drain and serve hot.

Makes 8 large or 16 small empanadas

Tuscan Kale Salad

Kale is a nutrient-dense green. I can almost feel my body sighing with relief when I eat this salad. The garlic and lemon juice make it a winter mood enhancer, a stream of artificial sunlight. The salad is a menu favorite at Marlow & Sons, as well as a staff favorite.

4 whole cloves garlic
¾ to 1 cup olive oil
2 to 3 tablespoons lemon juice
Salt and freshly ground black pepper
1 large parsnip, peeled and thinly sliced
1 to 1½ bunches Tuscan kale
¼ cup toasted walnuts, crushed
¾ cup grated Parmesan cheese

Preheat the oven to 450°F. Cover the garlic cloves with oil and simmer over very low heat until soft, about 30 minutes. Purée the cooked garlic with the lemon juice and about ½ cup of olive oil. Season with salt and pepper.

Toss the parsnip in a little bit of olive oil, sprinkle with salt and pepper, and roast it in the oven until it is just cooked, about 8 minutes.

Remove the ribs from the kale and slice into ¾-inch-wide ribbons. In a large bowl, toss together the kale, walnuts and ½ cup of the Parmesan. Add enough lemon-garlic vinaigrette and more Parmesan to create a creamy consistency. Serve immediately.

Serves 6 to 8 as a side

~ Sean Rembold ~

MARLOW & SONS (BROOKLYN, NY)

Sean Rembold is executive chef in the kitchen that set the standard for Brookyn's local sourcing. Rembold starts his meals in the pastures and rows where the ingredients grow. Marlow & Sons' general store and restaurant has made "hyperlocal" cool by serving Rembold's exceptional food.

What was your favorite food as a kid?
I was quite partial to bologna and cheese on Rainbow bread with Miracle Whip.

What was the first meal you made that you were proud of?
Getting to cook for my parents in Campagna in 1997.

What three adjectives describe your cuisine?
Simple, seasoned, and seasonal.

What book most influences your food, cookbook or otherwise?
Larousse Gastronomique.

What chef do you most admire?
Chef John Foster, director of Sullivan University's culinary program.

What music do you like to hear when you cook?
I mix it up but lately, the Shipping News.

What is your favorite hangover meal?
High-quality over-easy eggs with hot sauce.

What is your favorite midnight snack?
A pint of beer.

What restaurant in the world are you most dying to try?
Le Dauphin in Paris or The Willows Inn on Lummi Island, Washington.

What kitchen utensil is most indispensable to you?
Wooden spoon.

Who do you most like to cook for?
Regular customers, for sure.

If you could do one other job, what would it be?
Teach literature at Ole Miss.

What do you most value in a sous chef?
Loyalty.

What one food would you take with you to a desert island?
My wife's favorite food is bread, and hopefully, she would be there with me. So some high-quality loaves from either Tartine in San Francisco or Roman's in New York would do us just fine.

What is your favorite guilty-pleasure treat?
Entenmann's Devil's Food Crumb doughnuts. Not organic. Not natural. Not even close.

What most satisfies your sweet tooth?
A rye whiskey at Hot Bird in Brooklyn.

What would you eat at your last meal, if you could plan such a thing?
Purnell's Old Folks Bratwurst on rye with yellow mustard. Followed by a ripe peach.

Cheeseburger or foie gras?
Cheeseburger. Is that not the unanimous choice?

What's your favorite place (and what is your favorite thing to order) for:

Happy hour?
Lucky Dog on Bedford Avenue in Brooklyn.

Splurge meal?
Asador Etxebarri in Spain. Just two plane rides and a two-hour drive away.

Late-night/after-work meal?
Not a huge fan of late meals. I'd rather have a nice pint of beer or a glass of Ploussard from Arbois.

A cup of coffee?
For many years I've been a fan of Verb Café's coffee in Brooklyn, especially the iced version.

A greasy-spoon meal?
Not too greasy, but I love the food and mellow vibe at Great Jones Café in New York City.

Groceries?
I enjoy walking through the Farmers' Market at Fort Greene Park in Brooklyn.

Mémé

Mémé's family meal is truly a family meal. Chef and owner David Katz lives upstairs with his wife and two sons and they often glide and totter downstairs to sup with the restaurant's staff. It was hard not to go into auntie mode and spend my whole afternoon just taking photos of the kids. The meatloaf was also a terrific study, if not quite as adorable. You can't fault the meatloaf.

David's family is Moroccan Jewish. Mémé is what he called his grandma, his family speaking French, as most Moroccans do. The food that David grew up eating is the inspiration for what he cooks now. And the restaurant feeds his family, literally and figuratively. So this was a place I couldn't miss. Even his two little boys sat still and gobbled up the meatloaf and the creamy macaroni.

> ## OFF THE MENU
>
> Mémé Meatloaf
>
> Creamy Macaroni
>
> *Suggested wine:*
> Merry Edwards Olivet Lane
> Pinot Noir 2008 or
> Russian River Valley
> Pinot Noir 2008

No bargaining to finish one more bite at this dinner table.

David is rapturously enthusiastic. This is a quality I forget I miss until I am in its presence. He offered me a tour of the farmers' markets of Philadelphia, suggested more places I should visit than I could even write down, and asked myriad questions about cooks in other cities. In making my cookbooks and in running a national organization, the Butcher's Guild, I get to be a Johnny Appleseed of conversations. Cooking is a head-down job and the long hours can build a tunnel around you that leads only to and from the kitchen. By living upstairs, David could have compounded this isolation. But the sweetness of his curiosity gave it all a fairy tale lilt in its old worldliness. Any mémé would approve.

ABOVE: Chef David Katz manages his son and his supper.

Mémé's Meatloaf

Though this dish is a classic, it was not in my parents' repertoire, so I don't cook it with the benefit of muscle memory. This recipe hits all the sentimental chords and you barely have to don an apron. It is fast, straightforward, and the dish will be clean before it leaves the table.

2½ pounds ground beef, 80/20 lean/fat ratio
1 small yellow onion, minced
1 clove garlic, minced
½ cup grated Parmigiano-Reggiano cheese
2 eggs
4 tablespoons ketchup, plus extra
1 to 2 tablespoons Worcestershire sauce
¾ cup bread crumbs
2 tablespoons chopped fresh parsley
½ tablespoon fresh thyme
1 teaspoon soy sauce
Salt and freshly ground black pepper

Preheat the oven to 350°F. In a large mixing bowl, combine all the ingredients and 4 tablespoons of the ketchup. Form the mixture into a large loaf and place on a sheet pan lined with parchment paper. Rub some extra ketchup all over the top and sides of the loaf in a thin layer. Season with salt and pepper.

Bake for 45 minutes to an hour, until internal temperature is 140°F. Remove the meatloaf from the oven and let rest for 15 to 20 minutes before slicing and serving.

Serves 6 to 8

Creamy Macaroni

A good reminder that people are really not that hard to please. This dish is very simple, yet you will be hard-pressed to find someone who doesn't absolutely adore it. The egg and cheese give it enough protein to let it stand alone with a crisp salad.

1 pound elbow macaroni
4 medium eggs, beaten
1 stick unsalted butter, softened
1 cup grated Parmigiano-Reggiano cheese
Salt and freshly ground black pepper

Fill a large pot with enough salted water to cover the pasta by 2 to 3 inches. Bring to a boil. Add pasta and cook through, about 7 to 9 minutes. Drain the pasta in a colander and return it to the pot. Turn the heat down to very low and drizzle in the beaten eggs while mixing vigorously with a wooden spoon or rubber spatula. Add the butter, cheese, salt, and a generous amount of pepper, and stir until butter has melted. Serve immediately.

Serves 6

⌒ David Katz ⌒

MÉMÉ (PHILADELPHIA, PA)

Chef and owner David Katz has made use of his Moroccan Jewish upbringing to build his personal culinaria. One of *Esquire* magazine's Best New Restaurants of 2009, Mémé is already a Philadelphia phenom.

What was your favorite food as a kid?
Corn. Peaches. Pork chops.

What was the first meal you made that you were proud of?
Pasta with olives and tomatoes.

What three adjectives describe your cuisine?
I just make simple food.

What book most influences your food, cookbook or otherwise?
Culinary Artistry by Andrew Dornenburg and Karen Page.

What chef do you most admire?
Martin Picard.

What is your favorite ingredient?
Salt.

What music do you like to hear when you cook?
The Misfits, Minor Threat, The Smiths, Steel Pulse, Motörhead, John Coltrane, Stan Getz, the Clash, Elvis Costello . . .

What is your favorite hangover meal?
Cheeseburgers and milk shakes.

What is your favorite midnight snack?
Candy, chocolate, and Chinese food.

What restaurant in the world are you most dying to try?
Chateaubriand in Paris.

What kitchen utensil is most indispensable to you?
Fish spatula.

If you could do one other job, what would it be?
Wine importer.

What do you most value in a sous chef?
Toughness.

What food trend would you most like to erase from the annals of history?
Cupcakes and using the word "sexy" to describe food.

What one food would you take with you to a desert island?
Pork.

What is your favorite guilty-pleasure treat?
Cheesesteak with Cheez Whiz and American cheese.

What would you eat at your last meal, if you could plan such a thing?
A dry-aged bone-in strip steak with a bag of Funyuns, and a Miller High Life.

Cheeseburger or foie gras?
Seriously? Foie gras—no question.

What's your favorite place (and what is your favorite thing to order) for:

A splurge meal?
Morimoto in New York City.

Breakfast?
Dutch Eating Place in Philadelphia.

Pastry?
Dunkin' Donuts.

A late-night/after-work meal?
Shiao Lan Kung in New York City.

A cup of coffee?
My apartment.

A greasy-spoon meal?
Ruby's in New York City.

Kitchen equipment?
Previn Inc. in Philadelphia.

Ice cream?
Capogiro in Philadelphia for gelato.

Chocolate?
Kee's in New York City.

Michael's Genuine Food & Drink

MIAMI, FL

Michael's Genuine in Miami and Grand Cayman is very modern. The food is an idea as much as it is nourishment. The menus change daily, a reflection of the restaurant's philosophy-that food should come from ingredients sourced at small, local farms and can be affordable for most everyone. Chef Michael Schwartz puts his philosophy into action through projects such as Wholesome Waves, Roots in the City, and Chefs Move to Schools. Of course, it's much easier to sell a philosophy when it is delicious.

This rigatoni is sentimental for the red-checked-tablecloth era of Italian-American food but has the freshness of our contemporary expectations. I made it once for a friend who has given up gluten and adapted it by using brown rice rigatoni and frying the eggplant without breading. It worked beautifully. This recipe also instructs on the basic tomato sauce, which can be modified for particular tastes with the addition of chili flakes, little nibs of salami, or a dash of cream.

Thinking beyond the twenty-four-hour cycle is hard for restaurants and requires a dutiful passion. It is this passion that entitles Schwartz's restaurant to be called "a shining star" by the *New York Times*.

OFF THE MENU

Baked Eggplant
and Rigatoni with
Homemade Ricotta

Suggested wine:
Au Bon Climat Pinot Noir
Santa Barbara 2008

Baked Eggplant and Rigatoni
with Homemade Ricotta

Try adapting this pasta dish to the season you're in. Fresh peas in spring, or dark greens and mushrooms in winter—almost anything in your garden—can find comfort in the welcoming arms of rigatoni with marinara.

¼ cup plus 2 tablespoons extra-virgin olive oil, plus more for drizzling

1 small onion, coarsely chopped

3 cloves garlic, coarsely chopped

Sea salt and freshly ground black pepper

6 large heirloom tomatoes, about 4 pounds, cored and cut into chunks

3 large fresh basil leaves, thinly sliced

1 pound dried rigatoni

Canola oil for frying

2 large eggplants, sliced in ¼-inch-thick discs

½ cup all-purpose flour

2 eggs, beaten

2 cups bread crumbs

1 cup Homemade Ricotta (page 194)

One 8-ounce ball fresh mozzarella, sliced

½ cup grated Parmesan cheese

¼ cup thinly sliced fresh basil

Preheat oven to 350°F.

Heat a large pot over medium-high heat and add 2 tablespoons of the olive oil. When the oil is shimmering, add the onion and garlic. Cook and stir until the onion is soft, about 5 minutes, and season with salt and pepper. Add the tomatoes and their juices. Bring to a boil, then reduce the heat and simmer until the tomatoes begin to break down into a chunky pulp, about 5 minutes. Toss in the basil leaves and simmer about 20 minutes. Adjust salt and pepper. Stir the remaining ¼ cup olive oil into the tomato sauce, remove from heat, and purée the sauce with a hand blender.

Bring a large pot of lightly salted water to a boil. Add pasta and cook until al dente, about 10 minutes. Drain and set aside in a large bowl.

Heat 2 inches of canola oil in a cast-iron skillet over medium-high heat. Dip eggplant slices in the flour, then the egg, and lastly the bread crumbs. Working in batches, fry eggplant for 2 minutes per side or until lightly browned. Place on paper towels to drain. Eggplant absorbs a lot of oil, so you may need to add oil as you fry.

Pour the sauce over the pasta and toss to thoroughly coat. Pour rigatoni into a 9 x 13-inch baking dish. Top with a layer of the fried eggplant, a layer of ricotta and a layer of mozzarella slices. Bake for 30 minutes. Remove the dish from the oven and turn the setting to broil. Sprinkle the dish with Parmesan and broil for 5 minutes, or until the cheese has melted and browned at the edges. Sprinkle with basil, drizzle with olive oil, and serve.

Serves 8

Homemade Ricotta

1 gallon whole milk, preferably
  organic
1 quart buttermilk
1 tablespoon kosher salt, or more
Zest of 1 lemon, finely grated
½ cup heavy cream

In a heavy-bottomed nonreactive pot,* combine the whole milk, buttermilk, and salt over medium-low heat. After about 20 minutes, you will see steam start to rise from the milk; at that point give it a gentle stir with a metal spoon. Use a thermometer to check how hot the milk mixture is, and aim for 170°F to 180°F. Slow heating is best for making curds. Don't rush the process. After about 10 more minutes, curds will begin to rise to the surface (the curds are the clumpy white masses). Once you see curds floating, cook for 5 more minutes. At that point the curds will begin to sink, and that means it is time to strain the mixture.

Line a colander with a large piece of cheesecloth that has been folded over a couple of times. Set the colander in the sink. Pour the curds into the cheesecloth, leaving as much of the whey (the liquid) in the pot as possible. Gather the edges of the cloth, tie or fasten into a knot, and tie the bundle to the faucet; let the curds drip into the sink for 5 minutes.

Transfer the curds to a food processor and add the zest, cream, and more salt if desired. Pulse the ricotta until smooth. If you aren't going to use it immediately, store it in an airtight container in the refrigerator. Try to eat it within two days; it really is best the first day you make it.

Makes about 1 quart

* Use clean stainless-steel pans and utensils. Wooden spoons or any pot or utensil with remnants of strong food flavor will impart that taste to the cheese.

～ Michael Schwartz ～

MICHAEL'S GENUINE FOOD & DRINK (MIAMI, FL)

Michael Schwartz's mission is bigger than Michael's Genuine, though it finds its most direct home there. He is an advocate for food systems that benefit everyone from the grower to the eater, and partnered with Roots in the City Farmers' Market to bring the Nourishing Neighborhoods Double Value Coupon Program to the Miami area. He is also the author of a cookbook and is the 2010 James Beard Foundation's Best Chef South.

What was your favorite food as a kid?
Pizza.

What three adjectives describe your cuisine?
Fresh, simple, and pure.

What book most influences your food, cookbook or otherwise?
Zuni Cafe Cookbook is pretty important to my point of view as a chef.

What chef do you most admire?
Alice Waters. Her simple approach to food and focus on using fresh, local ingredients influenced my culinary philosophy.

What is your favorite ingredient?
If I had to pick one—tomatoes.

What music do you like to hear when you cook?
The music I like to hear when I eat—jazz.

What restaurant in the world are you most dying to try?
Eating at the country house of chef Francis Mallmann (author of *Seven Fires*) in Argentina would be pretty killer.

What is your favorite hangover meal?
Meat, probably a juicy hamburger.

Who do you most like to cook for?
My family.

If you could do one other job, what would it be?
Farmer.

What do you most value in a sous chef?
Balance.

What food trend would you most like to erase from the annals of history?
The trio. And foam.

What one food would you take with you to a desert island?
Indian River citrus from the Indian River District in Florida.

What is your favorite guilty-pleasure treat?
Ice cream.

What would you eat at your last meal, if you could plan such a thing?
A Caja–China-style whole roast pig.

Cheeseburger or foie gras?
Cheeseburger.

What's your favorite place (and what is your favorite thing to order) for:

Happy hour?
Bar Boulud in New York City, for pâté, terrine, charcuterie, a burgundy, and I'm happy.

A splurge meal?
Prune in New York City, and spoil me with a Parmesan omelet, marrowbones, and pork-shank confit.

Breakfast?
The Breslin in New York City, for yogurt or oatmeal.

A cup of coffee?
Stumptown double espresso.

A greasy-spoon meal?
Clarke's Miami Beach for corned beef, cabbage, potato, and grainy mustard.

Chocolate?
Chocolats Valrhona.

Michael's on the Hill

WATERBURY, VT

Michael's on the Hill was an early adherent to the "buy local" ethos, and chef/owner Michael Kloeti offers up the produce of Vermont in the heightened sensory reality of fine dining. The restaurant is in a circa 1820 farmhouse, and the regional food Kloeti prepares, down to the lamb-centric staff meal, could have been served at a candlelit harvest feast the day the house was first occupied.

In my family, which has one culinary foot in the northern Italian region of Lombardia, polenta is the starch of choice. At our gatherings, we serve it in the traditional way—on a wooden platter with very low sides. It rolls just to the very edges of the dish and cools evenly.

> ### OFF THE MENU
>
> ~
>
> Navarin of Lamb
>
> Creamy Polenta
>
> Ramp Gremolata
>
> *Suggested wine:*
> HDV Belle Cousine 2004
> or Owen Roe Sinister
> Hand 2009

The stew for staff meal translates perfectly to a dinner party menu, as it requires little last-minute fussing or individual plating. It even benefits from being cooked the night before. This way you can be drinking a glass of wine already when your guests begin complimenting the steam-drifts of aroma.

The ramp gremolata elevates the navarin from comforting to elegant. It is meat's best companion—a condiment worth mastering. As Kloeti suggests, you can alternate ramps with the season's brightest allium. Like most condiments, you may as well make extra for use with leftovers, like a cold lamb leg and roasted red potato lunch, or stir it into olive oil to pour over butter lettuce.

Navarin of Lamb

This stew is a wintry comfort, lush with the reduction of red wine. Like most stews, it gathers strength overnight, so if you are inclined, make it a day ahead and reheat while you prepare the polenta. The vegetable ingredients are sweet, as is the polenta with its cream and garlic enhancements. A strong crack of pepper at the table is just the thing.

3 pounds lamb stew meat, shoulder or shank, cut into 1-inch pieces
Salt and freshly ground black pepper
3 sprigs rosemary
10 sprigs thyme
¼ cup extra-virgin olive oil
¾ pound onion, medium dice, about 2½ cups
¾ pound carrot, medium dice, about 2½ cups
¾ pound celery root, medium dice, about 2½ cups
24 small cloves garlic
2 bay leaves
2 cups dry red wine
5 cups beef or lamb broth
1½ tablespoons chopped rosemary
1½ tablespoons chopped thyme
1½ tablespoons chopped parsley

Season the lamb with salt and pepper. Tie the rosemary and thyme together with a piece of twine.

Heat the oil in a large sauté pan over high heat and sear the lamb on each side until it is brown on all sides. Remove the lamb and set aside.

Add the onion, carrot, celery root, and garlic to the pan and sauté over high heat for an additional 5 to 10 minutes, until brown. Add the lamb, rosemary-and-thyme bundle, bay leaves, and wine; cook until the wine reduces by half, about 5 to 10 minutes. Add the broth and bring the mixture to a boil. Reduce the heat and simmer, partially covered, for 1½ hours, or until the lamb is fork tender. Let cool. Cover and refrigerate the stew several hours or overnight to increase flavor.

Before heating, remove the solidified fat from the top of the stew and discard. Reheat slowly, reducing the liquid until it gets to a sauce consistency and coats the back of a spoon nicely, around 30 minutes. Season with salt and pepper, and sprinkle the herbs on top. Serve the stew over Creamy Polenta, topped with a drizzle of Ramp Gremolata.

Serves 6 to 8

Creamy Polenta

I know, from a lifetime of kitchen duty, that constant stirring is the trick to clumpless polenta. Broil slices of leftover polenta the next day, stacked with lots of butter between each layer.

2 tablespoons unsalted butter
¾ cup chopped onion
4 cloves garlic, chopped
4 cups whole milk
2 cups chicken broth
2 cups cornmeal
1 cup Parmigiano-Reggiano
½ cup chopped fresh rosemary, thyme, and parsley
Salt and freshly ground black pepper

Heat the butter in a Dutch oven or other heavy-bottomed stockpot over medium-high heat. Sauté the onion and garlic until the onion is translucent, about 5 minutes. Add the milk and broth, bring to a boil, and turn the heat down to a simmer. Whisk in the cornmeal and simmer for 25 minutes, stirring constantly. Add the cheese and herbs; season to taste with salt and pepper.

Serves 6 to 8 as a side

Ramp Gremolata

Classically paired with osso buco alla Milanese, this gremolata is the salty and sour to red meat's rich and round.

4 ounces ramp leaves (substitute leaves from any member of the onion family, such as leeks or scallions)
Zest of 2 lemons
5 or 6 anchovy fillets
1 cup extra-virgin olive oil
½ teaspoon salt
Freshly ground black pepper

Put all ingredients into a food processor and blend until they are incorporated. If you prefer, you may incorporate the ingredients using a mortar and pestle.

Makes about 1 cup

⌒ Michael Kloeti ⌒

MICHAEL'S ON THE HILL (WATERBURY, VT)

Swiss chef Michael Kloeti is a true citizen of Vermont now. His ownership of Michael's on the Hill extends to involvement in Vermont Fresh Network, Local First Vermont, and Slow Food, and has earned him the first Vermont Chef of the Year ever selected by the Vermont Hospitality Council.

What was your favorite food as a kid?
Bread and sausages.

What was the first meal you made that you were proud of?
A cheese omelet that I made for my parents' breakfast.

What three adjectives describe your cuisine?
Local, flavorful, and simple.

What book most influences your food, cookbook or otherwise?
My go-to cookbook while I was training was Eugen Pauli's *Classical Cooking the Modern Way. The Food Lover's Companion*, which is a culinary reference book, is definitely one that I always have on hand.

What chef do you most admire?
Chefs who understand that the guest and the ingredients are more important than their ego.

What music do you like to hear when you cook?
I listen to everything from classical to eighties hits in the kitchen. The faster we need to move, the quicker the tempo!

What is your favorite hangover meal?
Before I got too smart to get hangovers, I loved eggs Benedict and espresso.

What is your favorite midnight snack?
That is dinnertime for me! A rib eye steak topped with local bleu cheese, a big salad, and a nice bottle of red is perfect.

What do you most value in a sous chef?
A sous chef who is such an extension of me that food quality and professionalism stay at its optimum level whether or not I'm in the kitchen.

What one food would you take with you to a desert island?
A whole pig.

What is your favorite guilty-pleasure treat?
Grand Marnier 150.

What would you eat at your last meal, if you could plan such a thing?
A perfectly braised short rib and pommes frites, but *what* is actually less important to me than *with whom*.

Cheeseburger or foie gras?
Cheeseburger with foie gras!

What's your favorite place (and what is your favorite thing to order) for:

Happy hour?
Sushi Zen in New York City, for "Chef's Choice" and some great sake.

A splurge meal?
Au Pied de Cochon in Montreal, Canada, for stuffed pig foot with foie gras and pouding chômeur.

Breakfast?
Home with my family. My wife makes the most perfect breakfast—buttermilk pancakes with Vermont maple syrup, sausage, and strong coffee.

Pastry?
Bossard Bakery in Brütten, Switzerland. This is the local bakery in the town where I grew up. My two boys and I would definitely get a nussgipfel, a flaky hazelnut pastry.

A cup of coffee?
Black Cap Coffee House in Stowe, Vermont.

A greasy-spoon meal?
Istanbul Döner Kebap in Winterthur, Switzerland, for the best lamb döner kebab, with lots of spicy, garlicky sauce.

Groceries?
Fairway in New York City.

Chocolate?
I love Vollenweider Chocolatier in Zurich, Switzerland. We make an annual family trip to their store.

Northern Spy Food Co.

I photographed the cover of this book at Northern Spy. The process of making *Off The Menu* involved a rapid, nationwide solo trip best served by packing light. But for the cover shoot, I did what is normally unfeasible and brought equipment. The crew of this small East Village neighborhood joint ate their staff meal under hot lights while I leaned over the table from a ladder, one hand propped on the ceiling, the other holding a rented lens valued higher than my car. Yet they still managed to be naturally at ease with one another. When I am taking photos, the subjects often assume their private conversations are being recorded. They're not, although I do of course eavesdrop. But the Northern Spy folks just spoke to one another, without guile or self-editing.

Northern Spy is a creature of New York. You can get enough covers every night because people eat so late. That is to say, this restaurant, with few tables, serves a lot of people. Which makes serving and cooking a balletic feat. The kitchen has room for two people to work and a small area where chef Nathan Foot lays eyes and hands on every dish before it goes out; he is the last person to touch every plate.

The paucity of space in a kitchen is made up for

OFF THE MENU

Spicy Pork
and Tomato Stew

Suggested beer/wine:
Captain Lawrence
Kölsch Beer or
Shinn Estates Red N.V.

with time. If there is only two feet of counter space and you need four feet, someone gets two feet until they are done and then the next person gets those same two feet after. In practical terms, it means Chef Foot is always afoot. Northern Spy Food Co. keeps its prices low so that people can come often, and it doesn't become an anniversary restaurant. But there is the madness of Foot's classic technique in every dish. You may never even know the rigor of the steps that went into the dish or that Foot worked hours for that extra step. Except, with every bite, you do know.

This staff meal had a fair dose of theater in it. After a day that started more than a few meals ago, the crew was tired. The servers probably would have slouched over their closing paperwork for the night, eating a bite in between all the satisfying equations that account for tips and taxes and sales. And with me hanging like Damocles' sword over the table, I am sure it was less than relaxing. But restaurant people are troupers. Chef Foot had created a meal that is just absolutely correct, perfectly comforting in its robust warmth; salty, savory, and dense, a buttress against thoughts of trudging home through the almost empty neighborhood. And at least they got to sit down.

Spicy Pork and Tomato Stew

Chef Nathan Foot devised this staff favorite to use up all of the trim from the whole pig the restaurant butchers once a week. It can marinate throughout service (or during your workday) and then get thrown in a pot to simmer once the pace starts to peter (or when you get home). Garnish with fresh cilantro and serve with rice and beans. Or use as the base for a taco, on a small, soft corn tortilla with queso fresco, creamy black beans, and pickled jalapeños.

½ pounds pork trim or boneless pork butt, cut into 1-inch pieces
½ large onion, julienned
3 cloves garlic, sliced
1 jalapeño, seeded and sliced
1½ tablespoons paprika
1 teaspoon cayenne
1 tablespoon ground coriander seed
1 tablespoon ground fennel seed
1½ tablespoons salt
½ tablespoon ground black pepper
2 tablespoons canola oil
1 cup beer
3 cups hand-crushed tomatoes
2 cups chicken stock
Salt and freshly ground black pepper
½ cup chopped fresh cilantro

In a large bowl, combine the pork with the onion, garlic, jalapeño, and spices. Toss to coat and let the pork marinate in the refrigerator overnight.

Heat the oil in a large, heavy-bottomed pot over medium heat. Cook the pork-and-vegetable marinade until the spices have formed a toasted coating on the bottom of the pot, about 8 to 10 minutes. Deglaze with beer and reduce by half. Add the tomatoes and stock, and season with salt and pepper. Simmer until the pork is tender, about 1½ to 2 hours. Adjust the seasoning. Garnish with cilantro and serve with rice, beans, or tortillas.

Serves 6 to 8

～ Nathan Foot ～

NORTHERN SPY FOOD CO. (NEW YORK, NY)

Nathan Foot has a spot so intrinsic to New York's Lower East Side, it's striking to learn that he accumulated most of his cooking experience in San Francisco. At Campton Place, Elizabeth Daniel, Masa's, Jardiniere, Myth Restaurant, and others, Foote prepared fancy food in big kitchens. Every bit of that expertise is flooding out of his tiny line at Northern Spy.

What was your favorite food as a kid?
My mother's griddled hot-dog sandwiches with mayo, sliced yellow onion, and sour dill pickle on Pepperidge Farm bread.

What was the first meal you ever made that you were proud of?
Shortly after graduating culinary school I cooked a Christmas dinner for my mother and some family friends that everyone seemed to really enjoy—that was particularly satisfying.

What three adjectives describe your cuisine?
Clean, simple, and honest.

What book most influences your food, cookbook or otherwise?
Essential Cuisine by Michel Bras.

What chef do you most admire?
Any chef who can still cook on the line and manufacture his or her own cuisine. At the end of the day, we chefs are really just cooks with better pay rates.

What is your favorite ingredient?
Salt: kosher to cook, and sea salt to finish (Maldon and Fleur de Sel).

What music do you like to hear when you cook?
I always liked classic rock: Led Zeppelin, Van Halen with Diamond Dave, Lynyrd Skynyrd.

What's your favorite hangover meal?
Something greasy like eggs and sausage from a diner usually works.

What restaurant in the world are you most dying to try?
Michel Bras's Laguiole in Laguiole, France.

What kitchen utensil is most indispensable to you?
My knives—a chef's knife, paring knife, and a boning knife—all used every day.

Who do you most like to cook for?
Our loyal local customers.

If you could do one other job, what would it be?
It's hard to imagine doing anything else, but I guess as long as it's not sitting at a desk I'd be happy.

What do you most value in a sous chef?
Loyalty, commitment to our craft, and tough skin.

What one food would you take with you to a desert Island?
I'd bring a chicken that laid eggs every day.

What is your favorite guilty-pleasure treat?
I don't have guilt about food, I also don't have a sweet tooth. I do like Jameson and cheap American beer, though.

What's your favorite place (and what is your favorite thing to order) for:

Breakfast?
Wherever I'm cooking at the time, I make good eggs and we always have fresh bread—soft scramble with toasted bread.

Late-night/after-work meal?
In San Francisco, I used to go to The Grubstake and get "The Nugget," a bacon-cheeseburger with a fried egg.

Cup of coffee?
I'm not picky about coffee, it's the function I'm usually more interested in.

Ice cream?
Any bodega with Ben & Jerry's: I dig their flavors and they don't skimp on the fat.

Nostrana

Nostrana is Italian for "ours." When I came to staff meal, chef/owner Cathy Whims was in Italy, soaking up inspiration for her regional Italian cooking and receiving the Leccio d'Oro award, which honors one restaurant in the world every year for eloquent presentation of Montalcino wines. I was sorry to miss her, but I have experienced her hospitality before. It is a gracious thing and it involves charcuterie and pizza and just the right glass of wine.

I had originally met Cathy while traveling to make my first book, *Primal Cuts: Cooking with America's Best Butchers.* She buys whole animals from local farms and cures meat for salumi. This flexibility to use up a whole animal, to wait months for something to cure, to use the peppers available that day at the market is very popular now. And it is, perhaps, no more popular anywhere than in Portland. Except maybe Italy.

In the specificity of my task to suss out the great staff meals, I have learned that restaurants with wood ovens win in the categories of variety and quantity. In a commercial kitchen, the ovens, counter space, range, and each second are all meted out with precision and a mind to scarcity, especially in the moments right before service. The wood oven cooks so hot and is so ample that it is no grave decision to throw something in for two or ten minutes and take it back out. Nostrana is illustrative of this observation, with a frenzy of dishes passing to and fro. Some were little leftovers—like putizza, a brioche-like sweetcake stuffed with walnuts, figs, and chocolate that was just pitching over the point of fresh. Some were staff-meal classics, like fettuccine with tuna and a chicken stew with peppers; some were menu items quick to prepare, a few pizzas—one with meat, and the Margherita.

Portland is a place where artists and artisans go to make their own scene. Over salad and pizza luganega, we talked about my camera choice and the benefits of living in Philly vs. Seattle. These were traveled people, people with interests and skills outside of food. And having an interest in food is also much more natural there. My cab driver turned down his Lenny Bruce CD to chat, and he gave me a list of hip farm-to-table restaurants much longer than I had dreamed of receiving from him. This is true everywhere, of course, people are surprising and wonderful—but in Portland, this new idea of farm-fresh food as a facet of the good life is much more on the tip of everyone's tongue. It is Bohemian there, stridently and sweetly.

OFF THE MENU

⁓

Pizza Margherita

Fettuccine with Tuna

Suggested wine:
Cameron Arley's Leap
Pinot Noir 2008 or Abbey
Ridge Pinot Noir 2008

BOTTOM: Samantha Smith, assistant bartender, at staff meal.

Pizza Margherita

Pizza Margherita is the primordial pie: dough, sauce, cheese. Once you have mastered this, Little Bird, you can move on to more exotic toppings (like ricotta from Michael's Genuine's family meal). San Marzano brand tomatoes are a chef favorite, if they are on the shelf at your local store. The pizza stone is unwieldy and extremely hot, so don't be afraid to enlist a sous chef.

Pizza Dough (page 207)
1 pound fresh mozzarella balls
Flour, for sprinkling
28-ounce can San Marzano crushed
   tomatoes
⅓ cup extra-virgin olive oil
Cornmeal, for sprinkling
1 bunch basil, for garnish

About 1 hour prior, place a pizza stone on the highest rack of your oven and preheat the oven to its highest setting, 500°F to 550°F. The stone needs this time to preheat.

Drain the mozzarella balls, pat dry with a towel, and cut into ⅓-inch slices.

Shape a piece of dough into a 9-inch circle on a well-floured baker's peel. Spread a thin layer of the crushed tomatoes over the dough, leaving a ½-inch border. Place a quarter of the mozzarella slices on top and drizzle with a bit of olive oil.

Carefully pull the rack a bit out of the oven and sprinkle a layer of cornmeal on the stone. Line up the far edge of the peel with the far edge of the stone; tilt the peel, jerking it gently and pulling back, to transfer the pizza to the stone. Bake until the pizza crust is golden, about 8 to 12 minutes. Carefully slide your peel under the pizza to remove it from the oven. Garnish with basil leaves and serve immediately. Repeat for the remaining four crusts.

Makes four 9-inch pizzas

Pizza Dough

3½ cups all-purpose flour
1½ teaspoons salt
One .25-ounce package active dry yeast
3 tablespoons extra-virgin olive oil

In the bowl of a heavy-duty mixer, add 3 cups flour, salt, and yeast and stir to blend. Add 1¼ cups lukewarm water and the olive oil, and mix with dough attachment until just blended. Switch to a dough hook and knead at medium/low speed for about 5 minutes, or until dough cleans the sides of the bowl and gathers smoothly around the dough hook. Remove dough to a lightly floured board. Knead about a minute or less by hand to bring together.* Place the dough in a lightly oiled bowl, turn to coat it, cover with plastic wrap, and leave it to rise, 60 to 90 minutes, until it doubles in bulk.

Turn dough out onto a lightly floured board and divide into quarters. Form each quarter into a ball, trying not to handle and deflate it too much. Place balls spaced apart on a floured tray or sheet pan and dust the tops with flour. Cover with plastic wrap and let rise until dough doubles in bulk, about 1 hour.

The dough is now ready to be formed into pizzas. On a well-floured baker's peel, gently form and stretch each ball into a circle. Try not to deflate. Top as desired and always drizzle with olive oil before cooking. Use the peel to slide the pizza onto your preheated pizza stone in the oven.

Makes four 9-inch pizza crusts

* Alternatively, the dough can be mixed in a bowl and kneaded by hand for about 10 minutes until smooth.

Fettuccine with Tuna

A quick recipe to quench a pasta craving. Do not skimp on tuna. You want a canned or jarred tuna that is still the texture of preserved fish, not watery Chicken of the Sea. Cook only for the 5 minutes called for, so the tuna doesn't get overcooked.

3 tablespoons extra-virgin olive oil

6 oil-packed anchovy fillets, drained and chopped

2 cloves garlic, minced

¼ cup finely chopped fresh parsley

1 cup chopped fresh tomatoes

2 tablespoons pine nuts, lightly toasted

Salt and freshly ground black pepper

1 pound fettuccine

12 ounces tuna in olive oil, drained

Fill a large pot with generously salted water and put over high heat to boil.

Heat the olive oil and anchovies in a large sauté pan over medium heat. Cook a few minutes, until the anchovies start to dissolve, stirring and mashing with a wooden spoon. Add the garlic and parsley and stir for 1 to 2 minutes, until garlic is fragrant. Add the tomatoes and pine nuts and season with salt and pepper. Cook on high heat for about 5 minutes and reduce the heat to low.

Add the fettuccine to the boiling water and stir well with a wooden spoon. Add the tuna to the sauce and flake it with a fork, allowing it to remain on the heat for about 5 minutes. When pasta is al dente, drain it in a colander and add it to the sauce. Toss well and serve immediately.

Serves 4

~ Cathy Whims ~

NOSTRANA (PORTLAND, OR)

Chef and owner Cathy Whims has spent years cooking in fabled Italian kitchens. It shows in her authentic cuisine. Nostrana was the Oregonian's Best New Restaurant in its opening year, 2005.

What was your favorite food as a kid?
Pizza—it was romantic and brought my family together.

What was the first meal you made that you were proud of?
I prepared a whole shad for my parents in my first apartment in college, and made shad roe as an appetizer.

What three adjectives describe your cuisine?
Rustic, gutsy, and reassuring.

What book most influences your food, cookbook or otherwise?
The Classic Italian Cookbook by Marcella Hazan.

What chef do you most admire?
The home cooks of Italy.

What is your favorite ingredient?
Anchovies and olive oil.

What music do you like to hear when you cook?
The Rolling Stones.

What is your favorite hangover meal?
Something healthy to make me feel better about myself, and more wine to make me feel better.

What is your favorite midnight snack?
A glass of wine and Parmigiano-Reggiano.

What restaurant in the world are you most dying to try?
Peppe Zullo in Foggia, Italy.

What kitchen utensil is most indispensable to you?
My most beloved item is my travertine marble mortar and pestle that I lugged back from Italy, but I couldn't cook without my Bob Kramer ten-inch chef's knife (well, I could cook, but it wouldn't be as much fun).

Who do you most like to cook for?
Other professional cooks.

If you could do one other job, what would it be?
Professional dancer.

What do you most value in a sous chef?
That she or he embrace and love Italian regional cuisine.

What food trend would you most like to erase from the annals of history?
Truffle oil—it is so fake and overpowering.

What one food would you take with you to a desert island?
Baccalà.

What is your favorite guilty-pleasure treat?
Ketchup squirted on an index finger with the refrigerator open.

What would you eat at your last meal, if you could plan such a thing?
I don't think I could eat.

Cheeseburger or foie gras?
Neither—truffles or a good hot dog.

What's your favorite place (and what is your favorite thing to order) for:

A splurge meal?
Le Calandre in Padua, Italy.

Pastry?
A croissant at Café Besalu in Seattle.

A late-night/after-work meal?
Bar Avignon or Navarre in Portland.

A cup of coffee?
Andrea Spella's Spella Caffe, roasted by his hand in Portland.

A greasy-spoon meal?
It's not too greasy, more fatty—Podnah's Pit Barbecue in Portland.

Groceries?
Pastaworks in Portland.

Ice cream?
Giolitti in Rome.

Chocolate?
Alma Chocolate in Portland.

Osteria Stellina

The hamlet of Point Reyes Station is nestled along the primordial coastline of Northern California. It is a place to regenerate, which has something to do with the positive ions in ocean air and the hypnosis of waves. There is agriculture, aquaculture, and a few movie stars. There is also the only restaurant in Marin County to receive a three-and-a-half star rating by the *SF Chronicle*'s revered Michael Bauer.

Osteria Stellina, located on the single street that makes up downtown Pt. Reyes, certainly has a captain at the helm, but its grace lies in the permeability of its outer membrane. The restaurant is breathing in Pt. Reyes and breathing out Pt. Reyes.

Restaurant culture can be isolating. When I waited tables in Manhattan I remember weeks of seeing few other people than my co-workers. Stellina's terroir is about people, as much as it is about ingredients. The employees here are members of the community. Rhonda, who runs Stellina's coffee bar, lives on a ranch that provides beef for the restaurant and where I once spent an afternoon castrating calves with the rancher and Stellina's chef/owner Christian Caiazzo. There is something wholesome about the staff here. They see daylight, they pick vegetables, they have rosy cheeks.

> ### OFF THE MENU
>
> Margarita's Chili Verde
>
> Crème Fraîche Coffee Cake
>
> *Suggested wine:*
> Pey-Marin Vineyards
> The Shell Mound Riesling
> Marin County 2010

The staff meal I shared with them was one oft-invoked by employees, a green chili called up like siblings discussing mom's pecan pie. The chili, like many family meals, has a few qualities that make it work: it is a one-pot dish, it is nourishing, and it uses inexpensive ingredients and the leftover things, the over-abundant things. Many chili recipes call for pork butt, but in Stellina's iteration, the pork leg is used. Since Stellina uses whole animals from local farms, it is often left with leg to use before it can bring in another hog.

The day of lunch the table was set with a pot of chili verde, locally made tortillas warmed in the oven and crusty hunks of bread. A new in-house baker had finally perfected his sourdough recipe and in a cross-cultural coup, it sopped up the tomatillo-dense stew perfectly. At one end of the table was Chef Caiazzo, casually filling in the staff on this week's crops from the farm he started at his home to supply the restaurant. At the other end of the table was Mark Pasternak, the farmer from Devil's Gulch Ranch, who had raised the meat that was braised. The back kitchen door creaked on occasion, steam sifting out and salt air sneaking in.

OPPOSITE: Chef Christian Caiazzo (bottom right), Margarita (bottom left), and farmer Mark Pasternak at the head of the table.

Margarita's Chili Verde

This is a homey, family recipe that Margarita, a prep cook, often had as a child in Michoacán. The restaurant before Stellina was a white man's version of a Mexican restaurant and the only highly regarded dish was Margarita's chili verde. She has even won a local cooking competition with it.

2 cups olive oil for frying

5 pounds Niman Ranch or other local pork butt, or fat part of the leg, trimmed of all but 10 percent of the outside fat and cut into 1½-inch chunks

2 heads garlic, chopped

Salt and freshly ground black pepper

1 large yellow onion, diced

1 large bunch cilantro, coarsely chopped

Salsa

5 pounds tomatillos, peeled from paper but not skins, raw

2 to 6 fresh jalapeños

4 cloves garlic, peeled

1 large yellow onion, peeled and quartered

Use a large, heavy-bottomed pot suitable for slow-frying and stewing. Heat the oil over medium-high heat and add the pork, garlic, and salt and pepper before the oil is too hot. Bring to a boil and lower to a simmer. (The entire mixture should be at a bubbly simmer.) Slow-fry the pork in the oil for approximately 1 hour. When the pork has a bit of brown color, and has been cooked well on all sides, remove about 90 percent of the oil. Add the onions and cook for 2 minutes.

While the pork is cooking, prepare the salsa. Put the tomatillos, jalapeños, garlic, and onion with 4 quarts water into a large container. Using a hand mixer, coarsely chop all ingredients together. The mixture should be chunky and not too fine.

When the pork, garlic, and onion mixture is ready, add the salsa and cook for approximately 1½ to 2 hours longer at a good simmer. Check the seasoning a few times while cooking and add salt and pepper to taste. Check the doneness of the meat at 1½ hours. The pork should be well braised and easy to bite through; the tip of a small knife should be easy to insert into the meat and withdraw. The meat should be "falling off the bone" tender.

Check the seasoning again for a final time, then add cilantro to finish. Serve with bread, rice, or warm corn tortillas.

Serves 8 to 10

Crème Fraîche Coffee Cake

Chef Caiazzo also owns a coffee stand in Point Reyes Station that bustles fine, locally roasted coffee all morning out of Toby's Feed Barn. And serves perfect baked goods, sweet and savory. This rich coffee cake is a favorite and I make it for Christmas breakfast.

1 cup pecans or walnuts

¾ cup dark brown sugar

2 teaspoons ground cinnamon

2 eggs

2 cups crème fraîche or full-fat buttermilk

1 tablespoon vanilla extract

2 sticks unsalted butter, chilled, cut into 1-inch cubes

1 tablespoon lemon zest

1 tablespoon baking powder

½ teaspoon salt

2 cups granulated sugar

3 cups all-purpose flour

Preheat the oven to 350°F. Spray a 9-inch bundt pan evenly and thoroughly with nonstick cooking spray; set aside.

To make the topping: spread nuts on a sheet pan and toast in the oven until lightly browned, about 5 minutes. Make sure to keep an eye on the nuts so they do not burn. Once toasted, coarsely chop the nuts and combine with the brown sugar and cinnamon. Set aside.

To make the batter: whisk together the eggs, crème fraîche, and vanilla in a small bowl. Set aside. In a stand mixer with a paddle attachment, cream together the butter, lemon zest, baking powder, and salt at low speed for 2 to 3 minutes, until softened. Add sugar and mix at medium speed for 3 to 4 minutes, until light and fluffy, scraping down sides occasionally. Turn mixer to low and add the egg mixture a few tablespoons at a time until incorporated, scraping occasionally; then add the flour in 3 batches, continuing to scrape sides after each addition.

Pour half of the batter into the prepared pan and spread evenly. Sprinkle half of the topping on the batter, then pour the remaining batter over that. Sprinkle the remaining topping on top. Bake for about 1 hour, until firm to the touch and a fork comes out clean.

Let cool completely before removing from bundt pan.

Serves 8

∽ Christian Caiazzo ∾

OSTERIA STELLINA (PT. REYES, CA)

Christian Caiazzo is a chef's chef. Having worked at many seminal restaurants, he seems to have a connection with every cook he meets. Postrio, Lascaux, Globe, and NYC's Union Square Cafe are a few lines on his resume. He also owns the coffee bar in Point Reyes Station, which serves Italian pastries out of a kiosk in Toby's Feed Barn.

What was your favorite food as a kid?
Lobster.

What was the first meal you made that you were proud of?
Seafood chowder at my first restaurant job, when I was fifteen, at a country club.

What three adjectives describe your cuisine?
Italian, savory, seasonal.

What book most influences your food, cookbook or otherwise?
Roast Chicken and Other Stories by Simon Hopkinson.

What chef do you most admire?
Alice Waters.

What is your favorite ingredient?
Parsley.

What music do you like to hear when you cook?
Led Zeppelin.

What is your favorite hangover meal?
Noodles, spicy soups, and pho.

What is your favorite midnight snack?
Nuts.

What restaurant in the world are you most dying to try?
Noma in Copenhagen.

What kitchen utensil is most indispensable to you?
Spoon.

Who do you most like to cook for?
My girlfriend.

If you could do one other job, what would it be?
Barista.

What do you most value in a sous chef?
Trust in the vision.

What food trend would you most like to erase from the annals of history?
Fusion.

What one food would you take with you to a desert island?
Pasta.

What is your favorite guilty-pleasure treat?
Twizzlers.

What most satisfies your sweet tooth?
Good doughnuts.

What would you eat at your last meal, if you could plan such a thing?
A twenty-seven-course tasting menu.

What's your favorite place (and what is your favorite thing to order) for:

Happy hour?
The Old Western Saloon in Point Reyes Station, where I live. It also happens to be the only place in town.

A splurge meal?
Combal Zero, just outside Turin, Italy.

Breakfast?
Boulette's Larder in the Ferry Building in San Francisco.

Late-night/after-work meal?
Yuet Lee in San Francisco.

Cup of coffee?
Four Barrel in San Francisco.

Greasy spoon?
Pork Store Cafe in San Francisco.

Grocery store?
Eataly in Turin, Italy, and New York City.

O Ya

The level of hospitality that garlanded me at O Ya still warms my memory. I spent one of the coldest days I have ever experienced snug in the kitchen and behind the sushi bar learning and talking and observing. Boston does not rank as one of the coldest cities in the United States, but to a Californian, at a certain point—cold is cold. Walking around the city in my idea of winter gear—jeans, boots, and a trench—had given me a bone chill. Tim and Nancy Cushman, the owners of O Ya, spent all day warming me up.

The first thaw came from watching their crew prepare staff meal, which happened in short intervals between hundreds of other things. They have the work of mise-en-placing a full kitchen as well as the sushi bar. Sushi can look like the simple assembly of ingredients, yet the ingredients are anything but simple. And, as you know from cooking anything beyond the simplest of meals, you don't make one dish and then move on to the next. You may chop everything first, get a pot of something going, prepare the salad, add to the pot, sauté the vegetables right before dinner. Once you spend a few years in a kitchen, commercial

> ### OFF THE MENU
>
> Potato Falafel Sandwiches
>
> Hummus
>
> Tzatziki Sauce
>
> *Suggested wine:*
> Elk Cove Willamette Valley
> Pinot Gris 2009

or home, this moves to the realm of innate prioritizing. So, occasionally a cook would call out to me, "I'm making the tahini!" or "I'm about to mix the falafel!"

The falafel are made with potato, rather than chickpeas—or garbanzo beans, as I grew up calling them. This is because O Ya uses potatoes on their menu and they don't always have chickpeas. Simple. And once you get the basic idea of what a dish is supposed to do, both in your mouth and chemically, while it is cooked, you can make these sorts of decisions. There were also gorgeous ends of fish fillets that aren't served in the restaurant because they are not *just so* when raw. And the menu is *just so*, beautifully.

Hospitality is a profound thing. To really offer all that you have to a guest is such an act of grace. I was in that grace when Nancy offered me dinner in the dining room; and again when I sat watching sushi chef Kawaguchi work and asked him all my many questions; and not least of all when we sat down together for staff meal and spoke the traditional Japanese prayer of thankfulness for the meal. Not a perk or an employee right, but a simple offering of grace.

TOP RIGHT: Chef Yukihiro Kawaguchi preps for dinner service.

Potato Falafel Sandwiches

Since O Ya doesn't always have chickpeas, they devised this falafel made of potato. It can be described as a meat-and-potatoes croquette but with Southeast Asian spices. This would also be tasty with ground lamb, if you have some of that in the house. Fill out pitas to your taste. I would add pickled beet and carrots and parsley, if it were my lunch.

4 large potatoes
2 tablespoons olive oil
1 pound ground beef
1 large onion, chopped
1 tablespoon kosher salt
Pinch of pepper
3 tablespoons curry powder
1 teaspoon ground cumin seed
1 teaspoon ground coriander seed
2 cups all-purpose flour
3 eggs
2 cups panko
Canola oil for frying
Sea salt

2 cups chopped iceberg lettuce
¾ cup diced English cucumber
¾ cup diced tomato
1 medium red onion, sliced
Pita bread, cut in half

Cut the unpeeled potatoes into chunks and boil until cooked through, about 20 minutes. Drain and mash the potatoes with a fork until smooth.

In a large sauté pan, heat the oil over medium-high heat. Sauté the beef and onion until beef is no longer pink, about 5 minutes. Add the salt and pepper and let the mixture cool.

Combine the beef mixture with the potatoes. Add curry powder, cumin, and coriander, and mix to combine. Form into multiple small balls and set aside.

Prepare a bowl of flour, a bowl of beaten eggs, and a bowl of panko. Dust each ball in the flour, dip into the eggs, and coat with the panko. Fry in a deep fryer or in 2 inches of oil at 350°F until golden brown, about 5 to 7 minutes. Drain on a rack or paper towels and sprinkle with sea salt.

Combine the lettuce, cucumber, tomato, and red onion in a bowl. Serve the falafel stuffed into the pita bread with the lettuce mixture. Top with Hummus and Tzatziki Sauce.

Serves 6 to 8

Hummus

Hummus is a low-cost way to add protein to your meal and you can also slather it on most anything to good effect. O Ya calls for canned chickpeas, or garbanzo beans, but you can also reconstitute dried ones by soaking overnight. This will sit happily in the fridge for a few days, so make extra and add it to lunches and snacks.

16-ounce can chickpeas
¼ cup extra-virgin olive oil
3 to 5 tablespoons lemon juice
2 cloves garlic
1 teaspoon salt
Pinch of pepper

Drain the chickpeas, reserving the liquid. Combine them with the olive oil, 3 tablespoons lemon juice, garlic, salt, and pepper in a blender. Blend until smooth, adding reserved chickpea liquid as needed. Taste and adjust lemon juice and salt. Serve immediately or cover and refrigerate.

Makes about 1½ cups

Tzatziki Sauce

Tzatziki is a cooling condiment. You can also serve it as a *meze*, or appetizer served with lots of other little tastes, like the hummus and falafel offered here. This is also right at home next to slices of grilled lamb or under a poached egg and a float of olive oil.

1 English cucumber
2 cups Greek yogurt
1 tablespoon finely chopped mint
1 teaspoon red wine vinegar
2 teaspoons lemon juice
½ teaspoon lemon zest
2 teaspoons kosher salt
Pinch of pepper

Peel, seed, and cut the cucumber into small dice. Combine all the ingredients in a bowl and mix well. Cover and refrigerate for at least 1 hour for best flavor.

Makes about 2½ cups

~ Tim Cushman ~

O YA (BOSTON, MA)

Tim Cushman's haute Japanese eatery in Boston is a darling of diners, both amateur and professional. Nearly every national and regional food writer has praised Cushman for his exquisite range of dishes and his adherence to the Japanese respect for ingredients.

What was your favorite food as a kid?
Fresh fish out of the river that ran through the backyard of my childhood home in Massachusetts: bass, trout, perch, pickerel.

What was the first meal you made that you were proud of?
It wasn't a meal, but when I was in fifth grade, I won a science fair when I made maple syrup from trees in my backyard.

What three adjectives describe your cuisine?
Full flavored, adventurous, and layered.

What book most influences your food, cookbook or otherwise?
Secret Ingredients by Michael Roberts.

What chef do you most admire?
Chef Michael Roberts was my first mentor in Los Angeles. He taught me to be inventive with ingredients and about building complete flavors.

What is your favorite ingredient?
Chilies—any kind. The hotter the better.

What music do you like to hear when you cook?
It really depends on my mood. Sometimes rock; sometimes jazz.

What is your favorite hangover meal?
Omelets and bacon and/or leftover pizza.

Who do you most like to cook for?
My wife, Nancy.

If you could do one other job, what would it be?
Play my guitar and tour internationally with a blues/rock band.

What do you most value in a sous chef?
A great palate, creativity, resourcefulness, and maturity.

What one food would you take with you to a desert island?
Pizza.

What is your favorite guilty-pleasure treat?
Ice cream.

What most satisfies your sweet tooth?
I don't have a sweet tooth. I'll take savory any day. I eat pizza for dessert.

What would you eat at your last meal, if you could plan such a thing?
A greasy pepperoni pizza.

Cheeseburger or foie gras?
Cheeseburger, rare to medium rare.

What's your favorite place (and what is your favorite thing to order) for:

Happy hour?
Noon Hill Grill in Medfield, Massachusetts, for craft beers, the best chicken wings, and chef John Straker's creative food.

A splurge meal?
Gibsons in Chicago for a big steak.

Breakfast?
Bourque Restaurant in Norfolk, Massachusetts, for eggs over easy and home fries.

Pastry?
Perfect cream puffs from any Beard Papa's.

A late-night/after-work meal?
La Taqueria in San Francisco for tacos.

A cup of coffee?
Blue Bottle Coffee at the Ferry Building Marketplace in San Francisco for cappucinno.

A greasy-spoon meal?
Red Wing Diner in Walpole, Massachusetts, for clam chowder and big bellied fried clams with tartar sauce.

Ice cream?
Ben & Jerry's Fudge Brownie.

Paley's Place

When Paley's Place first opened in 1995, it was located in a Victorian house so small that perishable ingredients had to be used up every day because there wasn't adequate refrigeration space in which to store them. This daily breathing in of farmers' market ingredients and breathing out of dishes made the restaurant a living thing. It also makes Paley's Place a forefather of Northwestern cuisine and Portland's farm-driven menus. It is hard to believe that anything that happened in the 1990s is an institution, but here we are.

Staff meal came by the hands of Patrick McKee, sous chef of Southern origins. There is something muscular and macho about this meal, which appeals to me. Pulled-pork sandwiches with coleslaw and Georgian-style barbecue sauce are at the center of the plate. The sauce is vinegary and a little sweet. The cheesy jojos threaten to colonize every inch of my appetite but I hold back by only eating them once I am nearly full. A jojo, for the uninitiated, is a battered and deep-fried potato wedge. These are mercifully unbattered but the blanketing of cheese gives them a mantle of over-indulgence worthy of the name jojo. "Whatever is left around

---

OFF THE MENU

Braised Pulled Pork
with Georgian-Style
Barbecue Sauce

Cheesy Jojos
with Ranch Dressing

Suggested wine:
J. Christopher Dundee Hills
Cuvée Pinot Noir 2007

---

here gets covered in cheese," chef and owner Vitaly Paley tells me. So the jojos are covered with cheddar cheese of nacho proportions. These will quiet the hunger of teenage boys, they are that forceful in their heartiness. And if you put some of that Georgian-style barbecue sauce on them, they are perfect. This collegiate aggressiveness toward hunger reminds me that staff meals often reveal the dark, secret side of a chef. The Paley's menu is French in influence and elegant and not covered in cheese.

Vitaly and his wife, Kimberly, have worked at fine New York restaurants such as Bouley, Union Square Café, and Chanterelle, but these seem almost too distant to mention. Paley's Place speaks for itself now, and the Paleys hardly need resumes. Kimberly sent me their very first menu, handwritten on notepaper imprinted with a French waiter holding a tray, with items like, for example, *suprême de pigeon au champignons sauvages*. Not so different from the French menus they prepare now, with *escargot à la bordelaise* and roasted bone marrow with garlic. In a town frothing with self-discovery, the consistency of Paley's Place is parentally warming.

Braised Pulled Pork
with Georgian-Style Barbecue Sauce

Pulled pork is a Southern classic and specifically beloved in North Carolina, where barbecue means pork. This is a version you can make indoors and then get that regional kick with the vinegary Georgian sauce.

5 pounds pork shoulder, cut into
   2-inch cubes
3 to 4 tablespoons pimentón
Salt and freshly ground black pepper
2 tablespoons rendered bacon fat or
   vegetable oil
3 medium sweet yellow onions,
   peeled and coarsely chopped
2 medium carrots, scraped and
   coarsely diced
5 large cloves garlic, finely minced
14-ounce can diced tomatoes
Bouquet garni: 3 bay leaves, a few
   sprigs thyme, and 2 tablespoons
   cracked black peppercorns,
   wrapped in cheesecloth
2 cups white wine
Georgian-Style Barbecue Sauce
   (page 225)
Hamburger buns
Favorite coleslaw

Season the pork shoulder with the pimentón, salt, and pepper, and cover and refrigerate for 2 to 3 hours.

Preheat the oven to 300°F. In a heavy, ovenproof sauté pan or Dutch oven, heat half the fat until almost smoking and sear the pork shoulder in batches to avoid overcrowding. Be sure to get a deep caramelization. Transfer the seared pork to a plate and set aside. Add the remaining fat to the pan and slowly cook the onions and carrots over medium heat until caramelized, 12 to 15 minutes. Add the garlic and cook briefly over low heat, about 3 to 4 minutes; then add the tomatoes and bouquet garni and slowly cook over medium heat until tomatoes are reduced by half. Add the white wine and reduce by half. Add the cooked pork with any juices that may have run onto the plate, cover, and cook in the oven for about 3½ hours, or until the meat pulls apart easily.

Allow the mixture to rest in the pan until cool enough to handle; discard the bouquet garni. Coarsely chop all the solids and combine with a few tablespoons of barbecue sauce.

Serve on soft buns topped with your favorite coleslaw and more barbecue sauce on the side.

Serves 8 to 10

Georgian-Style Barbecue Sauce

2 cups apple cider vinegar

1 cup white wine vinegar

1½ teaspoons Dijon mustard

2½ tablespoons freshly cracked black peppercorns

2 tablespoons red-pepper flakes

2 tablespoons salt

3 tablespoons dark brown sugar, plus extra for added sweetness, optional

Three 6-ounce cans tomato paste

5 tablespoons unsalted butter, diced

In a medium saucepan, combine all the ingredients for the barbeque sauce except the tomato paste and butter. Bring to a boil over medium-high heat, reduce to a simmer, and cook for 4 or 5 minutes. Add the tomato paste and cook on very low heat till thickened, and remove from heat. Finish the sauce with the butter. The sauce will be tangier when hot; it is supposed to be fairly tart. Add more brown sugar if a sweeter taste is more to your liking. Strain the sauce and allow to cool to room temperature before using.

Makes about 3 cups

Cheesy Jojos with Ranch Dressing

A jojo is a deep-fried potato wedge, sometimes battered. Here it is a rough-cut French fry, transformed into pub fare with gooey melted cheese and homemade ranch dressing for dipping. The Georgian hot sauce cuts the richness and a beer would not be out of the question.

Ranch Dressing

2 cups sour cream

½ cup apple cider vinegar

½ cup buttermilk

½ cup mayonnaise

2 tablespoons ground fennel seed

4 tablespoons dried vegetable flakes*

6 tablespoons chopped fresh parsley

Salt and freshly ground black pepper

Vegetable oil for frying

6 large russet potatoes, washed, dried,
   and sliced into ½-inch rounds

Salt

2 cups shredded sharp cheddar cheese

Combine all the dressing ingredients in a bowl, stir well to mix, and season with salt and pepper. Refrigerate if not serving right away. Dressing can be made a day in advance.

Fill a large stockpot a quarter of the way with oil. Heat over high heat to 325°F. Cook potatoes in batches until crisp golden brown. Drain on paper towels and season with salt. Transfer potatoes to an ovenproof dish or pan, sprinkle with cheese, and broil until cheese has melted. Serve immediately, with ranch dressing.

Serves 8 to 10 as a side

*Vegetable flakes are available online or easily prepared at home. To make your own, very thinly slice 1 large yellow onion, carrot, and fennel bulb and place into a large flat sheet tray lined with parchment. Dry in a food dehydrator or an 150°F convection oven for 6 to 10 hours until very brittle and dry. When cool, transfer to a food processor and pulverize into flakes. Store in an airtight container for up to 1 month.

～ Vitaly Paley ～

PALEY'S PLACE (PORTLAND, OR)

Vitaly Paley and his wife, Kimberly, opened Paley's Place in 1995 and have been collecting achievements ever since, from the James Beard Award for Best Chef Northwest to the Prince of Pork crown at Cochon 555's inaugural event.

What was your favorite food as a kid?
I ate everything as a kid. If I had to pick two, they would be potato latkes fried in goose fat, slathered with sour cream, and salmon caviar on black bread with butter.

What three adjectives describe your cuisine?
Bold, inventive, and gutsy.

What book most influences your food, cookbook or otherwise?
Larousse Gastronomique by Prosper Montagné. It is like a culinary bible to me.

What chef do you most admire?
My grandmother. Even though she was never a professional chef, she had a lot to do with developing my palate.

What is your favorite ingredient?
Currently a combination of ingredients: fennel pollen, piment d'Espelette, and persillade [chopped parsley and garlic].

What music do you like to hear when you cook?
When we need a little pick-me-up, it could be anything from Moby's greatest hits to good old-fashioned disco. If I need something ruminative it could be Glen Gould's version of the Goldberg variations, Keith Jarrett's The Köln Concert, anything by the Beatles, Jimi Hendrix, or Eric Clapton.

What is your favorite hangover meal?
Who eats when they are hungover?

What is your favorite midnight snack?
Nachos.

What restaurant in the world are you most dying to try?
El Bulli, Part Two, since I am too late for Part One.

What kitchen utensil is most indispensable to you?
My chef's fork.

Who do you most like to cook for?
Anyone who's hungry.

If you could do one other job, what would it be?
Bicycle tour guide in France.

What do you most value in a sous chef?
Loyalty.

What food trend would you most like to erase from the annals of history?
The rosemary sprig garnish in everything.

What one food would you take with you to a desert island?
Sushi.

What most satisfies your sweet tooth?
Chocolate.

What would you eat at your last meal, if you could plan such a thing?
Sushi or anything Mexican.

What's your favorite place (and what is your favorite thing to order) for:

A splurge meal?
St. John in London, for deviled kidneys on toast.

Pastry?
Pierre Hermé in Paris for macaroons.

A cup of coffee?
Home, made in my Bialetti [stovetop espresso maker].

A greasy-spoon meal?
The Stepping Stone Café in Portland for huevos rancheros and a spicy Bloody Mary.

Groceries?
Food Front Cooperative Grocery in Portland.

Kitchen equipment?
Sur La Table or In Good Taste in Portland for all kitchen gadgets and small wares.

Ice cream?
Street gelato vendors in Rome.

Chocolate?
Li-Lac Chocolates in New York City for a mixed box of truffles.

Perla's Seafood & Oyster Bar

AUSTIN, TX

Austin, Texas, is a city that suits me well. It is quirky, entrepreneurial/DIY, and has an eclectic and magnetic music scene. These are all qualities that also describe the city's food culture, which includes a cadre of food trucks, the good kind of dives, and barbecue joints galore. There is also Perla's, serving simple preparations of seafood that is sought out daily with an obsessive dedication to freshness.

Austin-born chef Larry Mcguire's culinary approach of unfettered simplicity is a step away from the general tendency towards complexity. Esquire Magazine praises Perla's: "Everything on the menu is done with such surprising care that it actually defines simple."

Staff meal is often a keyhole to what the base food yearnings of a kitchen are. Frittata Ranchera is a Tex-Mex craving, if I've ever seen one. With all the oysters flying around at Perla's you may forget it is Austin to the bone. But it is-down to the grill smoke ambling through the patio.

Frittata Ranchera is just the thing to make for overnight houseguests. The work of this meal is all up front, and unlike most egg dishes, it will still be tasty later. Revive with a quick drizzle of good olive oil and a sprinkle of fresh chopped cilantro.

OFF THE MENU

Alejandro's Frittata Ranchera

Suggested wine:
Cliff Lede Sauvignon Blanc 2010

Alejandro's Frittata Ranchera

This dish causes massive delight on a Sunday morning. The combination of potato, egg, and cheese makes it fuel enough for a day of active leisure. Adjust the heat of the salsa to suit your own predilection for tongue tingling.

1 Idaho potato, diced
5 tablespoons canola oil
Salt and freshly ground black pepper
3 jalapeños, sliced
1 poblano pepper, sliced
1 red bell pepper, sliced
½ Spanish onion, sliced
6 whole eggs, whisked
1 cup shredded cheddar cheese
About 12 flour tortillas
½ bunch cilantro, chopped

Salsa
4 jalapeños
5 Roma tomatoes
3 cloves garlic
½ red onion, diced
Salt and freshly ground black pepper
1 bunch cilantro, chopped

Preheat oven to 400°F. On a sheet pan, coat the potato with 3 tablespoons of the oil, season with salt and pepper, and roast until tender, about 20 minutes. Set aside.

For the salsa, bring a lightly salted pot of water to a rapid boil. Add the peppers, tomatoes, garlic, and onion, and cook for five minutes. Drain the vegetables and purée in a food processor to your desired consistency. Place in a bowl and season with salt and pepper. Fold in the cilantro and set aside.

Heat a rondeau or large sauté pan over medium-high heat and add the remaining 3 tablespoons of oil. Sauté the peppers and onion until the onion is slightly translucent, about 5 minutes. Add the eggs and stir to evenly incorporate ingredients; fold in the potatoes. Keep the mixture on medium-high heat for about 5 minutes, until the bottom sets. Take off the heat. Season with salt and pepper, and top with the cheddar cheese. Place in the oven and bake until the cheese is melted, about 5 minutes.

Meanwhile, warm the tortillas in a griddle or pan with a bit of oil and reserve, covered in a kitchen towel. Remove the huevos rancheros from the oven, top with cilantro and serve with the warm tortillas and salsa.

Serves 6 to 8

Pok Pok

"Pok pok" is the phonetic Thai description of the sound of pestle hitting mortar. Andy Ricker's Pok Pok is just as kinetic. Portland has become a destination for food tourists and professionals alike. Pok Pok is not exclusively the reason why, but the elements that make it great are the very principles of Portland's popularity. These elements are: profound focus on a specific cuisine, ingredient-driven food, prices matched to an economy of under-employed creatives, and a hipster aesthetic in a DIY package. And the food is really, really delicious. As in: you will think about it for days.

Pok Pok has focused on street food and managed to de-coagulate the American iteration of Thai food. Thai has gone the way of many Asian cuisines in our to-go commerce and become listless and fixed. Pok Pok has no Pad Thai. Right away we are starting fresh. There are thousands of Thai dishes, and finally someone has reminded me of this.

"Mama Phat is the standard noodle dish." Andy Ricker describes the evening's staff meal and its etymology with a scholarly clarity. His knowledge is not haphazard, it is the research of an eager acolyte. "MAMA is the brand of noodles, but like *Kleenex*, the name of the brand has become the name of the thing. *Phat* means fried." Dinner is an enormous round platter of long noodles plus the kitchen sink. "We use scraps of every leftover: red pork, game hens, chicken, then we tart it up with garlic, chives, fried shallots, peanuts, fish sauce, oyster sauce, palm sugar syrup." This is something you would order at a food cart in Thailand and though it might be slightly different every day, it will always be essentially the same.

Like most noodle dishes, there is a ritual of personalization at the table. Thais set out *khruang phrung* with meals, which comprises three or four sauces to season your own bowl: *naam plaa phrik* (fish sauce with green chilies), *phrik naam som* (rice vinegar with chilies), *phrik phon* (dried crushed chilies), and *naam tam* (sugar).

As someone who segregates their sweet and savory pretty strictly, I questioned the sugar bowl on the table. "The more sugar you add, the hotter you can make it," a veteran server explained.

OFF THE MENU

MAMA Phat

Suggested beer:
Rogue's Morimoto
Soba Ale

MAMA Phat

This simple noodle dish proves that a recipe's degree of difficulty is not a direct correlative to its excellence. Made with packets of instant noodles that are ubiquitous in Thailand, Pok Pok's MAMA Phat is a brilliant 30-minute meal. Since I grew up in an Italian-American kitchen, it is still thrilling for me to add in a dash of fish sauce or a cup of bean sprouts. This recipe will be an introduction to the exoticism of Thai cooking for the uninitiated and damn satisfying for the connoisseur.

6 packages MAMA Oriental-Style Instant Noodle, pork flavored

1 packet seasoning mix from instant noodles

2 tablespoons fish sauce

2 tablespoons oyster sauce

1 tablespoon granulated sugar

4 tablespoons pork stock or water

½ cup vegetable oil

3 shallots, thinly sliced

1 cup ground pork or sliced pork shoulder

1 cup julienned white onions

2 tablespoons thinly sliced garlic

2 cups julienned napa cabbage

1 cup bean sprouts

1 tablespoon chopped Thai chilies

¼ cup chopped fresh cilantro

Cook the noodles in boiling water until soft, about 2 minutes. Drain and set aside.

In a small bowl, combine the seasoning mix, fish sauce, oyster sauce, sugar, and stock. Set aside. Heat a wok over medium heat and add the oil. When it begins to smoke, add the shallots in two batches until light golden brown, about 3 to 5 minutes per batch. Transfer with a slotted spoon to paper towels to drain.

Pour off all but 2 tablespoons of oil from the wok and stir-fry the pork over high heat 3 to 5 minutes, until no longer pink. Add the onion and garlic and stir-fry a minute, then add the noodles, cabbage, bean sprouts, and chilies and stir-fry another minute. Add the sauce and stir-fry until well combined and most of the liquid has been soaked up by the noodles. Serve immediately with fried shallots and cilantro sprinkled on top.

Serves 6

‿ Andy Ricker ‿

POK POK (PORTLAND, OR)

Chef and owner Andy Ricker is expanding the palates of PDXers with his many ventures in Asian eats. His endeavors include Pok Pok, Pok Pok Noi, Whiskey Soda Lounge, Pok Pok Som, and Ping. He is James Beard Foundation's Best Chef Northwest 2011.

What was your favorite food as a kid?
Indian food.

What was the first meal you made that you were proud of?
Hamburger glop: macaroni with hamburger and tomato sauce.

What book most influences your food, cookbook or otherwise?
Thai Food by David Thompson.

What chef do you most admire?
David Thompson.

What is your favorite ingredient?
Fish sauce.

What music do you like to hear when you cook?
At the restaurant, none—music is distracting in a professional kitchen. At home, I often listen to Al Green.

What is your favorite hangover meal?
Vietnamese noodle soups.

What is your favorite midnight snack?
Peanut butter on toast.

What restaurant in the world are you most dying to try?
ABC Kitchen in New York City.

What kitchen utensil is most indispensable to you?
Mortar and pestle.

If you could do one other job, what would it be?
Tugboat captain.

What do you most value in a sous chef?
A great palate and the ability to get what I am talking about.

What food trend would you most like to erase from the annals of history?
Truffle oil.

What one food would you take with you to a desert island?
Avocados.

What is your favorite guilty-pleasure treat?
Ring Dings.

What most satisfies your sweet tooth?
Mangoes.

What would you eat at your last meal, if you could plan such a thing?
Laap meuang: Northern Thai minced-meat "salad" with pork cracklings, offal, and blood mixed in with the spices, served with bitter herbs and sticky rice.

What's your favorite place (and what is your favorite thing to order) for:

A splurge meal?
St. John Restaurant in London.

Breakfast?
Bacon sandwich and house-cured kippers at St. John Bread & Wine, London.

Pastry?
A croissant from Little T American Baker in Portland, Oregon.

A late-night/after-work meal?
Salad and lamb sandwich at Victory Bar in Portland.

A cup of coffee?
Stumptown in Portland.

A greasy-spoon meal?
Tom's Restaurant, Division and 39th, in Portland.

Groceries?
New Seasons Market in Portland.

Kitchen equipment?
Woeng Nakhon Kasem market in Bangkok.

Chocolate?
Xocolatl de David in Portland.

Restaurant Eugene

ATLANTA, GA

"I want to see these guys cook," Linton Hopkins, chef and owner of Restaurant Eugene tells me. "Instead of micromanaging, I want them to come to me with ideas." Linton encourages his cooks to make staff meal without a script. They are cooks, after all. "In this generation, so many people don't know how to make a biscuit."

Linton's original recipe for Gumbo Ya Ya calls for mojo—you'll have to make your own. It is clearly in his dish and just as evident in our conversation; his language is poetic without being pre-edited. This man is in touch with his mojo. "Chefs need to follow their own path and look within; I don't give a shit what other cooks are doing."

He does give a shit about the food system and so does his staff. His director of Hospitality and Fruition, Judith Winfrey, is also a farmer and chapter leader of Slow Food Atlanta. Hopkins has surrounded himself with people who are thinking about food as pleasure as well as about food as an industry that can benefit all its participants. "Sustainability means trust," he tells me, and I understand that he trusts the farmers who supply his restaurant, and his customers trust him.

Gumbo Ya Ya has other ingredients besides mojo; it is rich and smoky with the inclusion of andouille and tasso, two Southern standards in meat processing. This recipe is thickened without okra, which may be a selling point for some, okra being a divisive ingredient. Plus, you will then know how to make roux, which is helpful to know in any sauce-thickening emergency.

Dessert is clafoutis, which is one of my beloved standards. Like a tart, once you know the basic procedure, you can improvise on the filling. Pantry-common ingredients and your fruit overstock create a beautiful dessert. You will make it again and again, and people will come to expect it but love it no less. It is also perfect with milky coffee in the morning or as a snack with tea.

"We live in a culture where cooks eat fast food. I'm so sick of the celebration of fast food." Hopkins is well regarded by other chefs, someone whom people listen to. I'm so glad.

OFF THE MENU

~

Gumbo Ya Ya

Clafoutis

Suggested wine:
Peay Scallop Shelf Estate
Pinot Noir 2008

Gumbo Ya Ya

Chef Linton learned to make this recipe from an old Cajun who insisted that it isn't gumbo unless you add "mojo." Mojo is something that makes it your own. It could be a piece of fennel, sarsaparilla root, or bundle of sage.

3 onions, small diced

2 green bell peppers, small diced

6 celery stalks, small diced

1 stick unsalted butter

½ cup (¼ pound) duck fat

½ pound all-purpose flour, about 2 cups

1 head garlic, minced

3 tablespoons plus 2 teaspoons Creole
  seasoning

1 cup port wine

3 tablespoons peanut oil

2 pounds smoked andouille sausage, sliced
  thickly

1 pound tasso ham, cubed

2 pounds boneless chicken thighs, cubed

2 cups chopped tomato

¼ cup Worcestershire sauce

3 quarts chicken stock

2 quarts veal stock

Bouquet garni: 2 sprigs thyme, 2 bay leaves,
  12 black peppercorns, and parsley stems
  wrapped in cheesecloth

Mojo (you have to find your own)

½ cup chopped fresh parsley, save stems

Salt and freshly ground black pepper

Dash of Tabasco

Minced scallion, for garnish

Divide the "holy trinity" (the onion, green bell pepper, and celery) into thirds: one third for broth, one third for the roux, and one third to be sautéed. To make the roux, melt the butter (without browning) and duck fat in a cast-iron pan over low heat, and slowly stir in the flour. Stir the roux over low to medium heat until dark in color: it will begin to smell like peanut butter when it is done. Add a third of the holy trinity, a third of the garlic, and 2 teaspoons of the Creole seasoning to the roux. Stir until combined and let it cook for 3 minutes. Carefully add the port and stir. Set aside.

Heat the oil in a large sauté pan over high heat. Sauté the sausage until golden brown, about 5 minutes. Remove it and reserve, leaving the fat in the pan. Add tasso and sauté until golden brown, about 5 minutes. Remove the tasso and reserve, again leaving the fat in the pan. Repeat for the chicken.

Add the second third of the holy trinity and the remaining two thirds of the garlic to the fat in the pan, and cook over medium heat until soft and beginning to color, about 10 minutes. Add the tomatoes, the remaining 3 tablespoons of Creole seasoning, the Worcestershire sauce, and the chicken and veal stocks. Bring to a boil and let simmer for 10 minutes; then add the reserved meats, the last third of the trinity, the bouquet garni, and your mojo.

While the soup base is still simmering, stir in the roux in small amounts, adding more when the last bit is incorporated. Roux must be warm in order to dissolve lump free. The starch in roux is activated when the liquid comes up to a boil, so add just enough to slightly thicken the mixture. It will continue to thicken as it cooks. Let the gumbo cook over medium heat for 30 minutes, making sure to skim off the fat from the top of the soup occasionally. Add parsley. Adjust seasoning with salt, pepper, and Tabasco.

Serve with minced scallion on top. You can also add cooked seafood such as shrimp, crabmeat and crawfish tail meat, and rice, if desired.

Serves 6 to 8

Clafoutis

Here is a recipe for the arsenal of go-to desserts, because it is much easier than it tastes. I can make a clafoutis from memory and often do. This is the platonic clafoutis. It warms well to stone fruit and most traditionally to cherries.

3 eggs
⅔ cup granulated sugar
1 vanilla bean, split and pulp scraped out
¾ cup crème fraîche
¾ cup milk
½ cup all-purpose flour, sifted
Confectioners' sugar, for dusting

Preheat the oven to 350°F.

Place the eggs, sugar, and vanilla-bean scrapings in the bowl of a mixer. Whisk until smooth and the whisk leaves a short trail, about 5 minutes. Add crème fraîche and milk and whisk until smooth. Add flour and whisk until smooth.

Pour into a greased 9-inch pie or baking dish. Bake for 20 minutes, until the edges have browned and the clafoutis has set. Dust with confectioners' sugar and serve warm or cool.

Serves 6 to 8

Siren Hall

Siren Hall was a gift of remoteness. I had vowed to make this book without a car and was rewarded with more domestic train rides in a few months than the rest of my collective years. But northern Michigan has joined the chef conversation, so I rented a car in Detroit and headed north. Mario Batali had bought a house in Traverse City, and a spotlight shone on the region. A region that is just glorious in the summer, the locals told me. It was January when I visited.

Despite the many feet of snow and the vindictive wind, Elk Rapids is very clearly a sweet town. I could imagine it thawed in summer, Fourth of July bunting on the 19th-century facades, small but well-maintained sailboats in the harbor, a brass band in the gazebo. Though I couldn't help but lay a transparency of in-season over the uninhabited main street, there was a benefit to being the only guest in town. The first payoff came at Guntzviller's Taxidermy, which houses a spectacular museum of preserved animals in tableaus of their natural habitat. Being the only guest gave the opportunity for a guided tour from Voss Guntzviller.

The apex of off-seasonality was at Siren Hall, a stunning restaurant of stark whites punched with

---

OFF THE MENU

Pork and Vegetable Stir-Fry with Scallion Basmati Rice

Napa Cabbage Salad

Suggested wine:
Chateau Grand Traverse Lot 49 Riesling 2009

---

sculptures of lake fish in iridescent hues. "During the summer, we work insane hours and you can't wait for it to be over," shared Michael Peterson, the chef and owner. "But then in the winter, you are counting the days until summer." Sitting at the long bar and enjoying the pre-shift meal with the employees, I felt lucky to be there in the winter. We lingered over the Thai meal of basil-inflected salad and gingery pork.

The conversation turned to staff meals of yore. "Sometimes popsicles can be all that you need for a morale booster." Clearly that is a summer treat. "We have one famous meal we call the Gut Bomb." (Quick recipe for the brave and voracious eater: mash stale hamburger buns and chili to create a batter; put hot dogs on a stick and cover in batter; deep fry.)

I was keen to try the local wines, being a native of California's wine country. The charming manager and sommelier brought out a Riesling that galloped right along next to the Thai meal. I can see how the extremity of the seasons can leave you with a grass-is-greener feeling, as a restaurateur. But as a guest, I couldn't imagine a bad time to be cozied up to the bar at Siren Hall.

BOTTOM: Chef Michael Peterson at the end of the bar for family meal.

Pork and Vegetable Stir-Fry
with Scallion Basmati Rice

This recipe utilizes the trim from a pork-tenderloin dish on Siren Hall's menu and could also be used for trim in your house—any strips of meat that are suitable for stir-frying. This staff meal was so lauded by the crew, it ended up on the menu. The lime juice adds a treble note to make the dish sing and it is well accompanied by the napa cabbage salad.

Marinade

2 tablespoons finely julienned fresh ginger

1 tablespoon sliced fresh garlic

2 tablespoons soy sauce

2 teaspoons granulated sugar

1 tablespoon fresh lime juice

1 tablespoon canola oil

1 pound pork tenderloin, cut into strips

2 tablespoons canola oil

1 medium head bok choy, finely sliced

1 to 2 red bell peppers, julienned

¼ cup hoisin sauce

¼ cup chicken stock

½ cup peanuts, toasted and crushed

Salt and freshly ground black pepper

4 cups cooked basmati rice

½ cup finely sliced scallions

Soy sauce, optional

Sriracha or hot chili sauce, optional

Stir the marinade ingredients together in a bowl. Add the pork and toss to coat. Cover and refrigerate overnight.

Heat a large sauté pan over medium-high heat and add the 2 tablespoons canola oil. Add the pork, with marinade, and sauté 1 to 2 minutes, stirring often. Be careful not to burn the garlic. Add the bok choy and red pepper and sauté 3 to 5 minutes, until the pork is just cooked through and the vegetables are still crunchy. Add the hoisin sauce and enough stock to make a nice consistency. Do not cook hoisin too long, or it will become overly rich and salty. Add the crushed peanuts and toss quickly to combine. Adjust the seasoning.

Place stir-fry on a bed of the basmati rice laced with the scallions. Serve with soy sauce and sriracha on the side.

Serves 4 to 6

Napa Cabbage Salad

This salad is *just so* and doesn't need a thing. But you can also pile it with additions and take it anywhere on the continuum from condiment to entrée. Chunks of leftover barbecued chicken, almond slivers, sliced skirt steak, and seared tuna are all possibilities. The vinaigrette is also a marinade for proteins desirous of an Asian palate.

2 tablespoons rice vinegar
1 teaspoon granulated sugar
1 tablespoon fresh ginger juice
1 tablespoon soy sauce
1 tablespoon sesame oil
½ cup canola oil
1 small napa cabbage, finely shredded
1 to 2 cups baby spinach
1 to 2 carrots, peeled and julienned
½ cup fresh cilantro

Whisk together the vinegar, sugar, ginger juice, and soy sauce in a mixing bowl. Slowly drizzle in oils while whisking.

Combine the vegetables and cilantro in a large bowl. Lightly dress with vinaigrette and serve.

Serves 6 as a side

~ Michael Peterson ~

SIREN HALL (ELK RAPIDS, MI)

Michael Peterson attended the Culinary Institute of America, as well as Paris's Le Grenadine, before returning to his place of origin in northern Michigan. He is now the executive chef (and co-owner, with his wife, Rebecca) of both Lulu's and Siren Hall.

What was your favorite food as a kid?
Fresh doughnuts and cider.

What was the first meal you made that you were proud of?
Braised short ribs with potato parsnip purée—served to my parents when I was twenty three at my first restaurant.

What three adjectives describe your cuisine?
Fresh, varied, and crafted.

What book most influences your food, cookbook or otherwise?
Culinary Artistry by Andrew Dornenburg.

What chef do you most admire?
Charles DeLargy, who drilled me.

What is your favorite ingredient?
Fennel seed.

What music do you like to hear when you cook?
Led Zeppelin.

What is your favorite hangover meal?
Poached eggs and bacon with hash browns.

What is your favorite midnight snack?
BLT with avocado.

What restaurant in the world are you most dying to try?
Alinea in Chicago.

If you could do one other job, what would it be?
Fine woodworking.

What do you most value in a sous chef?
Honesty and perseverance.

What food trend would you most like to erase from the annals of history?
Garnishes in the seventies such as the tomato rose and zucchini boat.

What one food would you take with you to a desert island?
Lemons.

What is your favorite guilty-pleasure treat?
An olive burger from Slabtown Burger in Traverse City, Michigan.

What most satisfies your sweet tooth?
Marshmallow Fluff.

What would you eat at your last meal, if you could plan such a thing?
Pasties from Muldoon's, Michigan.

Cheeseburger or foie gras?
Foie Gras, with a side of foie gras.

What's your favorite place (and what is your favorite thing to order) for:

A splurge meal?
Fruit de mer tower from Balthazar, New York.

Breakfast?
The maple sausage from Bubby's in Tribeca, New York.

Pastry?
Any Parisian almond croissant.

A late-night/after-work meal?
Sushi and sake from Red Ginger in Traverse City.

A cup of coffee?
Ethiopian beans from Moka in Bellaire, Michigan.

A greasy-spoon meal?
Homemade toast from Round's in Traverse City.

Groceries?
Parmesan peppercorn bread from Zingerman's Deli in Ann Arbor, Michigan.

Kitchen equipment?
Saucepans from Mary's Kitchen Port in Traverse City.

Ice cream?
Black cherry from Higgins Store in Alden, Michigan.

Chocolate?
Walnut from Murdick's Fudge on Mackinac Island, Michigan.

Tabard Inn

WASHINGTON, DC

"Hotel guests are people that are okay with the quirkiness of a one-hundred-year-old building," Chaim the bartender tells me as he sets up for the lunch shift. I ask him if he has many drink orders to fill at lunch. "People adopt the international vibe and have a glass of wine at lunch." This is a lunch spot in the neighborhood of World Bank headquarters and Embassy Row, after all. *When in Rome . . .*

The bottom floor of Tabard Inn is a very busy restaurant serving very busy people, in several dining rooms and an outdoor garden with a living roof. A living roof, by the way, is a green space on top of a building that naturally insulates. Most of the square footage of the inn, which occupies two row houses just off Dupont Circle, is in hotel rooms, all different from one another and from most other hotels. The look is Parisian Flea Market meets Colonial design. Wrought-iron beds and big ottomans with charming paintings of unknown subjects.

Tabard Inn is especially dear in its setting five blocks from the White House and the accompanying palpitations of politics. There is a feeling of escape in the dining room, or at least of mutual indulgence.

OFF THE MENU

Wild-Boar Ragu

Suggested wine:

Claiborne & Churchill
Pinot Noir 2008

Everyone here is having a good long lunch. Every room feels like a nook, especially the Brown Parlor, fitted out in chinoiserie, and the rooftop deck, with brick walls high enough to keep the whoosh of the street out of view.

There are whole sections full of regulars here. One regular even gave herself a job. She occupies a stool at the end of the bar, a junction where people are always wondering which way to turn for the restroom. So she made a sign that she hangs on her back, which directs customers the right way while she enjoys her lunch. She was also invited to the Christmas party.

Though there are many old timers on the Tabard Inn staff, the crew I met at family meal were youngbloods. We ate spaghetti with wild-boar ragu and an unpretentious green salad. I love this meal because it is so familial. How many nights did I eat this very thing at home as a kid, albeit with ground beef instead of wild boar? I did not, however, ever have a meat sauce as enjoyable as chef Paul Pelt's. And this is the linchpin of this book—a simple, quick dish, which can be so much more delicious, consistent, and nourishing if you know how to make it like a great chef would.

Wild-Boar Ragu

Boar meat is gamey and sweet and has all the bristle and tusk of the animal itself. (If it doesn't happen to be boar season or you haven't the slightest clue where to procure a boar, you can use pork butt instead.) Boar is especially suited to a tomato-based ragu, which softens the flavor and distributes the fat into a sauce bordering on stew. My family serves this over polenta, as is traditional on our bit of earth in Northern Italy, but it is right at home on spaghetti, as it was served to me at Tabard Inn.

3 onions, diced

3 carrots, diced

3 ribs celery, diced

4 anchovy fillets

3 cups red wine

4 ounces pancetta lardoons

1 tablespoon chopped fresh rosemary

1 tablespoon chopped fresh marjoram

Salt and freshly ground black pepper

1¾ pounds wild boar shoulder or pork butt, cut into 1-inch chunks

1¾ pounds ground wild boar shoulder or ground pork butt

3 cups chicken stock

2 cups diced tomatoes

2 tablespoons tomato paste

2 teaspoons crushed chili flakes

1 cup heavy cream

In a food processor, pulse the onions, carrots, celery, and anchovy. Set aside.

In a small saucepan over medium heat, reduce the red wine to half the amount, about 15 minutes. Set aside.

In a large skillet over high heat, slightly brown the pancetta and strain off most of the fat. Add the vegetable-and-anchovy mixture, rosemary, marjoram, and salt and pepper. Sauté until the vegetables are soft, about 5 to 8 minutes, then add the meat, reduced wine, stock, tomatoes, paste, and chili flakes. Simmer until meat is tender, about 2 hours. Add the heavy cream and adjust seasoning. Serve the ragu with pasta or polenta.

Serves 6 to 8

～ Paul Pelt ～

TABARD INN (WASHINGTON, DC)

Paul Pelt has risen from line cook to lunch chef to executive chef at Tabard Inn. Over the years, he has focused his culinary odyssey on learning many traditions, most voraciously the foods of the African Diaspora, which feeds the soul of the Tabard menu.

What was your favorite food as a kid?
Shrimp fried rice.

What was the first meal you made that you were proud of?
Polish sausage and French fries.

What three adjectives describe your cuisine?
Two sum it up: diverse and venturesome.

What book most influences your food—cookbook or otherwise?
Thai Street Food by David Thompson.

What chef do you most admire?
Martin Picard.

What is your favorite ingredient?
Lemon.

What music do you like to hear when you cook?
Rock. Hendrix.

What is your favorite hangover meal?
Pizza.

What is your favorite midnight snack?
Carnitas.

What restaurant in the world are you most dying to try?
St. John (Fergus Henderson and Trevor Gulliver) in London.

What kitchen utensil is most indispensable to you?
All-Clad saucier.

If you could do one other job, what would it be?
Music appreciation teacher.

What do you most value in a sous chef?
Endurance.

What food trend would you most like to erase from the annals of history?
Foam.

What one food would you take with you to a desert island?
A whole cow.

What is your favorite guilty-pleasure treat?
Foie gras.

What most satisfies your sweet tooth?
Ice cream and chocolate.

What would you eat at your last meal, if you could plan such a thing?
Barbecue spare ribs.

Cheeseburger or foie gras?
Cheeseburger.

What's your favorite place (and what is your favorite thing to order) for:

Happy hour?
Home, for club soda.

A splurge meal?
Komi in D.C. for everything.

A late-night/after-work meal?
Kaz Sushi Bistro in D.C. for everything.

A greasy-spoon meal?
Jimmy T's Place in D.C.

Groceries?
Harris Teeter in D.C.

Ice cream?
Cold Stone Creamery.

Chocolate?
Schakolad Chocolate Factory.

Tavolàta

SEATTLE, WA

The dish served at Tavolàta's staff meal is something everyone should know how to make. For one thing, it has seven ingredients, which, depending on your proclivities, you may always have lying around. For another thing, it will remind you that cooking can make a dish more than the sum of its ingredients. That surprise makes this exquisite and makes you look like a genius, if you are ever in a mood that requires some buoying. Bigoli with Anchovies, Chilies, and Garlic, topped with fried bread crumbs, is a pasta dish that tastes as good ten bites in as it does with that first slurp. And if bread crumbs on pasta seems like overkill, it's only because you haven't had it.

Ethan Stowell is the chef/owner of Tavolàta and three other Seattle restaurants. He also owns Lagana Foods, which makes bronze-cut pasta, like the kind Tavolàta prepares for service each day. He is busy, I mean to say. But he made dinner for his employees this night and he made this dish, which is his personal favorite thing to eat. Tavolàta has staff meal after service, so it has the joviality you hope an Italian restaurant's would have. One long table, open bottles of wine tipped into juice glasses, and platters of sliced salumi making the rounds.

The post-work high is a well-known phenomenon in the restaurant industry. After being "on" for several hours and whipping around, driven by a set of constantly shifting priorities, it is nearly impossible to instantly unwind. In my early twenties, I usually met this elevated pitch with a night on the town. This gets expensive and exhausting with age. Sitting down to a meal with coworkers seems like the perfect antidote. Some revelry and grousing and nourishment are just the right combination to enjoy and then exhaust the post-shift restlessness.

I lived in Seattle in the late 1990s and there was no Tavolàta then. Since that time, restaurant culture has changed to the more regional and ingredient-driven cooking that celebrates a man like Ethan Stowell. On a visit back a few years ago, I had a king's feast at Tavolàta. After dinner, I was so sated and elated that I couldn't find my car. One might owe it to my horrible sense of direction. But I blame the anchovies, chilies, garlic, and fried bread crumbs.

OFF THE MENU

Bigoli with Anchovies, Chilies & Garlic

Suggested wine:
Long Shadows Poet's Leap Riesling 2009 or Scott Paul La Paulée Pinot Noir 2007

Bigoli with Anchovies, Chilies & Garlic

This dish will have you eating out of Tupperware at 1 A.M., if there happen to be any leftovers. It is made of things that are easy to always have on hand, so it is perfect for throwing together à la minute. It is rather spicy but the chilies balance the anchovies, so try it before you tinker with the heat. A big bowl of it needs no accompaniment, except a splash of wine in a juice glass and maybe a plate of olives and salumi.

Fried Bread Crumbs
2 cloves garlic, smashed with knife
¼ cup olive oil
½ pound bread slices, stale or lightly toasted
Kosher salt

1 pound bigoli pasta
¾ cup olive oil
3 cloves garlic, sliced
2 teaspoons chili flakes
12 oil-packed anchovy fillets, drained and chopped
Packed ¼ cup chopped fresh parsley

Put the garlic and oil in a saucepan over low heat. Allow to infuse for about 5 to 6 minutes. Meanwhile, put the bread slices in a food processor. Pulse to chop, then process for 1 to 2 minutes, or until finely ground. Add the crumbs to the garlic oil and cook over low heat for 2 to 3 minutes or until crumbs have toasted and absorbed the oil. Season with kosher salt. Crumbs will keep in an airtight container for about two weeks.

Bring a large pot of salted water to a boil. Add pasta and cook according to package directions, less 1 minute.

While the pasta is cooking, heat the olive oil over medium-low heat in a large sauté pan. Add the garlic, chili flakes, and anchovy. Cook gently, stirring occasionally, until garlic is soft and anchovy fillets melt into the oil, about 5 to 6 minutes.

When the pasta is done, drain and tip into sauté pan. Add parsley and toss well. Divide among four deep bowls and top each with a tablespoon or two of bread crumbs. Serve immediately.

Serves 4

THE ESCOFFIER QUESTIONNAIRE

∼ Ethan Stowell ∼

TAVOLÀTA (SEATTLE, WA)

Ethan Stowell is the executive chef and owner of almost the entire restaurant scene in Seattle: Tavolàta, How To Cook a Wolf, Anchovies & Olives, and Staple & Fancy. Most recently, he created Lagan Foods, bringing bronze-cut pastas to retailers.

What was your favorite food as a kid?
I grew up eating very well. We had three boys in our house and dinner was usually served family style. The mustard-crusted leg of lamb my dad made was amazing.

What was the first meal you made that you were proud of?
Shake 'n Bake chicken. I was about eight and the recipe was out of the *Walt Disney Cookbook*. I still have the book, it's probably the most stained book I own.

What three adjectives describe your cuisine?
Thoughtful, adventurous, and determined.

What book most influences your food, cookbook or otherwise?
I would say the Culinaria cookbook series. It's a great combination of history, reference, and reliable recipes.

What is your favorite ingredient?
Anchovies. They are incredibly versatile. Tinned ones for pasta dishes or sauces and fresh ones for roasting or grilling. They also taste great.

What music do you like to hear when you cook?
Anything upbeat. I like to feel invigorated while I'm cooking.

What is your favorite hangover meal?
Rice steamed with cardamom, then mixed with a fried egg and a little soy sauce.

What kitchen utensil is most indispensable to you?
My white-handled spatula, I've had it for years.

Who do you most like to cook for?
My wife, Angela. No question.

If you could do one other job, what would it be?
Professional baseball player.

What do you most value in a sous chef?
Honesty. If you fuck up, I'm okay with it—just come clean.

What food trend would you erase from the annals of history?
Atkins diet. It made everyone think pasta is bad for you.

What one food would you take with you to a desert island?
Pasta, I can't help it, I love the stuff.

What is your favorite guilty-pleasure treat?
Brownies. A good brownie makes Ethan a happy man.

What most satisfies your sweet tooth?
Brownies, coffee ice cream, and Sour-Patch Kids. I know it's bad, don't judge!

What would you eat at your last meal, if you could plan such a thing?
Spaghetti with anchovies, chilies, and garlic.

Cheeseburger or foie gras?
If it's grass-fed beef, I'll take the cheeseburger.

What's your favorite place (and what is your favorite thing to order) for:

A splurge meal?
Vitello d'Oro. It's a small restaurant in a northeastern Italian town called Udine. It was the best meal of my life. Amazingly fresh fish and the best steamed potatoes I have ever had.

Pastry?
A warm croissant. Not reheated warm, I'm talking fresh from the oven warm. There is a place in Seattle, Cafe Besalu, that has the best croissants outside of Paris.

Greasy spoon?
I live in Seattle and "Dick's is the place where the cool hang out"—Sir Mix-a-Lot, 1988. A great burger.

Toro

Toro is way into their staff meal. At the very tip of the tail end of dinner service, staff meal is served up in the open kitchen. Everyone scampers into the back and finds an uninhabited spot to eat before the final acts of waiting on the remaining tables—a few dessert orders, the drop of the checks, the *Glad you came in tonight*s.

The tao of being in a kitchen is to be doing. The moment you stand in a kitchen without a job or a destination, you are in the way—irritatingly and constantly in the way. So there is a perverse pleasure in being in this kitchen, during service, while the entire crew stands still and enjoys a few moments of a meal together. The energy of a post-shift staff meal is more kinetic. This is a battalion—bonded, wounded, engaged—as opposed to the mess-hall feeling of a pre-shift staff meal. There are benefits to both choices, but as a guest, post-shift is much more fun.

Toro and the nearby Coppa are both owned by chef Jamie Bissonnette (as well as restaurateur Ken Oringer). When I say Toro is way into their staff meal, I may as well be saying that Jamie is way into their staff meal. Each night, Toro and Coppa compete, via

OFF THE MENU

~

Mise en Place Ramen

Suggested beer:
Narragansett's Lager Beer

photos on Twitter, for best staff meal. Every dish has an invented name: Bang Bang Brokli (sliced hot dogs with brocolli on a hot, hot skillet), Mise en Place Ramen. "Coppa usually wins because they have a really small staff and they end up eating a lot of leftovers from the menu," Jamie explains. With Toro's many mouths, meals must be made; there's no sharing of a few tortellini.

The competitive bonhomie between Toro and Coppa illustrates one of my favorite elements of staff meal—it is an arena of unfettered creativity, of loose ends and individuality. The menu of a restaurant, even if it changes daily, is made in a strict style. Cooks making this food come from all over the world and have mutable interests and tastes. So, if you work at Toro, you may not want to eat *pimentón* every night. You may not even want to look at *pimentón*. "We do a lot of Asian food for staff meal instead."

While the menu is a top-down set of decisions made for the public, staff meal is a conversation among cooks. "Dude, they're having wings and meatballs at Coppa tonight. Did you get a picture of this up on Twitter yet?"

OPPOSITE: Johnny Keeley, cook, grabs extra bowls for his fellow cooks.

Mise en Place Ramen

This dish is made with the remaining mise en place at the end of service, so at Toro, it varies from night to night. *Mise en place* means, literally "everything in its place," and culinarily, "all ingredients ready to be used for service." The technique in this recipe will be your guide to thinking of the ingredients as elements. You may not have bell pepper, so substitute another vegetable with sweetness, crunch, and vibrance. I rarely have pork belly confit, but maybe another salty, fatty meat to add richness. This is a "kitchen sink" recipe and very quick to prepare, if you have leftovers in search of a new identity.

1 tablespoon canola oil

1 clove garlic, chopped

1 cup diced red bell pepper

1 cup chopped scallions, white part

1 cup chopped or julienned vegetables: carrot, salsify, celeriac, or kohlrabi

3 or 4 packs of 32-ounce instant ramen with enclosed seasoning packets

8 ounces diced pork belly confit or cooked bacon

4 ounces chopped cooked chicken leg, breast, or wings

3 quarts chicken stock

Salt and freshly ground black pepper

1 cup mixed fresh herbs: parsley, chives, mint, chervil, but not rosemary or thyme

Heat the oil in a soup pot over medium-high heat. Add the garlic, red bell pepper, scallions, all the vegetables, and the contents of the seasoning packets from the ramen, and stir quickly for 1 to 2 minutes. Add the cooked meats and stock and bring to a boil. Taste and adjust seasoning. Turn off the heat, add the ramen noodles, and cover for 12 minutes. Uncover and finish by adding the mixed herbs. Serve immediately.

Serves 6 to 8

THE ESCOFFIER QUESTIONNAIRE

～ Jamie Bissonnette ～

TORO (BOSTON, MA)

Jamie Bissonnette is a James Beard Foundation's 2010 nominee for Best Chef of the Region and *Food & Wine*'s Best New Chef in New England for 2011. With acclaimed partner, Ken Oringer, Jamie has created two restaurants that never slow down. And he makes excellent headcheese.

What was your favorite food as a kid?
Butter, liverwurst, and brussels sprouts. Can you believe it?

What was the first meal you made that you were proud of?
Scrambled eggs with cheese and toast.

What three adjectives describe your cuisine?
Creative, delicious, and balanced.

What book most influences your food, cookbook or otherwise?
Anything by Jacques Pépin.

What is your favorite ingredient?
Salt.

What music do you like to hear when you cook?
Punk, ska, and hardcore.

What is your favorite hangover meal?
Bánh mì.

What is your favorite midnight snack?
Anything in a tortilla, pizza, or eggs.

What restaurant in the world are you most dying to try?
L'Astrance in Paris.

What kitchen utensil is most indispensable to you?
My knives and my Le Creuset Dutch oven.

If you could do one other job, what would it be?
Tour with a band.

What do you most value in a sous chef?
Honesty and drive.

What food trend would you erase from the annals of history?
Balsamic reductions.

What one food would you take with you to a desert island?
Eggs.

What is your favorite guilty-pleasure treat?
Kookaburra black licorice.

What most satisfies your sweet tooth?
Candy from South End Formaggio, Boston.

What would you eat at your last meal, if you could plan such a thing?
Caviar and tacos.

Cheeseburger or foie gras?
Cheeseburger.

What's your favorite place (and what is your favorite thing to order) for:

Happy hour?
Mac's Club Deuce, Miami.

Splurge meal?
Koy Shunka, Barcelona.

Late-night/after-work meal?
New Golden Gate, Boston, or San Loco Tacos, Miami.

A greasy-spoon meal?
O'Rourke's Diner in Middletown, Connecticut. Or for a burger: Tasty Burger, Boston.

Groceries?
Ming's Supermarket, Boston.

Urban Belly

Urban Belly is a noodle and dumpling shop. This is street food elevated by carefully sourced ingredients and the culinary skills of chef/owner Bill Kim, who has worked in some of Chicago's top kitchens. But unapologetically, it is street food, which dissolves the membrane between the dining-room menu and staff meal.

"They usually just eat whatever they want," says Bill, who regards his young employees as opportunities to spread some good in the world. Bill and his wife, Yvonne Cadiz-Kim, who co-own Urban Belly and the equally popular Belly Shack, don't have kids. Bill says this gives him the energy to be generous with other people's kids. Besides his crew, Bill works with a school garden project and other endeavors to introduce children to healthy eating habits in "food deserts" (pockets of industrialized areas where nutritious food is unavailable.)

Bill recounted a story from his former life in Charlie Trotter's kitchen. He had gone beyond his limits of exhaustion and his body staged a coup by passing out. As soon as he had regained consciousness, he got a pat on the back and a nudge back to the line. The machismo of the kitchen lost its appeal for Bill, right then and there. He wants to be happy, to have the energy to do beneficial work outside his restaurants, and he wants the same for his employees.

Brothy noodle soups are suited to a restaurant's family meal or a meal for your family, because much of the tinkering happens at the table. Every cook perfects their additions to the stock—chili flakes, soy sauce, fresh herbs. It happened to be the day before Super Bowl when I visited Urban Belly, and the kitchen had also prepared chicken wings, as a lark. They had been working on the batter and dipping sauces for the past week and this was it, this was the one.

Bill is someone with an admirable relationship to food. Flavor and process are important, of course; but the struggle is about creating local systems that work; systems that nourish everyone along the chain in body and in spirit. So far, he has two restaurants, a school garden, and many happy employees. It isn't about what he owns or will own but about growing a family of well-fed kids.

OFF THE MENU

Chicken Wings
with Bleu Cheese
and Asian Thousand
Island Dressing

Rice-Cake Stew

Suggested beer:
Goose Island's
Sofie Vintage Ale or
Three Floyds' Robert
the Bruce Scottish Ale

Chicken Wings
with Bleu Cheese and Asian Thousand Island Dressing

The rice flour in the batter creates a lighter coating than the traditional wing. While satisfying on their own, you may begin to think of the wings as sauce delivery mechanisms. Trying to pick your favorite dressing between the creamy bleu cheese and the tangy Thousand Island could take up the better part of an afternoon.

Bleu Cheese Dressing

1 cup mayonnaise

1 cup sour cream

6 ounces crumbled bleu cheese

4 tablespoons lemon juice

3 tablespoons sherry vinegar

Asian Thousand Island Dressing

1 cup mayonnaise

½ cup ketchup

4 tablespoons sesame oil

2 tablespoons minced garlic

2 tablespoons minced ginger

1 scallion, sliced

2 tablespoons fish sauce

2 tablespoons lime juice

Chicken Wings

24 to 30 chicken wings, split, tips discarded

1 cup all-purpose flour

1 cup rice flour

3 tablespoons paprika

3 tablespoons garlic powder

3 tablespoons chili powder

Pinch of salt

Canola oil for frying

Combine the ingredients of each dressing in a separate bowl and refrigerate until ready to serve.

Lay out chicken wings on paper towels and pat dry. In a large bowl, mix together the flours, paprika, garlic powder, chili powder, and salt. Toss a few wings at a time in the mixture, shaking off the excess before transferring them to a sheet pan.

Once all the wings have been dredged, deep-fry them at 350°F until golden and cooked through, about 6 to 8 minutes. Transfer to a cooling rack. Serve with the bleu cheese and Asian Thousand Island dressings.

Serves 4 to 6

TOP RIGHT: Line cook Benjamin Moeller and sous chef Cameron Waron taste test wings and rice-cake stew. BOTTOM LEFT: Chef Bill Kim at staff meal.

Rice-Cake Stew

Oval rice cakes look like slices of water chestnut and have the "mouthfeel" of rice noodles—chewy, gooey, and soft. Available in the frozen section of Asian grocery stores, rice cakes are defined more by their texture and the flavors they soak up than by their innate flavor. This stew, layered with ingredients of all notes, infuses every cell of rice cake.

2 quarts chicken stock

1 pint coconut milk

1 cup Thai sweet chili sauce

4 tablespoons sambal oelek chili paste

4 tablespoons fish sauce

4 tablespoons lime juice

1 teaspoon vegetable oil

1 red bell pepper, finely diced

2 to 3 cups 1-inch pieces of baby bok choy

2 packages firm tofu, diced into
 ½-inch pieces

1 pound Asian rice cakes

In a large stockpot, bring stock, coconut milk, sweet chili sauce, sambal oelek, fish sauce, and lime juice to a simmer; cook for 30 minutes. Meanwhile, heat vegetable oil in a small frying pan. Sauté pepper and bok choy in the oil until just tender, about 5 minutes, and set aside.

Add tofu and rice cakes to the stock. Cook until rice cakes are tender, about 5 to 7 minutes. In the last 2 minutes of cooking, add the sautéed vegetables to the stew to heat through. Serve immediately.

Serves 6 to 8

∽ Bill Kim ∾

URBAN BELLY (CHICAGO, IL)

Before opening Urban Belly and Belly Shack with his wife, Yvonne Cadiz-Kim, Bill fleshed out his impressive resume at Charlie Trotter's, Trio, Bouley Bakery and finally Le Lan. His addictive street food earned him The Michelin Guide's Bib Gourmand Award for 2011.

What was your favorite food as a kid?
Mom's fried rice.

What was the first meal you made that you were proud of?
A ramen with kimchee that I made for my mom when I was six years old.

What three adjectives describe your cuisine?
Creative, direct, and bold.

What book most influences your food, cookbook or otherwise?
Nina Simonds's *Asian Noodles*.

What chef do you most admire?
Pierre Pollin, currently an instructor at Kendall College, who gave me my first internship at Le Titi de Paris, in Chicago.

What is your favorite ingredient?
Fish sauce.

What music do you like to hear when you cook?
Anthony Hamilton.

What is your favorite hangover meal?
Coconut water.

What is your favorite midnight snack?
Sushi.

What restaurant in the world are you most dying to try?
Any ramen shop in Japan.

What kitchen utensil is most indispensable to you?
Microplane.

Who do you most like to cook for?
My wife, my mother, and my mother-in-law.

If you could do one other job, what would it be?
Forest ranger.

What do you most value in a sous chef?
Dedication and loyalty.

What food trend would you most like to erase from the annals of history?
Plating vertically.

What one food would you take with you to a desert island?
Rice.

What is your favorite guilty-pleasure treat?
Puerto Rican pasteles and *arroz con gandules* from La Bombe on Armitage Avenue in Chicago.

What most satisfies your sweet tooth?
Korean rice cakes with red bean paste.

What would you eat at your last meal, if you could plan such a thing?
My mom's short ribs and braised daikon, and my mother-in-law's lechon, Puerto Rican roasted pork.

Cheeseburger or foie gras?
Cheeseburger.

What's your favorite place (and what is your favorite thing to order) for:

Happy hour?
Balsan at the Elysian Hotel in Chicago.

A splurge meal?
Daniel in New York City.

Breakfast?
Ina's in Chicago.

Pastry?
Mindy's Hot Chocolate in Chicago.

A late-night/after-work meal?
Itto Sushi in Chicago.

A cup of coffee?
Urth Caffé in Los Angeles.

A greasy-spoon meal?
Cozy Corner Diner in Chicago.

Groceries?
Whole Foods.

Kitchen equipment?
Chicago Food Corp. [Korean market on Kimball Ave.]

Chocolate?
La Maison du Chocolat in Paris.

Vetri

There have been such a great many refractions of what an Italian restaurant is in the last ten years, which is good and right. But then there is Vetri, which holds that glamour of a time when it was just a little exotic to eat Italian food, an act of sophistication to have a glass of wine, a treat to eat out.

The floors creak but are polished; students live in apartments upstairs and share an entrance, coming and going all day with a nod; the tablecloths are ironed free of creases. It is just a classy place. The staff meal struck me as having great dignity. And not the fake dignity of a bow tie, but bone-deep dignity. That feeling came from Sal Vetri. Marc Vetri is the chef and owner of Vetri and three other restaurants, a group which also includes the Vetri Foundation, encouraging healthy habits in the youth of Philadelphia. Sal is Marc's father. He does prep in the kitchen and he prepares staff meal.

When I talked to Sal, I expected him to tell me had cooked his whole life and couldn't give it up. On the contrary, Sal had owned a fleet of jewelry stores, had served in the military, had been a stockbroker. He likes to keep busy and he likes being around his son.

OFF THE MENU

—

Sal's Chicken Cacciatore

Suggested wine:
Banshee Wines Sonoma
County Pinot Noir 2009
or Unti Grenache 2007

Sal sat me down in the dining room and told me his recipe. Recipe gathering is generally a game of chase. Busy chefs trying to apply numbers to their instincts. But of course, there's this other way of just sitting with Sal, as the dining room slowly becomes itself at the hands of polishing servers and vacuuming bussers. His chicken cacciatore recipe has a Sicilian version and a brown version. The brown version has Lipton onion soup packets in it.

Before we ate, Sal slipped into the kitchen, and some bit of conversation sent him into a torrent of loud, playful cursing. "He would die if he knew we could hear him. He would never talk that way in front of a lady." The young female server smiled.

We sat down to supper, five of us all together. The round table with ironed white linens, family-style plates of food, and the company of father and son. Instead of the usual question and answer, we swapped stories. Marc is sarcastic and warm. He is also humble. Humility is not necessarily a common chef trait, especially in a chef so successful. Having your father there, as a totem of pride, is the natural order. So distinct from the modern leave-taking of the nest—so classy.

Sal's Chicken Cacciatore

This was given to me verbally, and as I jotted it down, Sal offered a dozen tiny alterations or inflections of this version. You could add other vegetables or different herbs. You could forgo tomatoes altogether, as Sal sometimes does, and make a thick onion sauce with a Jack Daniels finish. Regardless of your touches, the technique is the backbone—without it, this dish won't stand. Brown the chicken and then let it cook in juicy, robust vegetables that will flavor the meat, as well as be flavored by it.

Olive oil
2 whole chickens, quartered
½ tablespoon unsalted butter
4 cloves garlic, minced
3 onions, small diced
2 stalks celery, chopped small
3 bell peppers, small diced
3 potatoes, small diced
1 tablespoon tomato paste
Salt and freshly ground black pepper
Pinch of red chili flakes
Two 28-ounce cans crushed tomatoes
1 cup Chianti or red wine
1 cup grated Parmesan cheese
1½ cups mushrooms, chopped small
1 teaspoon oregano (less if dried)
Fresh basil

Preheat the oven to 375°F. Heat a thin layer of oil in a pan; when it is glistening, add the chicken parts and cook until they are very lightly browned, flipping to brown every surface. If your pan isn't big enough, sauté in batches. Add the butter, half the garlic, a third of the onion, and the celery. Turn down the heat and cook until the celery is soft and the onion is transparent, about 10 minutes. Set aside.

Coat a saucepan with olive oil and when it is glistening, add the remainder of the garlic and onions. Cook over medium heat for about 5 minutes without burning the garlic. Add the peppers, then the potatoes, allowing them to get tender, about 5 to 10 minutes. Then add the tomato paste and season with some salt, pepper, and red chili flakes. Add the tomatoes and simmer gently for 15 minutes, then add the wine, Parmesan cheese, mushrooms, and oregano. Blend the sauce well and season, then combine the chicken mixture and sauce in a pan and cook, covered, in the oven for about 30 minutes. To serve, sprinkle with sliced fresh basil and more Parmesan.

Serves 6 to 8

THE ESCOFFIER QUESTIONNAIRE

ᴥ Marc Vetri ᴥ

VETRI (PHILADELPHIA, PA)

Marc Vetri is the chef and owner of Philadelphia's Osteria, Amis Trattoria, and now Vetri. With his Vetri Foundation, he stretches his interests toward food education as well, teaching kids healthy habits and "eatiquette." He also broke Iron Chef Michael Symon's crown in a veal battle.

What was your favorite food as a kid?
Cheese.

What was the first meal you made that you were proud of?
Greek baklava in the fourth grade.

What three adjectives describe your cuisine?
Simple, rustic, and creative.

What book most influences your food, cookbook or otherwise?
Le Ricette Regionali Italiane by Anna Gosetti della Salda.

What chef do you most admire?
Mario Batali.

What is your favorite ingredient?
Extra-virgin olive oil, pistachio, and artichoke.

What music do you like to hear when you cook?
Jazz.

What is your favorite hangover meal?
Breyers Mint Chocolate Chip ice cream.

What is your favorite midnight snack?
Cereal.

What kitchen utensil is most indispensable to you?
My hands.

If you could do one other job, what would it be?
Musician.

What one food would you take with you to a desert island?
Cheese and salumi.

Cheeseburger or foie gras?
Cheeseburger.

What's your favorite place (and what is your favorite thing to order) for:

Happy hour?
Margarita on the rocks with salt at Distrito in Philadelphia.

A splurge meal?
Blue Hill at Stone Barns in Tarrytown, New York.

Breakfast?
Morning Glory Diner in Philadelphia.

Pastry?
Mindy's Hot Chocolate in Chicago for the best pastries and desserts.

A late-night/after-work meal?
David's Mai Lai Wah on Race Street in Philadelphia for dumplings.

A cup of coffee?
La Colombe in Rittenhouse Square in Philadelphia for espresso.

A greasy-spoon meal?
Little Pete's diner in Philadelphia.

Groceries?
Whole Foods.

Kitchen equipment?
Prévin in Philadephia for professional equipment and Fante's Kitchen Shop for the rest.

Ice cream?
Capogiro Gelato Artisans in Philadelphia.

Chocolate?
Harbor House Candy Shop in Ogunquit, Maine for dark chocolate.

Woodberry Kitchen

BALTIMORE, MD

Woodberry Kitchen is showing off. Honestly, it's almost too much. With an uncompromised commitment to local sourcing, to whole-animal butchery, to empowered, scrub-faced cooks on a mission to prepare ethical food—the restaurant is a blazing star in the food-movement cosmos.

Most of the cooking happens in the wood oven in the dining area. But there are walk-in coolers and steel tables and freezers, all crowded with bodies taut with concentration. "We wanted to be able to use local tomatoes all year so we canned a ton. Literally, a ton," chef and owner Spike Gjerde tells me while climbing up to a high shelf and showing me jar after jar of canned tomato iterations: marinara, whole, crushed, salsa this way, salsa that way.

Continued explorations through the labyrinthine kitchen reveal expertly flash-frozen peas and beans and carefully cured meats. Every moment of each season has been captured and suspended at its fullest expression. This archive of freshly preserved edibles gives Woodberry's cooks an uncommon agility and freedom. It is one of the happier kitchens I have visited. I attribute this to Spike's trust in the process

---

OFF THE MENU

⁓

Roasted Whole Croaker
and Cabbage Slaw

Ricotta Pancakes
with Roasted Applesauce

Herb Biscuits and Cheese

Suggested wine:
Red Car Reserve
The Pearl Roussanne 2009

---

of experimentation and in his employees' talent. Cooking professionally is often grounded in a repetition of achieving consistent results through well-tested means. Kitchens where someone asks you to "do something with these tomatoes" are generally full of more content cooks than kitchens where they tell you exactly what to do. This less monarchical approach to kitchen management is becoming more familiar in America, as we move in generational increments away from the era of the French chef and his kitchen of perfection-seeking minions.

Snow began to fall outside as the Woodberry Kitchen staff sat down to eat. The meal was, thematically, the collaboration of many people. There is a place in the walk-in reserved for what will become elements of the staff meals: pancake batter left from brunch, a few fish that won't hold out another day, some bruised potatoes that need severe pruning. These imperfect gems were nimbly fashioned into a luxurious feast: whole roast fish, biscuits in cheese sauce, potato salad, pancakes with apples, pierogi on house-made kraut. The dishes prepared were like preservations in amber of seasons past.

TOP RIGHT: Sous chef Jill Snyder with ricotta pancakes.

Roasted Whole Croaker
and Cabbage Slaw

This is an easy summer preparation (or any season when you're keen to grill or use that wood-burning oven, if you're lucky enough to have one). Cooking fish whole makes it much easier to achieve a crispy skin and moist flesh. The classic slaw builds a crescendo of summer flavors.

Two 1½-pound croakers* or any fresh,
   firm-fleshed white fish, scored
1 lemon, sliced
1 cup fresh herbs: chervil, tarragon, and/or
   parsley
Sea salt, enough to season the cavity
   and exterior

Cabbage Slaw

1 medium (1½- to 2-pound) head cabbage,
   shredded
2 large carrots, shredded
1 handful chopped mixed fresh herbs:
   chervil, tarragon, and/or parsley
1½ cups mayonnaise
⅓ cup apple cider vinegar
Salt and freshly ground black pepper

Heat a wood-burning oven to 900°F or set a grill to high heat.

Combine all cabbage slaw ingredients in a large bowl until generously coated and thoroughly mixed. Set aside.

Dress each fish by salting the interior cavity, then stuffing it with lemon slices and herbs. Salt the outside of the fish and place the fish in an oiled pan or on the grill. Roast for 4 minutes per side. Fish should be firm and should flake easily. Serve with the slaw on the side.

Serves 4

*Atlantic croakers, also known as hardheads, yield delicate, lean white meat with a sweet flavor that ranges from mild to moderately pronounced. The croakers Woodberry Kitchen used were one of the many local fish they enjoy cooking with from the Chesapeake Bay.

Ricotta Pancakes
with Roasted Applesauce

These are Mother's Day, breakfast-in-bed-worthy pancakes, and the applesauce suits them beautifully. You could also slather them in maple syrup or butter and the contents of any of those jars of jam rattling around in your refrigerator door.

Roasted Applesauce

1 tablespoon unsalted butter

¼ cup packed brown sugar

3 large, firm green apples, peeled, cored, and cut into large chunks

1 teaspoon cinnamon

½ teaspoon salt

Ricotta Pancakes

1½ cups all-purpose flour

2½ teaspoons salt

2½ teaspoons baking powder

3 eggs, separated

1¾ cups Cherry Glen ricotta cheese (or see Homemade Ricotta on page 194)

1¾ cups whole milk

To make the applesauce, melt the butter and brown sugar over medium heat in a pan. Add the apples and stir occasionally, continuing to cook over medium heat until they begin to soften. Sprinkle in the cinnamon and salt. Continue to cook in the pan until the apples are well coated and ingredients are thoroughly mixed. Cook the apples to desired consistency, from chunky to saucy. Taste and add more salt if needed. Keep warm.

In a large bowl, sift together the flour, salt, and baking powder. Set aside. In a medium bowl, whisk the egg yolks, ricotta, and milk until smooth. Slowly whisk the wet ingredients into the larger bowl of dry ingredients. Set aside.

In a dry, clean bowl, whip the egg whites until soft peaks form. Fold the whites into the batter. Heat a griddle over medium heat. Using a 4-ounce ladle, pour the batter onto the buttered griddle for each pancake, spreading the batter a little with the ladle. Cook until tiny bubbles form on the tops of the pancakes and they look slightly dry; turn and cook the other side until golden. Serve immediately, topped with the warm roasted applesauce.

Serves 4 to 6

Herb Biscuits with Cheese

Everyone should know how to make a biscuit. The baked cheese and herbs in these make them decadent beyond the pleasure of sopping up whatever liquid is in sight.

3¾ cups all-purpose flour, plus extra
   for rolling
4 teaspoons baking powder
1 tablespoon salt
½ cup chopped fresh herbs: rosemary, sage,
   chive, and/or chervil
2 sticks cold, cubed unsalted butter
1¾ cups buttermilk, plus extra for topping
2 cups raw-milk cheddar cheese, shredded

Preheat the oven to 400°F. In a stand mixer with a paddle attachment, mix the flour, baking powder, salt, and herbs. Add butter all at once, continuing to mix at low speed until the butter is well incorporated and the consistency of the mixture is pea sized. With the mixer still running, add buttermilk in a steady stream and mix only until it is just combined (about 5 seconds). Do not overmix.

Roll or pat out the dough on a floured surface to 1½- to 2-inch thickness. Cut to desired size (an easy way to get a nice round biscuit is to use the opening of a drinking glass as a cookie cutter) as close together as possible to minimize scraps. Patch together scraps and cut again (the scrap biscuits will not be completely smooth on top). Chill for at least 15 minutes, until the butter is hard.

Place the biscuits on a baking sheet lined with parchment paper. Brush them with buttermilk and bake for 20 to 25 minutes. A few minutes before they are finished baking, sprinkle cheese liberally over the biscuits and continue baking just until cheese has melted and the biscuits are golden brown (biscuits often don't change color very much on top, so be sure to check underneath for the golden-brown color). Serve warm.

Makes 12 biscuits

THE ESCOFFIER QUESTIONNAIRE

~ Spike Gjerde ~

WOODBERRY KITCHEN (BALTIMORE, MD)

Spike Gjerde has been working with the local produce of Baltimore for more than twenty years. His early focus on great ingredients has made him a master of seasonality and earned him attention far beyond his food shed, including the notice of *Bon Appétit*, *Gourmet*, the James Beard Foundation, and the *New York Times*.

What was your favorite food as a kid?
A.1. Steak Sauce.

What was the first meal you made that you were proud of?
The meal I made for my parents the first time they came to Woodberry Kitchen.

What three words describe your cuisine?
Collaborative, intuitive, and ecological.

What book most influences your food, cookbook or otherwise?
At Swim-Two-Birds by Flann O'Brien.

What chef do you most admire?
Joseph Poupon, chef and owner of Patisserie Poupon in Baltimore.

What is your favorite ingredient?
Sea salt.

What music do you like to hear when you cook?
"Minimum Wage" by They Might Be Giants.

What is your favorite hangover meal?
A pillow.

What is your favorite midnight snack?
Clothbound cheddar on bread.

Who do you most like to cook for?
Our farmers.

What restaurant in the world are you most dying to try?
Itanoni in Oaxaca City, Mexico.

What kitchen utensil is most indispensable to you?
48-inch stainless steel oven peel, a tool we use in our wood-burning oven.

If you could do one other job, what would it be?
Teacher.

What do you most value in a sous chef?
Sharp knives and a sharper wit.

What food trend would you most like to erase from the annals of history?
Chesapeake Bay menhaden reduction fishery.

What one food would you take with you to a desert island?
Bread.

What is your favorite guilty-pleasure treat?
Hot dogs.

What most satisfies your sweet tooth?
Dark chocolate.

What would you eat at your last meal, if you could plan such a thing?
Everlasting gobstopper.

What's your favorite place (and what is your favorite thing to order) for:

Happy hour?
Alexander's Tavern in Baltimore for a Flying Dog pale ale.

A splurge meal?
Peter's Inn in Baltimore for garlic bread.

Breakfast?
An everything bagel with cream cheese from Greg's Bagels in Baltimore.

Pastry?
Pain aux raisins at Patisserie Poupon in Baltimore.

A late-night/after-work meal?
Korean barbecue.

A greasy-spoon meal?
A western omelet at Pete's Grille, Baltimore.

Groceries?
Marlow & Sons in Brooklyn, New York.

Ice cream?
The quince gelato at Dolcezza in Washington, D.C.

Chocolate?
Taza chocolate.

Zingerman's Roadhouse

ANN ARBOR, MI

Even if "Hi, my name is Sally and I'll be your server tonight" service isn't your style, you can't not like Zingerman's. I dare you. Zingerman's is a phenomenon. It is a restaurant that graciously serves satisfying food made with locally sourced ingredients; it is a website where you can order a chocolate-covered pie delivered to you; and it is also a book written by Ari Weinzweig that explains how every business can be a phenomenon of Zingermanian proportions.

Almost all of the restaurants in this book are white-tablecloth establishments. I wanted to share with you that everyday eating can be enhanced by knowing the sorts of things that fine-dining restaurants know: not to cook longer but to cook smarter, to think of your kitchen as a living thing, not something you have to resuscitate at every meal. Zingerman's is so beloved that it transcends its category, and I hope some of the cheeriness of my evening there comes bubbling up in the Cheddar Ale Soup, aka beer cheese soup, which remains mythical to me, even in its tangible existence,

> ## OFF THE MENU
>
> Chicken and Biscuits Casserole
>
> Cheddar Ale Soup
>
> *Suggested beer:*
> Flying Dog Brewery Dogtoberfest

even at my lips. Beer cheese soup! It seems too taboo to be real. Too wholly wrought from desire.

This meal, like Zingerman's menu, is about straightforward pleasure. That is the goal of most meals served at home, which is at the heart of the hominess in this dining room. Zingerman's also has a famous deli, the memories of which have choked up more than one chef in their recollection of it to me: the mustards, the breads, the corned beef. In New York or LA, this might not be so extraordinary, save for the commitment to making everything in-house, but in Ann Arbor, it is the catalyst for food awakenings. Valhalla with pastrami.

The staff is large and young, and there was something collegiate about the dinner gathering, maybe a whiff of the University of Michigan coming up the road. How lucky for the young employees here, to have this understanding of the connection between food and generosity of spirit, to carry with them into the rest of their lives.

Chicken and Biscuits Casserole

This casserole is a heartening meal that absorbs all the leftovers in your fridge. It is also a reminder that gravy and biscuits are excellent meal stretchers. Zingerman's makes this potpie-like dish with their left-over smoked chicken from the barbecue, but you can use any heaps of left-over roast chicken.

Chicken Gravy

2 sticks unsalted butter

2 cups all-purpose flour

3 quarts chicken broth

½ cup half-and-half

3 tablespoons chopped fresh thyme

5 tablespoons olive oil

3 pounds boneless, skinless chicken
  thighs or breasts

Salt and freshly ground pepper

1½ cups diced onion

1½ cups diced celery

1½ cups diced carrot

2 cloves garlic, minced

2 cups diced potatoes

1 cup frozen peas, thawed

3 tablespoons fresh thyme

¼ cup chopped fresh parsley

In a stockpot, melt the butter over low heat. Add the flour and cook, whisking constantly, until the texture smooths out, about 5 minutes. Slowly whisk in the broth and the half-and-half. Simmer for 30 minutes, stirring occasionally. Add the thyme in the last 2 to 3 minutes. Set aside or let cool and refrigerate in a container. (Extra gravy can be added to left-over casserole before reheating.)

Heat 2 tablespoons of the oil in a Dutch oven or heavy-bottomed stockpot over a medium-high flame. Season the chicken with salt and pepper. Working in two batches, brown the chicken well on both sides, 5 minutes per side, adding another tablespoon of oil with the second batch. Cut into ¾- to 1-inch pieces and set aside.

Add the onion, celery, and carrot to the pot and sauté for 10 minutes over medium-high heat. Add the garlic and sauté another 3 to 4 minutes. Add the chicken, 2 quarts of the chicken gravy, and potatoes and bring to a simmer. Partially cover the pot and simmer gently for 15 minutes. Stir in the peas and thyme, and adjust the seasoning.

While the casserole is simmering, preheat the oven to 375°F and prepare the biscuit topping. In a large mixing bowl, sift together the flour, baking powder, and salt. Using hands, add the butter to the dry ingredients and blend to pea-sized

Biscuit Topping
3½ cups all-purpose flour
1 tablespoon baking powder
1 tablespoon salt
2½ sticks unsalted butter, small diced and at
    room temperature
1½ cups buttermilk

crumbs. Make a well in the center of the flour mixture and add all the buttermilk. Using two fingers, gently knead for 5 minutes, leaving dough with flecks of butter.

Pour the casserole into a 15 x 10 x 2-inch baking dish. Break up the biscuit dough into balls the size of a golf ball and place on top of the casserole. Bake for 15 to 20 minutes, until the biscuits are golden and fully cooked. Allow to cool slightly and serve with chopped parsley sprinkled on top.

Serves 8

Cheddar Ale Soup

Beer cheese soup always seems like an untenable fantasy to me. Like someone just named their two favorite things and added soup—like "pizza pinot soup!" But it works magnificently and is as rich and complex as it sounds. And, happily, it goes great with a pint of ale.

1½ tablespoons of Liohori or other Greek extra-virgin olive oil

½ pound carrots, peeled and diced

½ pound onions, diced

½ pound celery, diced

1½ tablespoons chopped garlic

6 tablespoons unsalted butter

6 tablespoons all-purpose flour

2 tablespoons Dijon mustard

½ teaspoon celery seed

½ teaspoon chopped fresh thyme

¼ teaspoon cayenne

1½ tablespoons Worcestershire sauce

4½ cups milk

½ cup brown ale (Sprechers Pub Ale or Samuel Adams)

1 teaspoon salt

½ teaspoon cracked black pepper

1 pound Grafton 2-year-old cheddar cheese (or other fine Vermont cheddar), grated

In a large heavy-bottomed stockpot, heat the oil over medium heat. Add the carrots and sauté for 8 to 10 minutes. Add the onions and celery, sauté for 10 minutes; then add the garlic and sauté for another 5 minutes. Add the butter and allow it to melt. Stir in the flour and cook for about 8 minutes. Add the mustard, celery seed, thyme, cayenne, and Worcestershire sauce. Stir well. Slowly add the milk about one cup at a time, mixing each time until the milk is fully absorbed. Add the ale and ¾ cup water, stir well, and season with salt and pepper.

Let cool and refrigerate overnight for extra flavor. To serve, slowly reheat the soup, adjust the seasoning, and stir in the cheddar cheese just before serving.

Serves 6 to 8 as a starter

～ Alex Young ～

ZINGERMAN'S ROADHOUSE (ANN ARBOR, MI)

Alex Young is the executive chef at Zingerman's Roadhouse, the second restaurant in the Zingerman's family. The James Beard Foundation's Best Chef Great Lakes 2011 is in charge of sourcing excellent local products, as well as artisanal products from around the country, and then creating home-style food for the Ann Arbor set.

What chef do you most admire?
Julia Child.

What is your favorite ingredient?
Pepper.

What music do you like to hear when you cook?
My daughter's laughter.

What is your favorite hangover meal?
Ham and eggs.

What is your favorite midnight snack?
Toll House cookies and milk.

What restaurant in the world are you most dying to try?
Something in China, Thailand, or Mexico.

What kitchen utensil is most indispensable to you?
Chef's knife or tongs.

If you could do one other job, what would it be?
Race-car driver.

What do you most value in a sous chef?
The desire to walk into the fire.

What most satisfies your sweet tooth?
Chocolate cake.

What food trend would you most like to erase from the annals of history?
Frothing.

What one food would you take with you to a desert island?
Potato.

What would you eat at your last meal, if you could plan such a thing?
Meat and potatoes.

What's your favorite place (and what is your favorite thing to order) for:

Happy hour?
One of the forty bourbons at Zingerman's.

A splurge meal?
Manora's Thai on Folsom Street in San Francisco for duck with green curry.

Breakfast?
Two poached farm eggs with prosciutto di parma & Levain toast and cappuccino from Café Fanny by Alice Waters in Berkeley

Pastry?
Doughnuts from The Dexter Bakery on Main Street in Dexter, Michigan.

A cup of coffee?
Lighthouse Café in Dexter.

A late-night/after-work meal?
A gyro at the stand on 52nd & 6th in NYC or a taco from a stand at 24th & Mission in San Francisco.

A greasy-spoon meal?
Quad burger from Blimpy Burger in Ann Arbor, Michigan.

Groceries?
New York City's Chinatown for Peking duck, fresh fish, and dumplings.

Ice cream?
Chocolate, if I must, at the Dairy Queen with my kids.

Chocolate?
Askinosie Chocolate in Springfield, Missouri, for chocolate nibs.

Index

ACKNOWLEDGMENTS:

Eric, my home.

Lucie, my sous chef.

My passionate and brilliant publisher, Lena Tabori, who has so diligently pursued the good lessons food can teach us. And a heart-felt extension of that thank you to Emily Green, Gavin O'Connor, and Zach Hewitt.

Clark Wakabayashi, the designer of this book who has wrought such excellence from ideas.

Katrina Fried and Alice Wong, my editors, who have extended the definition of the role so far beyond its parameters that I am tempted to make up a new word to capture better their talent, dedication, and vision.

My hosts and friends in cities far from home, who made my travels so much richer: Rob and Allison Levitt, Nick and Kristen Chaset, Amelia Posada and Erika Nakamura, Erich Ginder and Sally Brock, Scott Worsham and Sari Zernich-Worsham.

All the cooks who prepared such wholesome and generous meals and all the restaurant staffs that slowed their schedules in graciousness to me.

Northern Spy, for being cover models.

Tia, co-founder of The Butcher's Guild, for giving me the freedom and encouragement to be a writer, as well as her partner.

My parents, for their endless support and encouragement.
—MG

Published in 2011 by Welcome Books®
An imprint of Welcome Enterprises, Inc.
6 West 18th Street, New York, NY 10011
(212) 989-3200; Fax (212) 989-3205
www.welcomebooks.com

Publisher: Lena Tabori
Associate Publisher: Katrina Fried
Project Director: Alice Wong
Project Assistants: Emily Green and Zach Hewitt
Recipe Testers: Rosy Harari, Paul Kim, Miriam Pinchevsky, Teresia Precht, and Alice Wong.
Copyeditor: Ellen Leach
Designed by H. Clark Wakabayashi

Library of Congress Cataloging-in-Publication data on file.
ISBN: 978-1-59962-102-9

FIRST EDITION
10 9 8 7 6 5 4 3 2 1
Printed in China

For further information about this book please visit online:
www.welcomebooks.com/offthemenu